Practical Wisdom

PETER LANG
New York • Washington, D.C./Baltimore • Bern
Frankfurt am Main • Berlin • Brussels • Vienna • Oxford

Practical Wisdom

ON THEOLOGICAL TEACHING AND LEARNING

Malcolm L. Warford, EDITOR

PETER LANG
New York • Washington, D.C./Baltimore • Bern
Frankfurt am Main • Berlin • Brussels • Vienna • Oxford

Library of Congress Cataloging-in-Publication Data

Practical wisdom: on theological teaching and learning /
edited by Malcolm L. Warford.
p. cm.
Includes bibliographical references and index.
1. Theology—Study and teaching. I. Warford, Malcolm L.
BV4022.P73   230′.071′1—dc22   2004006750
ISBN 0-8204-7263-8

Bibliographic information published by **Die Deutsche Bibliothek**.
Die Deutsche Bibliothek lists this publication in the "Deutsche
Nationalbibliografie"; detailed bibliographic data is available
on the Internet at http://dnb.ddb.de/.

Cover design by Sophie Boorsch Appel
Cover concept by Jon Michael Eberly

© 2004 Peter Lang Publishing, Inc., New York
275 Seventh Avenue, 28th Floor, New York, NY 10001
www.peterlangusa.com

Printed in the United States of America

Seek wisdom so that you may live
—Prov. 9:6, LXX

Table of Contents

PART THREE: THE WORK AHEAD: PRACTICAL GUIDELINES FOR MORE EFFECTIVE TEACHING AND LEARNING

Preface

The theological and educational perspectives expressed in these collected essays draw upon our varying experiences in theological education and our continuing learning in The Lexington Seminar: Theological Teaching for the Church's Ministries, a project supported by Lilly Endowment Inc. and sponsored by Lexington Theological Seminary.

At the heart of The Lexington Seminar is the relationship between the purposes of theological education and the institutional contexts in which these purposes are embodied in the seminary as a community of faith and learning. Each year since 1999, we have invited five theological faculties to become part of the Seminar. To date, thirty-five seminaries have joined the project. The schools have been primarily denominational seminaries committed to theological education that prepares leaders for the church.

In selecting these schools, we have tried to identify institutions that have demonstrated academic integrity, are stable enough to focus on this project in a sustained way, and are constituted of faculty and administrators who are committed to collaborative work to improve teaching and learning. Further, we have invited schools that are varied in denominational relationships and theological commitments, because we feel that calling together this kind of diverse community draws forth a lively conversation in which the significant questions of a student's learning, a professor's teaching, and a school's mission may be addressed.

THE SEMINAR PROCESS

After accepting an invitation to participate in the Seminar, the seminary deans spend a year working with their faculties to develop a narrative that expresses the kinds of questions in theological teaching and learning that most concern them. (See the process flowchart.) These narratives are brief stories that illustrate educational challenges confronting a school. Anyone who has been around institutions very long knows that the stories currently circulating in the life of the school provide a description of the school's reality that is difficult to summarize in any formal document. In fact, as Wayne Booth once suggested, "The life of any institution depends on the stories its members can bring themselves to tell each other" (1988, 13).[1] Moreover, the stories we tell always reveal more than we think we know. In discussing these narratives with colleagues from other theological schools, their meaning takes on new texture and significance, and unexpected avenues into understanding are often discovered. Readers who wish to gather a complete view of this lore should go to the Archives section of the Seminar's Web site—http://www.lexingtonseminar.org/—where all of the narratives may be found.

In June, a team from each of the five schools comes to Northeast Harbor, Maine, for a five-day conference focused on the narratives. The teams are composed of the president, the dean, and four members of the faculty. At this summer seminar, participants discuss the five schools' narratives, meet as teams, worship together, and have time for renewal. The seminar itself is constructed intentionally to provide the time and space needed to promote evocative conversation and reflection. School teams are encouraged to be together in ways that are not possible during the regular academic year.

Through the critical discussions of the June Seminar we seek to

- Affirm the teaching ministry of theological educators,
- Raise up and discern the diverse ways in which issues of teaching and learning present themselves in institutional contexts,
- Evoke new perspectives on the challenges facing individual schools, and
- Encourage faculty to make conversations about teaching and learning a crucial part of faculty life.

In focusing on the narratives prepared by each school, the June Seminar is an occasion for reflecting on the underlying assumptions and perspectives that illuminate issues in theological teaching and learning. It is a place where colleagues can learn from one another, both in gaining a wider sense of the issues that affect theological teaching and in gaining insight into a particular educational issue or concern that each school faces.

THE LEXINGTON SEMINAR
PROCESS

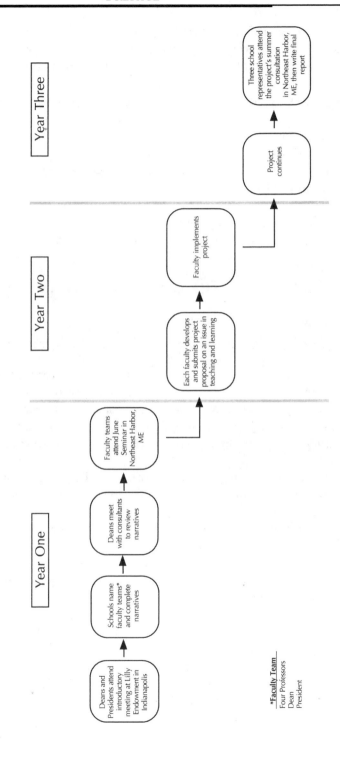

Year One

Deans and Presidents attend introductory meeting at Lilly Endowment in Indianapolis

Schools name faculty teams* and complete narratives

Deans meet with consultants to review narratives

Faculty teams attend June Seminar in Northeast Harbor, ME

Year Two

Each faculty develops and submits project proposal on an issue in teaching and learning

Faculty implements project

Year Three

Project continues

Three school representatives attend the project's summer consultation in Northeast Harbor, ME, then write final report

*Faculty Team
Four Professors
Dean
President

Following the June Seminar, the seminary teams refine the issue in teaching and learning which they have identified in their narratives and now want to address in an educational project over the next two years. While it is the responsibility of the team to do the initial work, the whole faculty in each institution is expected to be involved in selecting and designing the project itself.

From available studies on teaching, we recognize that the process of transformation involves the creation of a setting that allows for critical reflection and the emergence of principles that may shape educational projects. In this regard, implementing the Seminar projects and reflecting on their significance have often assisted faculties in taking additional initiatives to identify and address issues in teaching and learning. The final reports on the schools' projects that have been completed to date may be found in the Archives section of the Seminar's Web site (http://www.lexingtonseminar.org/).

THE COLLECTED ESSAYS

Although the writers have drawn upon a wide range of literature and experience regarding theological education, the essays in *Practical Wisdom*[2] refer often to the primary issues reflected in the schools' narratives and projects. At the time the essays were being written, only the narratives from 1999–2002 had been completed, so only those narratives were available for use as source material. Even though not every one of the narratives is referenced specifically in this book, every narrative did indeed inform the discussion of the issues.

Organized into three parts, the chapters provide ways of

- Rethinking the changing work and calling of theological teachers,
- Understanding the context of change in which theological schools now live, and
- Addressing the practical effort that has to be undertaken to deal with the challenges that schools face.

In all the chapters, the aim is to provide thoughtful perspectives on the issues and the practical implications for theological teaching and learning.

The writers of these essays represent the spectrum of theological traditions and cannot be pigeonholed into any one perspective. While we have tried to maintain a common tone to the whole book, we have at the same time tried to express the kind of diverse interpretations that characterize the Seminar itself. While there is a shared understanding of many topics addressed, the various points of view demonstrate a healthy unwillingness to conform to constricting unanimity.

ACKNOWLEDGMENTS

We are deeply grateful for the support of Lilly Endowment Inc., which has made possible The Lexington Seminar. The counsel and friendship of Craig R. Dykstra, Vice President for Religion, and John R. Wimmer, Program Director for Religion, continue to be crucial to all that we do. From the beginning and throughout the development of the project, Fred L. Hofheinz, former Program Director for Religion, was of singular significance in his guidance of the Seminar's purpose and program. In this regard, he made possible connections with The Keystone Conference: Theological Teaching for the Church's Ministries, which was created for Roman Catholic theological schools and led by Vincent Cushing, OFM, and Kevin O'Neil, CSsR, who were generous in their assistance as we developed The Lexington Seminar.

Lexington Theological Seminary has been the sponsoring institution for The Lexington Seminar, and for this hospitality we are very appreciative. Throughout its history, the seminary has been an institution known for its lively intellectual mission and for the service it has rendered in the education of leaders for the church.

We are also indebted to the significant editorial work of Kenneth Huggins. His attention to detail and his thoughtful recommendations throughout the writing and editing of the essays have been invaluable.

Finally, we want to express appreciation to the schools that have been part of the Seminar. The commitment that faculties, deans, and presidents have brought to this project has been significant for the whole enterprise of theological education.

Grateful acknowledgment is hereby made to copyright holders for permission to use the following copyrighted material:

Figure 1: Miley Nakamura, Mind Map of Lloyd Webber's Production. Reprinted by permission of Miley Nakamura.

Figure 2: Sue Lonoff, Sample Outline Based on Mind Map. Reprinted by permission of Sue Lonoff, Derek Bok Center for Teaching and Learning, Harvard University.

Figure 3: Derek Bok Center for Teaching and Learning, Harvard University. Sample Peer Response Sheet. Reprinted by permission of the Derek Bok Center for Teaching and Learning, Harvard University, and the President and Fellows of Harvard College.

Malcolm L. Warford
2004

Notes

1. All references may be found at the back of the book in the section entitled, "References and Recommended Reading."

2. The title came to mind based on comments made by Wendell Berry during a conference called "The Future of Agrarianism: *The Unsettling of America* Twenty-Five Years Later" (2002), organized by Norman Wirzba and sponsored by Georgetown College to discuss the significance of Berry's writings and ideas. In the context of these collected issues, I take "practical wisdom" to mean knowledge expressed in action, guided by a sense of faithful integrity, and oriented toward service—the good that may be done.

· MALCOLM L. WARFORD ·

Introduction

Teaching is often viewed as a solitary venture of self and subject, but on another level we know that both teaching and learning are a matter of relationships significantly shaped by the community in which they occur. For theological teachers, this community is the seminary, and today's seminary reflects the turbulent context of the church and society it is meant to serve. New student constituencies, multiple institutional commitments, and severe fiscal pressures, all occurring within a world of continuing change, present theological seminaries with challenges demanding meaningful response. But the responses are as mixed as those who offer them. Some theological teachers yearn for halcyon days in which schools express long-established traditions; others are more willing to embrace change but are unsure how. Still others are so overwhelmed by the sheer volume of their tasks that they have no time to address the critical issues facing their vocation, and all of us are confronted by the uncertainty of the future that stretches out before us.

The purpose of this book and the project out of which it emerged is to engage, in this context of change and uncertainty, crucial questions of theological teaching and learning. In framing these questions, we invariably return to four critical issues: diversity, formation, institutional identity, and assessment.

DIVERSITY: RECONSIDERING THE COMMONPLACES

The new student constituencies that theological schools are endeavoring not only to serve but to embrace reflect a wide spectrum of cultural backgrounds, personal histories, and theological commitments, and they are marked as well by formation in a culture in which the traditional foundations for learning cannot be taken for granted. Students come out of differing educational experiences that have shaped their forms of learning and self-understanding. They enter with varied abilities, uneven formation in the Christian faith, and the conviction that the seminary will fulfill their needs, no matter how diverse. Schools that once could take for granted that their distinctive theological traditions defined their essential reality now find it necessary to figure out how to maintain their heritage and yet at the same time express an ecumenical reality that is represented by increasing numbers of students.

At one time, seminaries dealt with the issue of diversity as a matter of accommodation; that is, the problem was defined in terms of how the school could make room for other perspectives and traditions. This approach no longer seems viable, neither on institutional nor on theological grounds. On the basis of institutional needs, most denominational seminaries cannot exist without recruiting students from other traditions, and these students cannot be viewed as guests but must be recognized as full participants in the life and ethos of the institution.

In responding to new constituencies and actively seeking their presence, seminaries are called to see their willingness to respond as a willingness to be transformed as well. How this transformation is discerned requires inquiry into the distinctiveness of each school's central theological stance and how this distinctiveness is sustained, revised, or made new in the midst of "strangers" who are now part of the household. Added to this theological and ecclesial work are the accompanying issues presented by the diversity of the students themselves in terms of ethnicity, culture, class, gender, age, and sexual orientation. Further, many students attend seminaries part-time, and a significant number of them are older adults who represent various places on the ideological spectrum. This enriches as well as complicates the wide-ranging educational backgrounds of theological students, especially as other entering seminarians come directly from college with the differing sensibilities and assumptions of contemporary youth culture.

Although students come with a commitment to ministry, their understanding of how they are to be prepared for this work and calling are often different from the traditional assumptions in theological faculties. Many students enroll in seminaries with what some observers have characterized as an "expectation for efficiency" in their theological education that will make it possible for them to juggle competing demands of employment and family commitments. This expectation, however, does not necessarily include the kind of time for study and reflection that lies closest to the hearts of most theological educators. A fundamental difference often exists, then, between the assumptions of faculty and students.

In an earlier generation, seminaries often recommended the kinds of courses that students seeking a theology degree ought to have taken before applying for seminary admission. Entering students, for example, who had little familiarity with the history of philosophy, were sometimes required to take a course specifically designed to help them meet this lack of philosophical background. Few theological seminaries today would find such a requirement possible.

The educational problems, however, are not just a matter of making up for a lack of knowledge in certain fields; instead, a more pervasive issue is that many students arrive without basic rhetorical and academic skills. The theological teacher's responsibility, or so it seems to many educators, has become more than just communicating a particular area of knowledge; it has become a responsibility to equip students with skills they should have acquired long before entering seminary—such basic abilities as comprehending a text, expressing a point of view, writing an essay, following standards of research and documentation, and knowing the elements of grammar and punctuation.

Such problems are widespread throughout higher education, and theological education, in this instance, reflects the larger cultural context. But theological education accepts another role beyond those which other institutions of higher education usually accept. Theological schools have come to expect to play an increasing role in a student's formation as a person of faith.

FORMATION: ADDRESSING ESSENTIAL QUESTIONS

The seminary is now required to be in itself a place of basic formation in the gospel as well as a community that equips men and women for the church's ministries. Protestant theological students often enter seminaries with limited experience in the life of a congregation and almost no knowledge of biblical and theological traditions. While this tends to be less so in theological schools where ecclesiastical endorsement is required before admission, it is an issue even in those schools. This trend represents a significant departure from a longstanding tradition in which the congregation was seen as the place of formation in faith. For generations, both the church and the seminary took it for granted that theological students were essentially formed in the practices of the Christian life through their nurture as children and youth in local congregations. They came to seminary having been shaped by Sunday schools, youth groups, college religious programs, and continuing family traditions of faith. In contemporary culture, however, this background applies only to some students because many have not been part of this ecology of Protestant ecclesial life. Seminaries, therefore, are increasingly responsible for an even larger proportion of students' spiritual formation. This new reality fundamentally changes the nature of what can be taken for granted in the classroom and raises critical questions about what is required for faithful teaching and learning.

These dynamics of theological teaching and learning are significantly shaped by the emergence of new technologies. The rapid rise of computers within theological education changes many of the fundamental patterns of education. In particular, this technological change is focused in the development of off-site learning programs that may take the form of television-linked classrooms in multiple locations and in the creation of Web-based courses conducted completely online. These trends are intensified by the establishment of "smart classrooms" that bring audio and visual resources into everyday coursework and in the redefinition and redesign of libraries far beyond that of providing access to printed texts and documents. The central question is what these new technologies and educational settings imply for the nature of formation. For example, how does an off-campus course require us to rethink our assumptions about community? Can we preserve a sense of community in the midst of distance learning? Must we reconstitute community in a different form?

While schools are interested in strengthening their educational programs through technology, many have not yet come to grips with the issues that are connected with this technological development. Some schools have seen technology as a way of extending what they are already doing, such as televising a traditional classroom. What schools are beginning to realize, however, is that technology is not neutral; it brings its own pedagogical assumptions and culture. How a school makes use of various technological possibilities is as much an educational issue as a technical one. For example, is it possible for televised presentations and electronically linked classes to increase the depth of students' learning and formation? There is a sense of possibility inherent within the use of computers and Web-based learning, but there is also the nascent realization that, like all technologies, these have to be guided by core educational values. The search for technologies appropriate for teaching and learning, the need for faculty education in the use of technology, and the desire to understand technology's impact on students' learning are just a few of the pressing challenges we face.

At another level, issues of formation in theological education are defined not only by the changing nature of students and the emergence of new technologies but also by the shifting style and ethos of seminary life. As denominational structures and programs have been reduced, local congregations and various ecclesiastical bodies have turned to seminaries for educational programs that were once the responsibility of other agencies or the local church itself. The cumulative effect of these changes has been to shift the taken-for-granted character of theological education. Diverse constituencies, distance learning, commuting students, and multiple programmatic commitments create a sometimes overburdened institutional context for faculty and students. It is a context that requires the rethinking of basic educational assumptions.

At the same time that theological schools face complex educational questions, the assumptions of theology itself have become more problematic. On any given faculty there is now significant theological diversity that makes it difficult to state curricular principles and agree on foundations for theological learning. Until the 1960s (and beyond that time for many theological schools), the seminary curriculum typically reflected a basic theological consensus. In the 1950s, one could look through the catalogues of many mainline Protestant schools and discern the outlines of a common theological perspective. The organization of the various fields of study, the flow of required courses, and the relative weight given to different disciplines expressed understandings of revelation, authority, and ministry that were largely shared by the faculty or at least held by a dominant majority. With the increased diversity of theological methods and models, this kind of unanimity in curricular assumptions and design is virtually impossible to achieve in most schools. How a faculty lives creatively and faithfully together with such diversity is a major and continuing question of institutional life.

This situation is complicated by the dramatic growth of religious studies as the primary influence in graduate theological programs. In this regard, doctoral candidates tend to be more prepared for teaching in a university department of religion than in a denominational seminary. Where once it was assumed that most, if not all, theological teachers would be ordained ministers who held the B.D. or M.Div. degree before moving on to doctoral study, that is increasingly not the case. The situation is made even more complicated by the fact that fewer theologians have served as parish ministers for any significant amount of time. While this new situation encourages a less clerical tone in theological education, it also means that younger scholars and teachers sometimes must be formed in basic pastoral understandings that once were taken for granted.

INSTITUTIONAL IDENTITY: ENGAGING MULTIPLE AIMS

All of these educational and theological issues are set within institutions that are often fragile and torn by competing needs. Out of the need to develop new sources of revenue and the effort to equip the church for ministry, theological seminaries find it difficult to avoid multiple and often competing programmatic commitments. Many schools are beginning to realize that, without necessarily intending to, they have become more like resource centers than schools defined primarily by practices of teaching and learning that require time for study and reflection. In this regard, a basic question that must be asked is at what point does a school move so far in the direction of programmatic overload that it loses its sense of distinct purpose?

One of the reasons the church at large is in significant difficulty is the absence of any real, sustained conversation about the essential theological issues that are the foundation of its life. When the church is so consumed by its own business that it cannot stop long enough to reflect on where it has come from and where it might be going, then it has forfeited its substance. The theological school is not the only place where this theological inquiry should occur, but it is an essential community for nurturing that conversation throughout the diverse ministries of the church.

This situation calls for a new intentionality about the use of faculty time as the seminary tries to respond to the concerns of the church, the expectations of the academy, and the changing culture of the school itself. As schools take on new institutional commitments to off-campus courses, distance learning, multiple degree programs, and various forms of continuing education, they stretch already slim resources. Many of the changes occurring in theological education are happening with little thought about the long-term consequences or the cumulative effect on existing programs. The assumption is that new programs can be added to existing academic commitments. But this often puts vulnerable institutions even more at risk.

Less than a generation ago, most seminaries were modest organizations of varying levels of competency. As institutions, they followed nineteenth-century institutional models in which the administration was, in effect, the president, who more often than not was a member and head of the faculty. A development director, sometimes called a vice president, and a secretary, if there was one, staffed fundraising efforts. Recruitment was handled informally, and public relations were the responsibility of whoever was available. Various student services were usually assumed by faculty or a part-time dean of students, but few institutions had created the kind of student services staff we now see. Maintenance issues were largely deferred, and the buildings and grounds staff focused on repairs, patching, and making do. The board of trustees met infrequently and was composed primarily of clergy and church lay leaders who were not necessarily key benefactors. Boards functioned as courts of appeal and places of general oversight, but little was expected by way of fundraising or policy development. The academic affairs of the school were the prerogative of the faculty, and the president supposedly took care of everything else.

These administrative patterns changed quickly when fiscal realities began to require new ways of operating, especially as denominational support diminished or, in many cases, disappeared entirely. More extensive administrative structures were required to handle the emerging expectations of congregations, various public relationships, and new constituencies of support. The role of the board of trustees grew as the seminary had to cultivate more direct contributions from individual donors and as the board itself became more aware of its own fiduciary responsibilities. These various dynamics of administrative growth soon began to upset the balances of power within the institution, and tensions emerged, especially as faculty felt that new staff appointments were taking over responsibilities long assumed by faculty members themselves.

There are, of course, variations in this complicated landscape. Evangelical schools tied to more conservative theological traditions have tended to prosper while more liberal mainline schools—with significant exceptions—have struggled with destabilizing forces. At the same time, theological schools of varying theological commitments that are located in regions of economic growth have been buoyed by this rising tide and generally find themselves in a much different institutional place than their peer schools in less dynamic regions. Differing though the landscape may be for particular schools and traditions, the increased levels of institutional change have contributed to the volatility of the environment in which most theological schools function, and each institution's struggle with identity—the definition of purpose and mission, the creation and abandonment of programs, and the endless search for fiscal stability—has profoundly affected the practices of teaching and learning.

ASSESSMENT: FIDELITY TO OUR INTENTIONS

Entwined with the three critical issues just discussed is a responsibility that all seminaries struggle to fulfill—educational assessment, the responsibility to ascertain what we are doing and how well we are doing it. Such an evaluative task is more complex than making a precipitate judgment about what is good or bad. For inherent within theological education resides the continuing and ethical obligation to learn how to do it better and more faithfully. Fulfilling this obligation is an expression of our fidelity to the vision that has called us into being as a community of faith and learning.

In one sense, the responsibility for assessment lies within the nature of religious commitment itself, and we can claim a certain theological impetus for our evaluative commitments. But the more immediate reason for the current emphasis on assessment comes from the public community, and most of all from the federal government itself. The regional accrediting bodies and the Association of Theological Schools (ATS) have had to be responsive to government requirements for measurements of institutional effectiveness and integrity of academic programs in their member institutions. Finances are attached to these expectations because government funding of various scholarship programs used by students depends on credible evaluative systems being in place.

The expectation for assessment is fueled also by increasing church concern about ministry programs and whether the money spent on theological schools is really worth the cost. In some denominations, the question is whether the schools themselves follow a sufficiently orthodox line; in others, the question is whether the curriculum is relevant enough for the contemporary practice of ministry. With increasing calls for nontraditional routes to ordination and the actual development of alternative models for theological education within denominations and local congregations, theological schools are often pressed to demonstrate effectiveness to church officials and donors.

In recent revisions of regional and ATS accrediting standards, assessment is a major component of decennial self-study reports. Schools have to demonstrate they have designed and implemented evaluation models. Expressing intentions is not enough; schools are expected to provide some kind of evidence that the stated goals of degree programs are being achieved. The aim here is not some expectation of perfection; instead, it is the assumption that theological schools will take seriously their responsibility for the quality and the faithfulness of their programs, institutional practices, and overall aims.

In a larger sense, assessment is not something apart from the vocation of teaching; it is of its essence. The difficulty, of course, is determining how such essential assessment is to be carried out. Some schools try to impose quantitative measurements that are often at odds with educational aims, while others try to avoid any measurement at all because they are not convinced that what exists can be evaluated. Sometimes assessment is reduced to an almost punitive level that demoralizes faculty and staff. In this regard, much needs to be done in creating forms of evaluation, especially course evaluation, that are occasions for learning and not some kind of political poll that measures popularity but misses the essential questions of theological education. Each school must define and implement its own distinctive means of assessment and then engage the learning from this evaluative process in a way that informs and reforms educational practice.

FACULTY WORK AND CALLING

Formulating faithful and workable responses to the issues of diversity, formation, institutional identity, and assessment is made even more difficult by the solitary nature of faculty life. While faculty often meet together, the practices of mutual learning are not all that common. In the midst of the activities and sometimes frenzied schedules of academic institutions, there is not much evidence of sustained collaborative effort on fundamental educational questions. However, in order to address the issues that have been named, it is crucial that faculty develop collaborative practices.

The irony is that while seminary faculties spend a lot of time together, this familiarity does not necessarily result in friendship, common learning, or awareness of each other's deepest commitments. For example, as the role of the various academic guilds has been strengthened in recent years, theological professors have tended to see others in the same scholarly field as their primary intellectual colleagues and not those colleagues with whom they serve on a given faculty. Many seminary faculties seem to have little sense that they share a common vocation. In this regard, Timothy Fuller (1989, 3) observes the following:

> Academic institutions, it would appear, are in varying degrees disintegrated communities of scholars. They remain places physically set apart for teaching and learning, but entering their premises no longer guarantees encounter with a self-understanding, however mysterious and complex it may initially seem, that gradually discloses a distinctive manner of activity that really does set them apart. What has been obscured, if not lost, is the idea of a school, a college, a university.

As Fuller goes on to suggest, this loss is not "that what is missing is an organizing, energizing goal for education" (3); instead, what is missing is the essential practice of teaching and learning—namely, conversations that matter. This description of education as conversation is identified particularly with the work of the British philosopher Michael Oakeshott.

Oakeshott (1989) argues that while academic institutions are not the only places in society where learning occurs, he asserts that these institutions should have "a special manner of engaging in the pursuit of learning" (97). This special manner was once cultivated by the fact that most faculty lived on or near school grounds. This proximity helped form these individual teachers and scholars as a community in which "a tradition of learning . . . [could be] . . . preserved and extended" (97). In effect, the faculty lived together in a "home of learning" (97). This kind of community was characterized most of all as a place of conversation (Fuller 1989, 12–13).

"The pursuit of learning," Oakeshott writes, "is not a race in which the competitors jockey for the best place, it is not even an argument or a symposium, it is a conversation" (98). The challenge to theological education is how to reclaim the school as a place of conversation sustained by colleagues who constitute a community of teaching and learning. Since most faculty now live off campus and follow not only the familiar commuting patterns of most in our society but also often share the fragmented consciousness and harried pace that characterize our culture, it is often difficult for faculty members to find time to be together in meaningful ways. Aside from reinstituting faculty housing on campus—an impracticality for most schools and no guarantee of collegial renascence—how can faculty, given today's social context, form a way of being together that approximates the collegial ideal we espouse but so often fail to embody?

In this regard, as Timothy Fuller suggests (3–6), we may need fewer new programs and more renewed intentionality about what we are already doing and how we can learn to do it better. This perspective, however, should not be read as an appeal to the past. For while some schools may be able to renew traditional residential and full-time models of seminary life, most will need to envision and establish contemporary forms that will give new expression to what we have valued most in the inherited structures of theological education.

Within the context of the Christian faith, the conversation that Oakeshott describes is most of all defined by *metanoia*, the change of mind and heart that constitutes the essential conversion of our lives. This kind of transformative learning is at the heart of all Christian education, and as such, theological education is called to understand its vocation within this context. Theological teaching is not for itself alone, but for the church's ministries. Sadly enough, though, far too many seminary graduates disparage their experiences as theological students and distance themselves quickly from the school as a significant community in their lives. For these, the seminary is removed from the congregation, and the theological teacher is marginal to their own sense of the Christian life. As pastors, they view their theological education as disconnected from what they do in ministry. We may know countless exceptions to this perspective, but we also know that it is a way of seeing that is prevalent throughout the church, and while our first inclination may be to respond defensively, we need to resist such temptation and engage the issue with energy and imagination—and with the understanding that the task of re-creating the relationship between the church's ministries and theological education is a collaborative effort that must be addressed by seminaries, congregations, and denominational structures.

The issue, actually, is as old as the idea of schooling itself. As Pierre Hadot observes (2002, 13), it began with the Sophists who "invented education in an artificial environment." While the earliest classical philosophical tradition understood knowing as lived experience rather than abstract thought, the Sophists created the school as the primary place for learning. The earlier emphasis on learning that occurs by formation in a community's life—its values, institutional practices, and traditions—was superseded by teaching and learning in the formal setting of the school. Ever since, we have struggled with reconnecting knowledge and experience in the kind of practical wisdom that shapes our souls and forms the practices of our lives. For theological teachers, these dynamics call us to rethink the nature of our work and reclaim the sense of calling that first led us to this vocation.

In a memoir of her father, James Hastings Nichols, who was a church historian and academic dean of Princeton Seminary, novelist Sue Miller (2003, 54) writes:

> After his death I will read a testimonial from a student describing his quiet, careful *listening* in his office hours, and I will recognize this extraordinary generosity. You never knew—never even had a sense of—what he put aside to give himself to your pressing concerns. But he was *there*. When you asked him to be, he was absolutely there.

For those acquainted with James Hastings Nichols, this description is easily recognizable as the person we knew at varying degrees of familiarity. It is the image of a scholar who was the kind of theological teacher many aspire to become. However, if testimonies of many current professors are true, and there is little reason to doubt them, it is increasingly difficult to approximate this ideal. The changing character of theological education, the growing multiplicity of institutional aims and programs, and the impact of diverse issues that press in upon theological teachers establish a situation in which our reach exceeds our grasp of the kind of teaching for the church's ministries that we would most of all want to embody. While earlier generations also faced issues of time and changing expectations, the context in which they functioned seemed more stable. It is now apparent that the increased pace of seminary life and the widening range of institutional commitments are eroding traditional patterns of faculty life and work.

Our hope for addressing this situation comes out of our vocation itself, and Sue Miller provides us with a clue for achieving that hope. As she speaks of her father—"he was patient and respectful—a born teacher, I think, because he was a learner himself" (60)—we are reminded of the essential connection between our teaching and our commitment to learning. It is this fundamental commitment that we must draw upon when we address the crucial issues we face as teachers in the church and as members of communities of teachers in particular theological seminaries. It is doubtful that external pressures will lessen significantly for faculties. If we are waiting for someone outside ourselves to change our situation, then that wait will be endless and frustrating with the predictable outcome being the increased fragmentation and isolation of faculty from each other and from the purposes of our lives. In order to renew the practices of theological teaching and learning, we must understand the shared character of these practices and the institutional contexts in which they find a home.

Most importantly, we must address the multiple issues that frame theological education through the sort of imaginative theological work, informed by educational research and practice, that constitutes practical wisdom. This is the aim of the authors of this book.

Rethinking the Work and Calling of Theological Teachers

· RAYMOND BRADY WILLIAMS ·

The Vocation of Teaching

BEYOND THE CONSPIRACY OF MEDIOCRITY

Teachers — Teaching
Students — Learning
0 discipline — Content

Three components of theological education—teachers and teaching, students and learning, and theological disciplines and content—form a developmental sequence in the career of many teachers, but it is a sequence that is too often broken by institutional rigidities, personal inclinations, and the guild structures of academic disciplines. Nonetheless, a shift of attention has accelerated during recent decades, and we are beginning to realize that our work and calling as theological teachers require a transformation of ethos and practice, both in the doctoral graduate schools that shape new faculty and in the theological schools that provide the enabling environment for excellent teaching and learning.

For generations the ethos of secular doctoral institutions was to focus, at the expense of teaching, on narrowly conceived research, and this ethos was duplicated in the majority of theological schools where it was neither relevant nor effective. Fortunately, schools are beginning to realize that it is essential to attend to the preparation of graduate students for careers as teachers, not just scholars, and to encourage theological faculty to place as much emphasis on their teaching as they do on their research. Furthermore, changes in the demography of students and their expectations require that faculty members attend to what and how their students learn. It is clear that pedagogical and assessment methods appropriate for previous generations are not adequate for the current generation of students. More effort must be put into understanding the learning process and adapting teaching methods to the insights of this improved understanding. Finally, despite the changes that schools are beginning to make in the preparation of future scholars and teachers, many old habits continue. The increasing disciplinary specialization and guild structures of graduate schools and the academy in general result in forms of knowledge that are often trivial, irrelevant, and dull. Students yearn for—and meaningful learning requires—integration, grandeur, breadth, and relevance.

TEACHERS AND TEACHING

The shift from a single focus on disciplinary content to the practices of teaching was marked on the national scene by the elaboration in 1990 of "the scholarship of teaching" by Ernest Boyer, then president of the Carnegie Foundation for the Advancement of Teaching. It was part of his attempt to transcend what he called "the tired old 'teaching versus research' debate" with a new definition of scholarship that reflected the full range of academic and civic mandates for faculty members. He posited four types of activity as true scholarship.

1. The *scholarship of discovery* is what most academics mean when they refer to "my work" as specialized research at the cutting edge of a discipline.
2. The *scholarship of integration* is research at the boundaries where fields converge that places specialized scholarship in larger contexts of meaning.
3. The *scholarship of application* is the connecting of the theory of a discipline to civic life as an aspect of the scholar's responsibility to transmit knowledge. Boyer suggests that scholars in all disciplines have a responsibility to interact with civic institutions and engage in public discourse, an idea which applies dramatically to theological teachers, who should cultivate an active engagement with lived religion in church and society that some scholars seek to avoid.
4. The *scholarship of teaching* builds on Aristotle's observation that teaching is the highest form of understanding (23).

Eugene Rice (1990), who helped design the new paradigm of scholarship, identified three distinct elements in the scholarship of teaching: first, a synoptic capacity to provide coherence and meaning; second, pedagogical knowledge to represent a subject in ways that transcend the split between intellectual substance and teaching process; and third, teachers' comprehension of the learning process.

The work of Boyer and Rice precipitated considerable discussion in some academic circles more than a decade ago, and many colleges, universities, and theological schools have started to place greater emphasis on teaching skills, although, unfortunately, this emphasis seems to be more apparent at the point of hiring than at times of tenure and promotion. Scholars joining faculties are often expected to present, not only their articles and book projects, but their teaching portfolios, philosophies, and evaluations. Accrediting agencies challenge theological faculties to implement assessment plans that include the scholarship of teaching. Scholarly and professional organizations, such as the American Academy of Religion and the Society of Biblical Literature, have developed committees, workshops, and programs to foster better teaching in the field. Several schools with doctoral programs have instituted seminars, mentoring, and courses on teaching for their graduate students.

The current president of the Carnegie Foundation for the Advancement of Teaching provides a significant elaboration of Boyer's work. Lee Shulman (1989, 13) uses the important and powerful pulpit of the Carnegie Foundation to sharpen the concept by establishing three characteristics of the scholarship of teaching: (1) It will entail a public account of some or all of the full act of teaching—vision, design, enactment, outcomes, and analysis. (2) It will be made public in a manner susceptible to critical review by the teacher's professional peers. (3) The resulting knowledge will be amenable to productive employment and development in future work by members of the academy.

Teaching has the greatest social impact of any scholarly activity in theology and religion. In thousands of locations and contexts, teachers daily engage students in public reflection on their subjects—and well beyond. Teaching is the work that provides justification for theological positions and salaries. Articles and books generally reach a few score specialists in narrow subdisciplines, whereas teaching affects hundreds of students who are thereby empowered to extend that influence into all areas of society. Work in developing courses and curricula and day-by-day teaching in various contexts do more to define and empower the academic disciplines of theology and religion than do other aspects of scholarship. The greater the distance between scholarly research and teaching, the more irrelevant both become. Hence, even though teachers occasionally speak of something else as "my own work," teaching is the defining work for professors, schools, and the professional disciplines.

Teaching and learning in theological schools is generally very good, better than in other disciplines and professional schools, so reflection about theological teaching can emphasize celebration and affirmation as much as remediation. This reflection is based on two assumptions: (1) no one wants to be a bad teacher; (2) every teacher, even excellent ones, can become better. A significant step toward addressing these two assumptions occurs when teachers engage in conversation with other good teachers, and the Carnegie Foundation has undertaken a study of teaching and learning for the preparation of clergy that will provide comparative data around which such conversations can take place. Those teachers who do not move forward fall behind, because expectations, learning styles, and contexts are constantly changing. Thus, it is sad when a teacher of great promise fails to improve and thereby loses luster, but it is a matter for rejoicing when excellent teaching is fostered, experienced, and rewarded.

Teaching is the last bastion of professional life that is conducted in relative secrecy—unobserved, absent of critique by peers, and without a mandatory refreshment of knowledge and skill. The classroom is the teacher's castle where colleagues hesitate to tread. It is protected both by academic freedom and by a "don't ask, don't tell" conspiracy of silence about teaching and learning and thus leads to an unhealthy privatization. Where little support for collaboration or collegial discussion about teaching exists, a situation often develops in which a strange double self-deception occurs. Most teachers are better at teaching than they feel they are and certainly than they feel called to be by God. Yet they are often not as good as they pretend to be. Such doubts and suppression of doubts result in several pathologies. Perhaps the worst is a flight from teaching to research and publishing, which, if done as an escape from teaching, leads to research that is dull and irrelevant. Neither fear nor pretense provides a solid base for good teaching and learning. Better than such self-deception is a systematic collaboration that will help faculty members come to a clearer understanding of their abilities as teachers and thereby improve their teaching skills.

Further, the privatization and pressures under which theological students and faculty work can lead to a conspiracy of mediocrity, which is the greatest single danger facing theological schools. It occurs when a silent and unholy pact is made between student and teacher that if the teacher does not expect very much from the student, the student will not demand good teaching from the teacher. The unfortunate reality driving the conspiracy is that teaching is one of the easiest jobs in the world to do poorly but one of the hardest to do well. The danger is that everyone will be satisfied with mediocrity, a state that is easy enough to achieve but which comes with great costs to both students and teachers.

The penultimate character of work in theological schools makes it spiritually frustrating and thus a fairly dangerous activity in which to engage. Few objective standards exist for judging the success or failure of a teacher's work. Each classroom is a private stronghold that teachers guard with misdirected ferocity, and yet their validation as teachers rests in the learning and formation of students and, ultimately, on the success of those who choose a path of ministry. But teachers will have no reliable means of predicting the outcome of their teaching until they knock down the walls of privatization and open up the castles of their classrooms to the invigorating light of collegial collaboration.

Implications for Practice

"We teach as we were taught" is the conventional wisdom. The statement contains some truth. Graduate education is a process of formation for future faculty members—a kind of professional training, though academics hate to think of it as such. Many new faculty members learn to imitate their graduate teachers, especially their doctoral advisors, reducing scholarship to research. They copy their teachers' lecture styles; they adopt their manner and questions in seminars. They begin their teaching careers trained in what could be called the observation method, copying through trial and error that which they have experienced. Such observation is a necessary but not a sufficient step in learning to teach. It is much like expecting a patient who has gone through many operations to get up from the table and begin to operate on other patients.

Fortunately, some graduate faculties have instituted apprenticeship programs, either formal or informal. Apprenticeship is a well-tested method by which most people throughout history have learned their special craft—parent to child, craftsman to craftsman, teacher to student. It assumes that graduate students who participate in active teaching with a skilled teacher will develop skills and a disciplined reflection on their experience. Reflection on teaching and learning by faculty and students in graduate school links basic research in the discipline with primary career goals in exemplary ways that avoids the unfortunate distinction between research and everything else that is one's career. The close linking of research and teaching enriches the results of research and enhances the quality and integrity of a teacher's life. The best graduate programs involve faculty and students in discussions of pedagogy, class sessions and course preparation, observations of teaching, and reflection, often in conjunction with the university's teaching and learning center.

The methods of observation and apprenticeship have met with more success than one might predict, but they alone are no longer adequate. Teachers and students no longer constitute homogeneous cultural groups. Theological students come from far more varied backgrounds and have far more varied life experiences than the students of previous periods. Teaching is more challenging, and more exciting, than it was a few decades ago. This new situation suggests that new approaches and greater attention to teaching and learning are required throughout a professor's career. An endemic problem with the apprenticeship method is that it is restricted to the pre-entry career stage as though teaching were a skill learned and thereafter applied rather than an art acquired through lifelong learning.

Collaboration in the art of teaching is more promising than either observation or apprenticeship (Shulman 1993, 6–7). Collaboration should be started early in doctoral study and should characterize the environment in colleges,
universities, and theological schools throughout a faculty member's career.
Apprenticeship for a brief period is a way to begin; collaboration with colleagues
throughout a career is the way to continue. Collaboration with colleagues
through structured discussions and projects is absolutely essential to the future
health and well-being of theological schools, faculties, and students. The goal
of collaboration is to enable colleagues to learn from each other and engage
in a common discourse about their life's work so that together they will
enhance the learning of their students.

The richest context for such collaboration is in local institutions, even
though it is surprisingly difficult to create a safe local space for discussions of
teaching and learning. Collaboration changes the discussion and evaluation of
teaching from summative judgments about salary, tenure, and promotion to
formative partnerships aimed at helping all teachers become better. It liberates
faculty members from the consumer mentality of institutions and the professional myopia of students and thus enables them to deal more creatively with
the particular missions of the institutions in which they teach. Moreover, collaboration enables teachers to return to the passions and virtues that led them
into teaching in the first place. Responses to recent works on the teacher's vocation by Parker Palmer and others reveal a yearning for reflection and discussion of the deeper issues of the teacher's calling.[1]

Collaboration in the art of teaching comes in many different forms. For
example, graduate faculty can gather in faculty meetings and at retreats to discuss ways of helping their doctoral students prepare for careers as teachers,
which in turn leads to faculty engaging in discussions with students about
course preparation, course syllabi, and the vocation of teaching. As another
example, a faculty member might invite a trusted colleague to discuss syllabi,
visit classes, and reflect about teaching. Such collaboration might develop
into a team teaching project that incorporates disciplined discussion of pedagogy and student learning. Further, deans can designate faculty meetings and
retreats for collaborative reflection about institutional mission, student learning goals, and teaching strategies. Larger schools can establish teaching and
learning centers; smaller institutions can affiliate with university centers or designate a faculty member to be a teaching fellow, encouraging and facilitating
reflection on teaching and learning. Faculty members can join workshops on
teaching and learning, such as those convened by the Wabash Center and The
Lexington Seminar, or they can develop workshops with their colleagues
(Barnes 1999). Faculty in a specific subdiscipline of theology and religion can
gather some guild colleagues to reflect on the challenges and mastery of teach-

ing a particular subject. Finally, deans and department chairs bear responsibility for regularly attending to the question, "What and how well are our students learning today?" They must work together to create an environment that encourages excellent teaching and learning for the benefit of their students.

Students and Learning

The first rule of good teaching is "Know your students!" And that means knowing how students in a class learn best and to what ends by clearly identifying their learning styles and their learning goals. It is increasingly important for teachers to understand and respond to these styles and goals, and yet at the same time it is growing increasingly difficult to achieve this understanding and make the appropriate responses, in part because the demographic profile of students is changing so rapidly. The demographic changes recorded on paper in the 2000 United States census are a lively presence in the classrooms of theological schools and universities, and these changes are likely to become more pronounced with the passage of time. Diverse learning styles, new ethnic and religious differences, new student expectations and market demands, age variations, and divergent theological commitments make classrooms and institutions exciting and sometimes conflicted places, leading faculty to fall into an odd kind of cynicism mixed with haughty self-congratulation: "I'm okay, you're okay, students are awful."

Theological teachers may know their students better than teachers in other secular institutions, but they often know the wrong things in the wrong ways. The openness and sharing characterized by some theological schools creates an ethos encouraging the lowering of boundaries and the sharing of knowledge about personal matters that is sometimes mistaken for answers to the questions that faculty really need to ask: How do these students learn? What goals do they seek? How can we enable their success?

It may be helpful to note why current students' experiences are so different from their teachers when they were students and why they may be resistant to what teachers are trying to help them learn. Many teachers were socialized in relatively stable social and religious contexts—cradle Christians, secure homes, liberal arts education, stable churches, relatively straight career paths. Teaching for such students was intended to pass them through a refining fire of doubt and criticism. Few students now enjoy such previous securities. Some arrive in seminaries with identities formed in the midst of postmodern struggles with fragmentation, broken homes, broken communities, broken churches, and broken worlds. Many craft a personal identity that is no assured thing, but is instead fragile and hard won, a personal accomplishment grasped desperately with faith. Other students come from strong and diverse communities, often minority communities with personal creeds and conduct foreign to those of most faculty members. Both groups of students may, with good reason, suspect that what teachers call transformation will separate them from all that they hold dear, even their faith.

A teacher attending The Lexington Seminar conference in Maine described the process desired for students as the movement from enchantment to disenchantment to re-enchantment, bringing to mind Paul Ricoeur's description of first naiveté, then the necessary critique, and then, God willing, a second naiveté (1967, 352). What is missing in these simple descriptions of the process is the pain and suffering that attend the transformation of students, pain and suffering that all good teachers remember, understand, and heed, and with which they must help their students cope.

W. E. B. DuBois captured the pain and suffering of transformation in "On the Coming of John," published in *Souls of Black Folks* ([1903] 1996, 230–251). Two Johns, one black and one white, returned home from northern colleges to the same small Southern town. Both curiously had become prodigal sons through education. The son of the local judge—white, aristocratic, and wealthy—arrived from Princeton to his anticipated state of privilege, though not without pain. The black son returned from a technical institute to be met at the railroad station by his family and church members and taken to the Baptist church for a joyous welcome. Pushed reluctantly behind the pulpit, he talked about things that had become important to him. But he had changed so much that he spoke in "an unknown tongue" learned at college and could not make connections with his people. He made the mistake of saying that the difference between Baptists and Methodists about baptism was not important. In response, an elderly black deacon stood up and "seized the Bible with his rough, huge hands; twice he raised it inarticulate, and then fairly burst into words, with rude and awful eloquence," but John "never knew clearly what the old man said." An awful chasm! John passed silently into the night. When his little sister joined him, John wept on her shoulder. "John," she said, "does it make everyone unhappy when they study and learn lots of things?" He paused and smiled, "I am afraid it does," he said. "And, John, are you glad you studied?" "Yes," came the answer, slowly but positively.

One message of the story is that everyone stands on the shoulders of their forebears to see more than those forebears could see. Teachers prepare students for an unknown future, and neither teachers nor students should forget that they do not learn in order to know; rather, they know in order to learn, which is always the forward movement in real education.

But never forget the pain involved. Remembering that pain should cause teachers to take off their dirty shoes when entering the classroom because they tread on holy ground.

A teacher's work is based on a fundamental ethical imperative that arises from a basic human characteristic: relationship. Humans are social creatures and cannot exist without social relationships that provide language, existence, and meaning. Each is impelled to intrude into the lives of others with word, touch, signs, and much more, and, moreover, to receive the other into a personal sphere of existence. Only so can one be human. It is part of the social contract. Each class of teacher and students constitutes a specialized interpretive community with its own rules, ethics, boundaries, and goals. Students and teachers enter into it willingly and, one hopes, with a sense of calling to human and social good.

IMPLICATIONS FOR PRACTICE

One of the narratives from The Lexington Seminar (Colgate Rochester Crozer Divinity School 2002)[2] refers to the need for "compassionate pedagogy," a concept teachers should ponder throughout their careers. The first challenge of compassionate pedagogy is to know the students and their learning styles and goals. The most important step is to move from the current emphasis on summative assessment that results in final grades, mailed after the opportunity for engaged learning ends, to formative assessment that helps faculty learn how to teach better and students learn how to learn better.

Adult learning, which is the context and focus of theological education, has been the focus of much research and reflection in the past couple of decades, and many useful resources on developmental stages and adult learning exist. Two books of particular value are *Intelligence Reframed: Multiple Intelligences for the 21st Century* (Gardner 1999) and *The New Update on Adult Learning Theory* (Merriam 2001). Further, theological faculties can and should participate in workshops and seminars on adult learning.

Research on diversity and the effect it has on learning styles has also begun to appear and should be used by theological faculty to help broaden their teaching strategies. Numerous classroom strategies are available to faculty members who wish to find out how their students learn, what their goals and aspirations are, and how well they are learning at any given point in a course. In fact, theological faculty are in a particularly sound position to make valuable contributions in the scholarship of teaching.

All such research and scholarly endeavors enable a teacher to better meet the first requirement for good teaching: "Know your students!"

DISCIPLINES AND CONTENT

Many of The Lexington Seminar narratives demonstrate a struggle with the character of the theological disciplines in search of the elusive virtues of integration and relevance. Students move from class to class and from assignment to assignment searching for the unity that will create from their courses a curricular relevance to lived religion that is the context for their life and vocation. Theological disciplines are mere skeletons of their former selves, being malnourished by narrow specialization, fragmentation, postmodern critique, and secularization in many theological schools and Ph.D. programs. Attention to the breadth, grandeur, and unity of the theological disciplines is essential to the integrity and relevance of theological teaching.

The study of theology and religion is the most compelling of all disciplines in higher education because it reveals fundamental aspects of value and commitment, encompassing all humans through time and place and engaging many critical methods developed and honed through the centuries of the Western tradition. These methods constitute a genealogy of disciplines, mansions of human creativity; they are our cultural and religious heritage, and their proper use and maintenance is crucial to individuals, church, and society, because throughout time, across space, and in every culture, religion has functioned to ground individual and group identity in a transcendent reality that anchors identity and preserves it.

Theological teaching and learning is at the apex of humane study because such teaching and learning develop directly out of a fundamental characteristic of humanity. Humans are creatures who create, bear, manipulate, and transmit symbols. As a species, humans are instinctually deprived, but they are culturally creative and social as a direct evolutionary necessity stemming from that deprivation. Hence, humans can inhabit a broad ecological niche stretching from the heavens to the depths of the sea. We humans create meaning and accomplish most of what we do culturally rather than instinctually. Our survival depends upon it. All forms of teaching and learning, especially as the acts of relatively free social beings, emerge from that basic human necessity to create and communicate meaning through culture. Hence, theological teachers are formative agents of a fundamental human capacity.

Religious and theological systems are universally generated out of that symbol-creating capability and that human striving for meaning and identity which makes theological teaching one of the most conservative and, at the same time, one of the most transformative of human activities. The creation of religious symbols testifies to a human striving for survival and meaning that requires us to transcend ourselves in all that we do. Religion and theology represent the self-reflexive aspect of human creativity that symbol creation makes possible and encourages. One might well argue in theological terms that this is what makes humans "in the image of God" and enables them to receive and interpret revelation from God. Alas, we bear this treasure in earthen vessels.

Religion's power arises by providing a transcendent basis for personal and group identity in relation to God and divine revelation. Most individuals and groups throughout human history have self-identified themselves in relation to a set of beliefs and practices, anchored in a transcendent realm, that encompasses their fundamental social relationships. The relevance of religion is demonstrated by the human tendency to couch their basic commitments, value systems, worldviews, and mores in religious terms. These enable believers to be, in their own and in God's terms, strong and good. Transcendence gives them the power to stand firm against many earthbound pressures to be "confirmed to this world." A sobering caution, however, is that this power can be divine or demonic and that the only antidote for the demonic is the divine. The only cure for bad, dangerous religion is good, salvific religion. That is ultimately what is at stake in theological teaching and learning.

The importance, breadth, and depth of both the content of the theological disciplines and the methods that have been developed to study them constitute the *raison d'être* of the theological teacher. Stephen Webb (2000) argues convincingly that the old distinction between research and teaching is a false one. He indicates that teaching itself is a way of researching the very ideas we are teaching, of experimenting with various modes of thought, of translating thought into practice. Teaching is not mere application; it is not a matter of distributing information that has been gathered elsewhere. Teaching itself affects the way we think, the way we research, the way we live. To teach is to reveal. To educate is to create ways in which self-revelation can enable the other to explore and discover new fields and new ways of thinking and being. Indeed, teaching is the highest form of understanding.

Four aspects of the understanding of religion are present in the apprehension of religious experience. The first is the primary religious experience often associated with myth, symbol, faith, discipline, and ritual found in faith communities. A second aspect is reflection on the experience in theological and pastoral work and in the legal and ethical prescriptions for community order appropriate to the theological seminary. A third aspect is critical analysis in a discourse in the academy about the first and second aspects that often distances the student from the specific traditions studied. The fourth aspect is evaluation and appropriation, either positive or negative, of what is studied for the living of one's own life and vocation. Each of the first three has its own primary social community: the church, the seminary, and the college. The fourth, of course, is at the heart of Christian discipleship.

The theological teacher in a seminary or divinity school is engaged in the richest study of religion at all levels from the perspective of commitment within a particular Christian tradition. These exalted claims for theologians of the church fly in the face of Kierkegaard's critique of those who think that they "go farther." Johannes de Silentio's dictum (Kierkegaard 1954, 21–25) criticizes those who think that the easiest thing in the world is to go farther than faith, to develop analytic and academic systems that will permit them to go farther than the first level of religious experience. It is not easy, but theological study reaches for the highest levels of human reflexivity about symbol, meaning, and identity creation. Thus, one might call the academic study of religion and theology the queen of the human sciences, striving toward the divine.

Theological teachers occupy a special place in the church as conservators, critics, and creators of a theological and pastoral tradition. They are always caught in a basic hermeneutical tension between what goes without saying in a church, what can be said, and what will be said. The tension between experience from the past and imagination for the future, between conservation of a heritage and the creation of new possibilities, must be worked out in the intellectual and religious biography of each theological teacher and student. Education is both celebration and quest, hence, the ambiguous position of teachers and students in any society and church as they are, at one and the same time, conservators in the custodial class and its institutionalized critics. Excellent theological teachers provide a space in which students can do their own thinking about the tradition and their vocation; they also provide resources and examples to assure that students do their thinking in the best of company.

To be sure, it is possible to structure and teach theological studies in a dull and lifeless manner by wringing out all passion, expansiveness, and significance, but that is more difficult with theology and religion than with most other subjects. Unfortunately, some teaching practices conspire to narrow the vision and reduce the effectiveness of theological education. For example, graduate study can be made increasingly narrow and irrelevant, church theologians can be stultified through guild professionalization, curriculum decisions can be governed by turf wars, inappropriate pedagogies can reduce an exciting discipline to rote learning, and ill-directed reward systems can encourage all of the above.

Theological teachers must enter through a narrow gate of doctoral study, and it seems that graduate study has become more deformative than formative, both personally and professionally, over the past few decades. Scholarships and fellowships provide smaller portions of the funding, so more students are forced to work at marginal, low-paying jobs to cover their costs. The opportunities for secure tenure-track teaching positions have been reduced, resulting in an increased competition for credentials that is often counterproductive. Increasingly narrow specialization limits vision. Graduate students are expected to present papers at scholarly meetings, publish articles, gain extensive teaching experience, and, if possible, sign a book contract before they are elevated slightly to the position of "junior faculty" with all the status liabilities that designation implies. Such deformation of candidates and younger colleagues in the profession appears to be a culture-wide experience shared by young lawyers, physicians, clergy, teachers, and others. The deserts of graduate education expand, and the promised land of entry into the profession grows more parched.

A significant goal of doctoral education should be to produce theological teachers and theologians of the church who are able to be faithful in their work of conservation, critique, and creation in a lively religious and theological tradition. Graduates also become public intellectuals who serve an increasingly important function to negotiate the role of religion and its institutions in the public sphere. That requires preserving a creative balance in graduate schools of the pastoral virtue of chastened, normative, faith-based proclamation and the academic virtue of neutral, objective investigation for its own sake. It is unfortunate that the role of the academic critic of religion is increasingly thought to require secular commitments by some who, at the worst, despise religion, disdain religious people, and denigrate the church, or at the least, are noncommittal.

It is particularly unfortunate when theological schools, created to house the theologians of the church and to educate ministers for the church, duplicate the ethos of secular doctoral programs. It is a shame when theological teachers and schools sell their birthright for a mess of pottage. Guild professionalization and identification directs the talents and creativity of theological teachers, through jargon and syntax understood by only a handful of like-minded colleagues, toward topics that bear little relevance to the life of the church, the faith of Christians, or the social good. These same guild identifications become the battle lines for curriculum discussions that are little more than turf wars, what one wag has called "the intramural sport of faculty." The pedagogical corollaries are obsessive coverage of huge amounts of data, learning styles based on information retention, and summative assessment of both faculty and students through objective tests or standardized measures. Thus theological schools adopt reward systems defined by guild expectations and preserved by status differentiations of entrenched, unimaginative faculty and administrators. Straining at gnats!

IMPLICATIONS FOR PRACTICE

A bleak and perhaps overdrawn picture of a starved discipline nevertheless points to some constructive steps that theological teachers and schools could take to preserve their birthright in the power and relevance of theological teaching for the church. Graduate schools could focus more intently on educating church theologians who are conservators, critics, and creators of a theological heritage. Changes in degree programs, curricula, and courses would focus the efforts of students more consonantly with the breadth and power of religion than narrow subdiscipline specialties. The theological teachers and theological schools would have to reexamine their reward systems to make sure that they reinforce rather than pervert the grand work of theological exploration and creativity and the grander work of preparing Christian ministers who can serve the church faithfully. Graduate programs rarely focus on integration and relevance, nor on pedagogy and teaching. Time and resources are needed to permit faculty to catch up with contemporary challenges and demands, which inevitably leads to a new focus on teaching. In fact, one of the discoveries of The Lexington Seminar is that attention to pedagogy not only reveals new ways of engaging students and understanding the vocation of the theological teacher, it also generates a renewed passion for the theological discipline itself.

CONCLUSION

The spotlight has shone on three elements: teachers, students, and theology as a discipline. What is next?

The spotlight could better illumine theological study if it moved back a bit to focus on the institution as the unifying agency for discipline, teaching, and learning. Note that this is not a call for one more fragmentation of the image, adding a fourth component separate from faculty responsibility. What is needed is a more unified image of the teaching/learning process. The focus should be on the theological school as a unified learning organization and an enabling environment for excellent teaching. The goal is to pull together the highest vision of the theological disciplines in the service of the church's mission, the excellence of diverse teachers who together see their work as teaching scholars and theologians in the church as one calling, and the aspirations and abilities of their students as learners so that they will in their work as ministers be conservators, critics, and creators of a lively and life-giving heritage. The goal is to provide an enabling ethos for excellent theological teaching and learning, a worthy mission for theological schools and a compelling vocation for theological teachers.

NOTES

1. See Palmer (1993; 1997; 2000), Daloz (1996), and Parks (2000).
2. All narratives cited in this book can be found in the Archives section of the Seminar's Web site: http://www.lexingtonseminar.org/.

·VICTOR KLIMOSKI·

Evolving Dynamics of Formation

In 1968 I began seminary training to become a Roman Catholic priest. Twenty of us from throughout the upper Midwest composed that year's entering class. All of us came from families of Northern European descent who were active in the local parish. Sixteen were from communities in which they were born and from the parishes in which they had been baptized. Eighteen of us had some level of pre-seminary training ranging from four to six years. Without looking at our transcripts, faculty knew we each had an undergraduate degree anchored in liberal arts with philosophy or theology as a major field of study. Most of us had completed extensive studies in Latin and Greek and could read French or German. We had a broad knowledge of the Bible, its history, and the principles of interpretation. We knew the major dogmas of the church and had been formed in the devotional pieties of Catholicism of the pre–Vatican II era. In addition to our knowledge base, we had well-developed skills in writing and knew how to turn out a properly structured research paper.

Seventeen of the twenty were twenty-three years old. The oldest was thirty, and only two had had a career prior to deciding to enter seminary. We all lived in the same residence hall, following a daily way of life with a rhythm that held us accountable to be in specified places at specified times—no exceptions allowed. We were disposed to learn from our faculty what sort of priests we should become and looked to them to help us interpret the meaning of the changes set in motion by the Second Vatican Council. Apart from the great cultural shifts that were beginning to occur, the entering class of 1968 was very much like the other sixty seminarians at St. John's Seminary in Collegeville who were much like the generations that had preceded them. The faculty could presume without knowing who we were as individuals that we shared a fairly common degree of intellectual and spiritual homogeneity. Further, they could presume that having been raised in and by the church, we were coming to Collegeville to gain insight into *why* we believed as Catholics—not to learn *what* we believed as Catholics.

This anecdote resonates across other denominational seminaries. While faculties are probably overly presumptive to believe that students several generations back were all at the same starting point, they are essentially correct in believing that most students shared a common foundation. Even the most casual review of seminary students today produces a different panorama. Seminary students today tend to be older and have a wide range of life experiences and lessons learned from other careers. They are increasingly diverse racially and ethnically, and nearly half are women. They may or may not have had a durable relationship with a parish or congregation prior to their sense of vocational call and may or may not have been raised in churched families or families that were intact. They often lack writing and research skills and approach the tasks of critical thinking defensively or with an attitude that every opinion is worthy because it is someone's opinion. Their undergraduate work reflects the national drift from a liberal arts core to specializations in fields not immediately germane to the study of theology. As they begin their seminary work, many of today's students are seeking information and skills needed to be a pastor and not a vision of the church and ministry in mission. As a result, theory is too quickly disconnected from practice.

This generation of students seems to have a fairly clear notion of the ministerial identity *they* will claim and the relationship *they* will have with the church. They often display a high sense of personal altruism but a low sense of interdependence. They are eager to minister but not disposed to lead, finding the work of one-to-one counseling or preaching or leading worship far more congenial than the public tasks of calling forth the ministries of the baptized or engaging the issues of the wider community. They are tentatively receptive to the wisdom of the faculty and are not at all reluctant to declare a scholar as unorthodox because she or he does not share the same view of the Bible or tradition that the student holds. Increasingly, seminary students live off campus, are trying to manage a marriage and family, sometimes have the challenge of single parenting, work at other jobs to support themselves, serve a congregation in some capacity, and worry about the debt they are carrying from their undergraduate studies. And, yes, they want to serve the church.

This composite picture, which may be overdrawn but touches on much we have heard in The Lexington Seminar, suggests that uniformity in students' backgrounds is generally gone. The narrative from United Theological Seminary of the Twin Cities (2001)[1] offers a good illustration. At the core of the story is a student's complaint about the final integrative exam. As she lays out her case, drawing on her own experience and that of other students she knows, we begin to see that the way in which this student, who is a thirty-year-old lesbian from an evangelical background and still uncertain about her denominational affiliation, understands and strives for integration is not the same as that followed by the divorced student in her mid-forties from a rural community who is a student pastor or the forty-year-old white male who tends to keep real engagement in the issues at arm's length or the older African American woman married to a pastor and very involved in her local Methodist church. Each is attending seminary for different reasons and each brings a distinct background that shapes his or her understanding of and ability to demonstrate "integration."

While the diversity and apparent unpreparedness of today's students to begin seminary study often evokes laments among faculty members, it does not mean that theological education is compromised. What it does mean, however, is that faculty must do more than just teach their topics—as they imagined they would do when they were in graduate school. As a character in the Bethel Theological Seminary (2001) narrative says to another faculty member, "Do you realize . . . that once I set a foundation for what we're doing, I only have time in a quarter to spend about ten minutes on each chapter of the Gospels? If I start stealing time from that to deal with these 'process things' [issues in students' lives that have become public], the students will leave here underprepared to do the kind of work they're going to be asked to do. Besides, they come here expecting to get a lot of content." While the student issues raised in the Bethel narrative are not new to seminary life—ideological rigidity and problems in a marriage—they represent the host of issues that push and pull at students as they enter the traditional, formal process of preparation for ministry. The resulting tension cannot be ignored and has encouraged a new look at the need for explicit strategies of formation.[2]

This essay explores formation as a point of focus in ministerial education. That focus obviously targets students, but my experience with participating schools in The Lexington Seminar suggests that formation needs to include the faculty as well. It is tempting to think of formation as a way to "fix" students who are differently and diversely prepared to study for the ministry. Faculty teams in the Seminar, however, have often discovered that their own formation is critical if they are to help their students form themselves for the work of professional ministry. In its summary of the Seminar experience, the team from Pacific Lutheran Theological Seminary (2001) noted that one insight they had gained about themselves as a faculty was that they happened to be a group of people who worked in the same building, but they had yet to form themselves as a community. This conclusion resonates with a principle point in this essay: Formation, if it is to have a transformative effect, cannot be relegated to a chaplain or the pastoral care office but must flow throughout the institution and find expression in the classroom as well as the chapel. In what follows, I offer a working understanding of formation, suggest six observations about formation as constitutive of seminary education, and explore implications for the work of teaching and learning.

THE CALL TO ATTENTIVENESS

As I listen to schools grappling with the challenges of formation for ministry and reflect on my own experience as a dean in a school where formation played a dominant role, I am drawn to the conclusion that formation is about processes and practices that sharpen one's attentiveness. *Paying attention* is an ancient admonition for those seeking wisdom in many religious traditions. Certainly, my life as a student at St. John's in Collegeville and now as a member of the staff has been formed in this call to alertness that is so much a part of the *Rule of St. Benedict.* Being attentive is important in all aspects of a person's growth and development. First and foremost, it means being attentive to the movement of God in one's life, through the Word, and in the tradition one bears. When we are advised to listen for God's voice, it means we need to be still. We need the ability to let go of our conclusions long enough to grasp the sorts of questions that should dog our steps. This aspect of attentiveness is key to cultivating spiritual depth of character and maintaining one's spiritual center in the midst of life's multiple demands.

Formation also includes paying attention to the expanding vision of a graced world discovered in the disciplined study of theology and scripture. The rigorous study of the Bible, church history, Christian teaching, or worship bring the learner and the teacher into intimate contact with a long tradition of seeking to understand God's self-revelation. While the canons of the Enlightenment and the German model of graduate training insist on an objective pursuit of the truth, the seminary classroom is always a place of wonder, of standing in awe before the mystery of God that we apprehend bit by bit. Alexander Schmemann has written that the study of theology is always an act of worship for it is an encounter with the very experience of the mysteries of God, and that encounter demands a response.[3]

Two other dimensions of formation have specific reference to students and bear on the formative work within the faculty. The first has to do with taking on the identity of a minister—not the external trappings and privileges of the office—but the profound sense of identity that comes from conforming oneself as a servant of the gospel. For some this boils down pragmatically to learning what a minister should do. It is a formulaic approach to ministry. When one *embodies* an identity as minister, however, it means subjecting one's preferences to gospel norms. It means learning that collaboration and interdependence are cultivated dispositions of the heart that require discipline to restrain oneself from bulling ahead on one's agenda despite the circumstances. Embodiment of identity means learning to "think like a minister," an adaptation of Schon's notion of reflective practice that draws one beyond a collection of skills to an artfulness attentive to time and place, persons and circumstances, and the wisdom of God's word ever present.[4]

Second, formation includes cultivating attentiveness to the expectations required for skillful public leadership. In recent years some have asserted that, as valuable as clinical pastoral education has been in seminary life, it has endorsed unwittingly a therapeutic approach to pastoral care that can shift attention from the community to the individual. Whether that is the case is perhaps debatable. What does seem clear is that candidates for the ministry find greater appeal in pastoral work that involves one-to-one relationships than in those aspects of ministry that include forming and sustaining a community of active believers, calling forth the gifts of the baptized, and empowering people for witness and service in the world. What it means to be a pastor cannot be disconnected from what it means to be a leader, and this is a matter for formation.

Six Observations about Formation as an Institutional Practice

Embedded in the notion of attentiveness are the core elements in the life of a theological seminary: academic training, pastoral development, and spiritual and human growth.

While there is little disagreement about the significance of the elements involved in preparing the church's ministers, there is no corresponding unanimity regarding how formation formally fits into a school's culture and ethos around these core elements or whether formation is primarily about personal spirituality and only secondarily related to academic study and pastoral training. Six observations I have gleaned from my experience and my work with The

Lexington Seminar might help inform the conversations that are certain to continue regarding the institutional character of formation.

1. Prepared Differently and Diversely

To suggest that we appreciate today's students as prepared "differently and diversely" for seminary studies is not an attempt to put a happy face on an unfortunate situation. In an ideal world, would St. John's School of Theology prefer that all its incoming students have the same academic and family backgrounds that my colleagues and I had in 1968? Probably. The study of theology and scripture in preparation for church ministry is enriched when people have a broad intellectual background that rests on a foundation anchored in the practices of the church. Focusing on what we might perceive as student deficiencies, however, can impede a faculty's ability to identify approaches that develop students' critical appreciation of Christian tradition and revelation. This is in part a pedagogical challenge that depends on a faculty's openness to new models of instructional practice suited for professional education in which preparation for ministerial practice is not viewed as intellectually compromised.

Although the renaissance in higher education for teaching excellence offers an abundance of resources, the starting point is learning from students themselves how they have been prepared. Claremont School of Theology undertook such a project as the faculty sought to understand, through their Lexington Seminar narrative (2000), the dilemma facing a fictional student who finds himself caught in the gray area between the deconstruction of his beliefs and the work of creating a new synthesis. In addressing the issues expressed in the narrative, the faculty recognized that they needed to understand more fully their students' sequence of theological education. Thus, they designed a process that invited a representative group of incoming M.Div. students to meet with two faculty members over the course of the year to describe what that process of taking apart and putting back together was like. Each session began with the simple request, "Tell us about your experience so far at Claremont." The faculty team listened, asking questions only when in need of clarification. The team then reviewed each interview and culled the themes for presentation to their colleagues. This example of faculty attentiveness takes seriously the experience of the students as a valid insight into the impact of the learning systems a school creates.

That said, the need to change attitudes from lament about what students often lack in background to an appreciation of what they bring to their work as learners does not suggest that standards should become thin as water. On the contrary, for formation to work faculty need to be clear on what it takes for a student to succeed academically, pastorally, personally, and spiritually as a ministerial leader in the church. All the listening in the world will not compensate for the absence in students of the requisite talent and disposition to respond.

2. Formation as a Way of Being a Seminary

For formation to be a transformative force in institutional life, it cannot be relegated to a department but needs to become a way of being a school. In the Bethel Seminary narrative cited earlier, the professor complaining about a suggestion that he help students process their personal issues retorts that it is not his job: "That's why we have a Student Life Office. You are the ones who should deal with these things." In one way he is correct, for schools need persons with special expertise in counseling students on personal and spiritual issues. Such persons are also a resource to faculty as they come to understand that as teachers they are formators. As the Bethel Seminary narrative shows, the manifestation of rigidity or the intrusion of personal problems cannot be compartmentalized. Such personal issues can easily shift the point of balance in learning situations and require attention. This does not mean that each faculty person needs to be a therapist, but he or she needs to be attentive to how personal matters affect encounters with course content and how he or she is frequently the person best situated to guide students to deeper insight into self and into the issues with which they grapple.

The pervasiveness of formation as a way of being a school can become chaotic if there is no consensus about the explicit criteria for determining what adequate preparation for ministerial leadership looks like. Faculty members each bring their own assumptions about what those criteria are. Some have criteria that are clear, specific, and—sometimes—non-negotiable. Others may only care that students do their work and not be disruptive in class. Still others judge adequate formation on the basis of whether they like or dislike the students personally: Could this person be my minister? That sort of variability does not contribute to the transformative potential of formation and sends a contrary message to students about the formative expectations of the school. Should students be able to demonstrate a capacity to draw critically on their studies in discussing and analyzing pastoral dilemmas? Do the ways in which students interact with one another, talk about one another, relate to faculty, administration, or staff matter? Is grade point average the sole determining criteria in assessing whether a candidate for ministry has demonstrated the capacity to exercise public leadership? Coming to agreement on such criteria is demanding work and accounts for the eagerness to delegate the "formation stuff" to a department or office. Doing so, I contend, keeps formation at the periphery of a school's life and encourages students to believe it to be as inconsequential as they perceive their teachers do.

When formation is a way of being a school, a notable shift occurs in the design of courses and field experiences. Faculty and administrators think of creative ways in which the work of the curriculum can explicitly embody the formation criteria the faculty determine are important for preparing the church's ministers. Connections are created and clearly modeled among the various courses and learning experiences that define a student's program of study so that she or he is constantly challenged to pay attention to how the various elements cohere. At The Lexington Seminar, the team from United Theological Seminary of the Twin Cities grappled with a common problem: How do we enable students notably different in their approaches to learning and formation to demonstrate integration? That question has engaged the whole UTS faculty in a discussion of what indicators are key signs of program integration. Examples of the indicators include the following:

- The student demonstrates accountability for his or her own learning process and decisions.
- The student is able to understand and articulate both the particularity of his or her own cultural, familial, religious, and personal stories as well as the resonance and dissonance with others' stories as social and cultural narratives.
- The student is able to articulate his or her own theology of ministry, drawing on core curricular areas.

More significantly, perhaps, is the fact that the faculty is considering the pedagogical implications of such a list. How will they teach differently so that students can gain the knowledge, skills, and abilities the indicators reflect? Thus, as a result of faculty consensus on its criteria, formation gains institutional footing and begins to reshape curricular design.

Finally, I contend that formation has become a way of being a school when the awarding of a Master of Divinity or pastoral ministry degree is contingent on the student's response to formation in all its dimensions—academic, pastoral, spiritual, and human development. That means that a student who carries a 4.0 grade point average but demonstrates few other attributes for pastoral leadership will not be able to complete the degree. If we offer no accountability for a degree as a sign of one's suitability for professional ministry, the degree is lopsided at best, misleading at worst.

3. FORMATION AND STUDENT RESPONSE

Those who work closely with formation report that few students come to seminary seeking formation. They may assent to the idea, but they begin to resist when it poses questions they would rather not hear or raises issues they would prefer to avoid. If formation includes being attentive to the movement of God in one's life and listening to the needs of the church, it is only natural that what the student imagines she will be as a minister may rub up against what the church actually needs in its ordained and professional ministers. The same holds true as the student begins to mark out how she or he will relate to denominational officials. Negotiating between personal preferences and desires and those of the larger community is part of the formational task. Can I be a pastor in situations in which people think and see the world differently than I do? Am I able to collaborate appropriately with denominational officers? Can I share leadership with members of my congregation as we work in partnership? Can I deal with the realization that my ways are not necessarily God's ways?

The answers to such questions are not always the ones that students want to hear. It is not easy to learn that some of one's behaviors have a negative impact on others and the community or to learn that one's view of the world, theology, ministry, the church, and what a pastor should do is incomplete or misinformed. Formation is about change, and change can be painful. As a result, faculties should not be surprised when students become disgruntled at being asked to take a closer look at their conclusions about the sort of minister they intend to be. Students like to be affirmed, but they also need to be attentive. A formative atmosphere, created and sustained by the faculty, makes both affirmation and challenge equally productive. But it may not make students immediately happy.

Because student satisfaction plays such a strong role in decisions about seminary life, schools may be hesitant about giving formational feedback. Will too much directness—even spoken out of love—motivate a student to switch schools? This is not a trivial question in an age when every tuition dollar is precious. But the resolution is not a matter of being more or less direct. The invitation of students into a formational process needs to be adult in every way possible so that there is mutual understanding from the very first day about how the seminary and the student work cooperatively to achieve the ultimate aims of formation. This includes ensuring that students and faculty share an understanding of what formation means—that it includes, for instance, both growth in the spiritual life (often the student's assumption) and demonstrated progress in attaining the attributes of one who will lead as a pastor. In its indicators of integration, United Theological Seminary of the Twin Cities clearly expects students to take responsibility for their own growth and development even while the faculty is poised to provide the intellectual, spiritual, and personal resources needed to support that process.

4. FORMATION AND ASSESSMENT

The assessment movement in higher education has made schools increasingly aware of the need to measure and justify what they are doing. That is a reductionist view of assessment, but it does help emphasize the need to determine whether what we do has the intended impact. Academic and pastoral formation lend themselves to measurability in ways that spiritual and human growth formation do not, which is why the efforts of a faculty to determine formation criteria are so important. Such criteria may be fairly broad. For example, consider the following criterion from a draft of *Indicators of Integration* developed by United Theological Seminary of the Twin Cities: "Demonstrates awareness of their personal strengths and limitations and takes responsibility for their own emotional health."[5] As faculty discuss how such a criterion might be manifested, members begin asking assessment questions. What will the student need to know? How might she or he act? How might students describe their growth as they move through the program? Who can help us see students in relationship to this criterion? Such a discussion may help faculty realize that a formation criterion sounds good but does not enjoy shared meaning within the faculty. Or faculty may discover that there are no ways to determine whether a student is responding to what the criterion specifies. Students may not know what the criterion means or what they should be doing in regard to it. This aspect of assessment analysis can have an invigorating effect on a school as it helps faculty think together about what they expect of students. Furthermore, as they examine the criteria they establish, faculty also reflect on what is happening in courses and other learning experiences that equip students to meet formation criteria.

5. FORMATION AND THE CHURCH

The church is sometimes a distant partner in the preparation of candidates for ministry. Some of that distance results from the implicit trust of the denomination in the expertise of the seminary. Some results from the seminary's reluctance to let the church become too deeply involved in the functions of the seminary. Formation, especially in regard to cultivating the identity of a minister as pastoral leader, is an excellent forum in which the seminary and the church can work closely together. Church leaders and denominational officers need to understand the challenges of seminary formation in all its dimensions and the reasons that standards are often rigorous and demanding. At the same time, seminary faculties need to be in intimate communication with denominational leaders, exemplary pastors, professional ministers, and lay leaders about the life of the church in the world-as-it-is.

In that dialogue, I contend, is the vision for new models of seminary formation that bridge the weary argument of whether students need more theology or more preaching. They need both in a way that equips them as agents of transformation in their congregations and parishes. To do that, seminaries need to have the full support of their constituents, and their constituents need to learn the costs of forming the type of pastoral leaders they seek. An example of a seminary that is attempting to maintain a healthy dialogue with its constituents is that of Pacific Lutheran Theological Seminary, which, as part of its project for The Lexington Seminar, invited bishops in its service region to be part of a lecture series, thus encouraging the bishops to meet with faculty and students and discuss issues the bishops face in their leadership roles.

6. Formation as a Lifelong Process

As formation matures in a school as a way of life, it should become evident that this way of being a school models a lifelong process, not just a procedure for being ordained or credentialed for ministry. Being attentive, obviously, is not a practice for students alone nor is it something one does only in the seminary. Among the benefits in being in a formation environment are that students ideally gain (1) the skills and disciplines for self-assessment, (2) an appreciation for the role of mentors, and (3) an openness to change and adaptation as they engage the work of ministry, attentive to the lessons it continually teaches about being a disciple, about creating community, and about being a leader who calls forth the leadership of others for the sake of the gospel. In a 1987 study of assessment of the professions, Joan Stark and her colleagues (Stark, Lowther, and Haggerty 1987) identified six clusters of competencies for professional development.[6] One of them was the degree to which graduates of a professional school were able to adapt to changing circumstances encountered in the practice of the profession. Someone has remarked that seminaries are excellent at helping students become very good seminarians. The speaker, a seminary professor, was not as sure seminaries were as skilled at helping them become excellent pastors and professional ministers. A view of formation as a lifetime process positions graduates to live a life of attentiveness because it has been in the rhythms of their experience since the time they were students.

IMPLICATIONS FOR TEACHING AND LEARNING

These six observations about formation relate in large measure to those processes and expectations faculties create for students as a way of helping them develop a pattern of life undergirded by a keen sense of attentiveness. Much of the conversation in seminaries today focuses on what we need to do for a population of students who have changed in some significant ways from those who preceded them twenty or thirty years ago. We know that students may not necessarily catch on as they proceed through the program, not because of their willfulness but more often because of the circumstances of their lives. As a character in the narrative of the Church Divinity School of the Pacific (2001) says to a student, "Preparation for ordained ministry is not only education and training, you know, but also formation. In fact, the traditional Anglican seminary approach has been described as 'formation by osmosis,' because so much of it has to do with studying and praying together in community."

In 1968, my classmates and I learned a great deal by osmosis. We dwelt together with sixty other seminarians in close quarters, following a common rhythm of life that taught us far more than we perhaps acknowledged. The osmotic approach no longer holds. The invitation to students to grow and change needs to be explicit, clear, and direct. Structures that served the osmotic phase of seminary training need to be reexamined and changed as radically as necessary in order that students might reap the greatest possible benefit from their experience in a formative environment.

The concern for the formation of students as pastors and ministers well equipped to lead congregations, deeply grounded in theology and scripture, trained in the arts of pastoral ministry, and committed to their spiritual and personal growth is an admirable addition to the agenda of seminary faculties. What we have learned in The Lexington Seminar, however, is that this concern does not stand alone as though it were a fix for students bearing deficits because of their backgrounds. Formation concerns reverberate throughout the system and have tended to lead schools participating in the Seminar to a new focus on the faculty itself.

Some of the participating schools offer dramatic examples of what happens. Eastern Baptist Theological Seminary (2000) came to the Seminar with a narrative filled with familiar concerns. How do we teach students to think theologically? How do we help students appreciate the value of the entire curriculum, especially the traditional disciplines, for ministry? How do we get students to buy in to our model of learning that proceeds from foundational courses to the treatment of more specialized topics? How do we engage students as the adult learners they are, some of whom are already serving congregations?

As the Eastern Baptist team processed its narrative in the Seminar, the focus shifted. Eastern was coming to the end of a major revision of its curriculum for which the questions noted above were very important. The faculty recognized that the design of the new curriculum had great potential. It would move from teaching-centered to learning-centered pedagogies, from a course-based to a competency-based curriculum, from reliance on GPAs and field evaluation to ongoing assessment and discernment throughout a student's time in the program, and from keeping spiritual and character competencies as external variables to making them integral to the curriculum itself. These are heady aspirations. As the time approached to implement this grand design, faculty began to ask, "Are *we* ready?"

> We were excited about the design and goals of the new curriculum, but in our hearts we really wanted someone else to deliver it. We weren't quite ready to give up old, familiar ways. We couldn't imagine what would take their place. We needed more than an engaging curriculum. . . . We needed to be converted as teachers and as learners. . . . We would need to go against ways of teaching and learning we had come to accept as good, necessary, and even right.

As a result of this insight into the faculty costs of designing a curriculum responsive to a changing student population, Eastern began to attend to the ongoing formation of its faculty. The school initiated a series of luncheons at which senior faculty nearing retirement were invited to reflect on their experience and the lessons learned. There were retreats and workshops designed to address needed faculty competencies if the curriculum was to achieve its purpose. The very first retreat, however, began by inviting faculty to reflect on how the change in curriculum would affect their spiritual and professional lives. In pairs, faculty members shared their anxieties about the changes they faced and prayed together over them. As a group, the faculty explored the range of costs associated with the changes that were ahead as they implemented the new curriculum and faced a series of dramatic institutional events. Issues they addressed included (1) accepting relationship as key to faithful teaching and learning, (2) learning the needs of students, (3) understanding the personal and institutional transformation required to begin new ways of teaching and learning, (4) relating to external partners, and (5) defining ways administrators could support the transition implicit in the new curriculum.

What Eastern has learned in this process has been underscored by several schools participating in The Lexington Seminar. Nothing of significance can happen in a school—including developing a vibrant formation environment—without cultivating significant personal and professional trust within the faculty itself. This may occur as a result of the day-to-day activities of faculty, but it is no more certain than "formation by osmosis." Too many stories are repeated by faculty in too many schools to deny that seminary life is often akin to being on a treadmill. Time is swallowed in great gulps by a host of activities, programs, and commitments that are individually good in their intent. Taken together, however, this host becomes oppressive. Small faculties spread themselves thin in efforts to be all things to those seeking theological knowledge and spiritual growth. A good portion of that responsiveness to needs stems from a spirit of altruism that one can only admire. But the truth of the matter is that many schools keep expanding programs and commitments in order to attract more students in order to raise more revenue in order to meet the rising costs of higher education. This is not a matter of being busy. For the most part, faculty understand that seminary life entails busyness. There is a difference, however, between being busy and feeling harried.

As schools wind themselves tightly with obligations that seem to multiply with little relation to one another, faculty disperse into those areas in which they have some measure of control. They dread meetings, they avoid volunteering for initiatives in which they might even have some interest, and they stop talking. What Eastern Baptist Theological Seminary discovered, along with several other schools participating in the Seminar, is that when space and time are provided for conversation, things happen. People begin to discover the depth of shared convictions, the real sources of disagreement and difference in perspectives, the network of support and encouragement that often lies dormant, and the capacity to get a lot of work done because the chatter of distancing oneself from the fray yields to substantial exchange of ideas, concerns, and—yes—feelings that reflect the richness of what it means to be people vocationally called to seminary teaching.

This has been the case for Associated Mennonite Biblical Seminary (2000) in its efforts to build faculty relationships. There faculty members have engaged a sustained discussion of how to define, nurture, and teach core concepts of Anabaptist/Mennonite theology in a school where a substantial percentage of students are not Mennonite. Weekly faculty luncheons organized around related topics have produced insight into the points of agreement and disagreement about what constitutes the Anabaptist/Mennonite tradition and vision. More importantly, such discussions have had a notable impact on faculty morale. As Associated Mennonite's president, Nelson Kraybill, stated in the seminary's project report, "Of my five years here, I experienced this past academic year as the one when the faculty most seemed to enjoy each other, came to faculty meetings in the best spirit, and seemed most energized for their work. . . . For the first time I have seen, faculty had a structured opportunity to learn what and how others teach."

Could this outcome at Associated Mennonite have occurred without a "structured opportunity"? Perhaps. But the general wisdom gained through the conversations encouraged by The Lexington Seminar indicates that such changes are most likely to occur with the aid of an intentional plan. Therefore, based on what we have learned during the course of The Lexington Seminar, I would propose the following strategies for consideration.

Develop a Faculty Formation Program

The process of developing a formation program for faculty requires a series of decisions. The first is a decision to address the obvious questions:

- Where will we find the time?
- How will we ever reach agreement on what to do or learn to enter into conversations that are not about business?
- How will this affect advancement to tenure and promotion?
- How will we get everything else done besides?

While these questions are important, they too often take on definitive value. The ability to respond to them rests, in part, on the second decision that the seminary must make: to decide to create the temporal space in which formation can occur, because nothing will happen if faculty formation is wedged in among everything else.

So how might space be created? One way is to declare a truce, such as Associated Mennonite Seminary did, on taking on any new initiatives for at least a year—no new grants, no new programs, no new external commitments. Such a truce tangibly declares a break in the pattern of continuing to do more. A truce, however, is temporary, so a third set of decisions must occur. The seminary must decide to develop criteria for evaluating which current aspects of seminary programming should continue and which should be brought to a close. This decision is painful, for advocates almost certainly exist for any activity the school is doing. But the time has come for schools to be increasingly intentional about deciding which of all the good things they might do they will do—given the available resources *and* their commitment to faculty formation. Without this sort of purposeful decision making, no space will be created, and faculties will continue to be fragmented and harried.

REEXAMINE THE IMPLICIT ROLE OF FACULTY

For the vast majority of theological schools, being faculty also means implicitly taking on administrative duties. It is the price paid for a model of governance in which faculty not only set administrative policy but do the heavy lifting to implement it. This approach emerged in a period when higher education moved from a paternal structure in which faculty relied on their administrators to do what was needed to keep pathways to classrooms, chapels, and libraries reasonably uncluttered. I am not arguing against the faculty's role in determining institutional direction and policies, but it is naïve to think that one can be fully engaged in the demanding work of teaching, in the development of one's scholarly expertise, and in service to church and community while also functioning in named and unnamed administrative roles in the web of committees that frame the average theological seminary.

Seminaries too often assume that their structure is inviolate. But the truth remains, despite the accrediting expectations of the Association of Theological

Schools, that there is no template. Schools are free to order the prescribed functions in ways that serve their core purposes. And as they are free, schools must be willing to challenge themselves with conversations about delegation, trust, accountability, and fluidity in structures and thus enable administrators and faculty to create the models of academic life that are best suited to the needs and realities of theological education and ministry formation.

TAKE ADVANTAGE OF OUTCOMES ASSESSMENT

While assessment can add a new layer of busyness to seminary life, its underlying principles are rich in potential. Faculties may sometimes argue that the ways they do things in the classroom are sacrosanct and bear directly on the quality of graduates. But how do they know that? What makes the difference between a "good" graduate and one who falls short? What *is* a good graduate in terms of her or his abilities to succeed and lead in the ministry? What specific components in the curriculum and the environment of the school have the most evident impact on whether a student responds to the opportunities offered or simply "gets through the program"? Faculties often hold on to practices and requirements out of an untested conviction that without them the curriculum will fail. As a result, few things really change, and the tendency is to tinker rather than make purposeful adjustments.

As faculties become increasingly skilled at constructing outcomes assessment plans, they will be far more able to determine what works and does not work in achieving institutional goals. They will be less swayed by anecdotal stories and better able to assess program impact at macro and micro levels. Outcomes assessment is not about customer satisfaction but about how what a faculty does affects what it seeks to accomplish. This level of objectivity—when it is based on queries and goals that faculty generate—enables purposeful, targeted decisions regarding curriculum and institutional life.

REDESIGN THE MASTER OF DIVINITY DEGREE

Paying attention to what outcomes data teach will eventually encourage faculties to radically re-envision the purposes and structures of the M.Div. degree. The current structures of that degree have been created for a student population that no longer exists. While some schools have done an excellent job interrelating the theoretical and practical aspects of this professional degree, too many schools still tend to treat attention to practical theology and ministerial arts as accommodations in the degree rather than as ways of knowing distinct and integral to the degree itself. Redesigning the Master of Divinity degree from the bottom up, a design in which the life of the church takes precedence, cannot occur without faculty members engaging their individual and corporate understandings of their educational tasks. They must ask themselves questions and seek out answers and solutions: How might a faculty construct a curriculum in consultation with seasoned pastors and other professional ministers? What pedagogical changes become necessary once we take seriously what we know about adults as learners? How do such changes disorient and intimidate people accustomed to being experts in their discipline and masters of their classrooms?

While there are technical aspects in redesigning a curriculum to be more responsive to emerging needs of the institution and the society it serves, a shift in the curriculum's underlying assumptions calls for adaptive work. As Heifitz and Linsky suggest (2002, 13), adaptive work is dangerous because it calls for "experiments, new discoveries, and adjustments from numerous places in the organization or community." That is why the next suggestion is particularly important.

DEVOTE SIX DAYS EACH YEAR TO DISCUSSIONS OF TEACHING AND LEARNING

Alverno College has earned a national reputation for the integral role of assessment it has established at every level of institutional life. Every course is keyed to core competencies related to the faculty's understanding of what a graduate of Alverno needs to know, to do, and to think. When one asks administrative leaders or faculty how the college has been able to maintain this labor-intensive commitment for more than twenty-five years, the answer is simple. Faculty meet in three annual institutes of three to five days each, the focus of which is to examine what faculty are doing, what they are learning, and how they teach differently as a result of student experience. Faculty "teach publicly" and are resources to one another in terms of pedagogy. In short, they take their formation as faculty as critically as they do their development as disciplinary experts. What the seminaries participating in The Lexington Seminar have overwhelmingly demonstrated is that substantive change in teaching and learning— indeed, in institutional life generally—will not occur until sustained conversations become integral to faculty life.

This realization is evident in the projects undertaken at Eastern Baptist Theological Seminary and Associated Mennonite Seminary. This was the case as well at Claremont School of Theology, where the effort to listen to M.Div. students led to a sustained process of faculty listening to one another because of what they began to hear from students. Sustaining conversations about pedagogy and the life of theological educators helps to surface the rich talent that exists in every faculty so that members can encourage and be resources to one another. Regular, public conversations about teaching and learning emancipate the classroom and particular courses as an individual's fiefdom. The curriculum in its entirety becomes the work of the faculty as a whole.

More importantly, discussions of the central work of the faculty as a community of teachers become a powerful path to faculty formation, for such discussions return frequently to core values about one's discipline, one's sense of vocation as a teacher, and one's vision of the church and its mission. There is no pretense that this will produce some form of homogenized harmony. There will be divergence, disagreement, and even struggle over what constitutes a "theological educator." But as the formative process for students seeking to be pastors for the church is challenging, so is the formation of a theological faculty a process unbounded by terminal degrees and faculty handbooks. Rather, it is a dynamic process of change and adaptation—the very thing we urge upon our students and can model for them.

DO LESS. TALK MORE. CHOOSE WISELY.

These suggestions for giving due attention to the formation of faculty are costly. Some of them run against the canons of faculty life as we know it. Some require a hard rethinking of the seemingly impenetrable structures that hold a school together. To encourage schools to do less may sound preposterously cavalier, especially to institutions that have concluded that doing more is the only way for them to remain viable. But the level of busyness evident in so much of theological education is ultimately counterproductive. This does not suggest that schools are failing to produce graduates who can respond adequately to the needs of the church. It does suggest that the quality of life is compromised when schools move from being busy to being harried.

The tiger that time has become will not be tamed easily. One powerful way in which it may be better managed is through sustained, substantial conversations about what matters. The design of The Lexington Seminar rests on its ability to provide time, space, and structure for discussions that seldom or never occur at home. As Lexington teams have returned to their home institutions and replicated in a variety of ways similar opportunities for discussion, they report that wonderful results occur. Faculty life and relationships become reinvigorated. People discover a new sense of common purpose and shared values. As in the case of Eastern Baptist Theological Seminary, faculty found courage to confront their anxieties about change and face up to a series of institutional crises that challenged their best thinking. However, talking more about what matters is not a magical balm that rids the institution of all blemishes and warts. As the final report from Claremont School of Theology (2000) illustrates so well, the quality of faculty conversations has significant impact but does not suddenly alter the complexity of complex people living in complex settings:

> We learned by conversational practice how to listen openly to positions that are different from our own. . . . An emerging discovery is that the most important tensions we experience are probably not going to go away. We will need to learn not only to live with them, but even to affirm and embrace them.

The renewed interest in the formation of seminary students is important for the reasons cited in this and other essays in this volume. Students have changed in ways that challenge faculty ability to engage them in deep learning about the Christian faith and the mission of the church. Taken seriously, formation as a process of learning and following the ways of discipleship is like a stone cast into a pond. The circles spread outward, and everything is altered. As faculties encourage their students to be attentive to their relationships with God, to their understanding of Christian tradition, and to their images of the professional minister and the contemporary congregation, faculties themselves will be challenged to pay heed to their own best advice. Formation wedged in after everything else is done meets a requirement; formation that reminds a community of learners to create space, to reverence time, and to drink deeply at wisdom's well is transforming.

NOTES

1. All narratives cited in this book can be found in the Archives section of the Seminar's Web site: http://www.lexingtonseminar.org/.

2. I recognize that formation is a category largely adapted from the Catholic experience, which itself emerged from the monastic tradition of guiding individuals into a particular tradition of Christian discipleship. Its use here and in the wider seminary world reflects the need to be more intentional about helping students acquire the knowledge, skills, attitudes, and dispositions that are needed for moving into a communal and leadership relationship with the church and local congregations.

3. See the chapter on "Liturgy and Theology" in Fisch (1990).

4. "The question of the relationship between practice competence and professional knowledge needs to be turned upside down. We should start not by asking how to make better use of research-based knowledge but by asking what we can learn from a careful examination of artistry, that is, the competence by which practitioners actually handle indeterminate zones of practice—however that competence may relate to technical rationality" (Schon 1987, 13).

5. This effort is being lead by Dr. Barbara Ann Keely, a faculty member of United Theological Seminary of the Twin Cities (www.unitedseminary-mn.org).

6. The six competencies are *conceptual competence* (theoretical foundations of the profession); *technical competence* (ability to perform tasks required of the profession); *contextual competence* (understanding the societal context of one's work and the ability to do a multi-perspective analysis of the environment); *interpersonal communication competence* (ability to

use written and oral communication effectively); *integrative competence* (capacity to meld theory and skills in response to specific situations); and *adaptive competence* (ability to anticipate and accommodate changes by gaining new knowledge, new skills, and a new focus on context for the sake of the church's mission).

·GRETCHEN E. ZIEGENHALS·

Faculty Life and Seminary Culture

IT'S ABOUT TIME AND MONEY

It is no great surprise that each year the seminary teams participating in The Lexington Seminar go home to their theological institutions eager to replicate the kind of time they experienced at the Summer Seminar in Northeast Harbor, Maine. Coming off the frenetic pace of seminary life, the teams feel honored by the peaceful seaside setting, the balanced rhythms of morning worship and working sessions, followed by communal afternoon leisure, and the time to process teaching and learning experiences in informal conversation with diverse colleagues. They long to share this kind of time with their faculties at home, and many teams use a portion of the grant money they receive from The Lexington Seminar for a faculty retreat that offers to their colleagues the kind of time experienced in Maine.

In reflecting on what he felt to be the most important aspect of the Seminar, one participant wrote, "Thank you for the hospitality, for the incredible site of this event, for honoring time and space, for thoughtful balance of work and play, which we rarely get to do in our academic life." Another wrote, "The pacing, which presumed and demonstrated that 'down time' contributes to productivity, was significant as a means of helping us begin to reflect differently on the debilitating effects of the relentlessness of our work at home."

As a consultant for The Lexington Seminar, director of The Women's Studies Program at Georgetown College, and the mother of four young children, I understand "the relentlessness of our work" to which the participant above refers, and I sympathize with the feeling of distress that such relentlessness creates. The distress we feel comes, in part, from the many expectations we face and from the guilt we feel when we pause long enough to admit that we cannot do it all. Throughout the meetings of The Lexington Seminar, a recurring lament has been the lack of time and money to accomplish multiple expectations.

As a direct result of increasing financial pressures, seminaries and their faculties are being pressed to take on more responsibilities and complete more tasks within time constraints that do not acknowledge the challenge of the increased duties. In addition, seminaries strain under the load of tense relations with the church; multiple campuses and programs; and students who, because of their diverse cultures, races, denominations, and educational backgrounds, require more time to acclimate and educate.

In an attempt to understand this quandary, the first section of this essay looks at the nature of time and money in seminary culture: How are seminary communities experiencing time? In what ways are seminaries diverging from earlier models? To what extent have diverse student bodies, more expectations of faculty, and increasing financial pressures precipitated this change? The second section examines seminaries' responses and questions: Can we gain more time and money through better time management techniques? What if we simply see the problems in new ways? If we set personal and institutional boundaries and limits, will we lose face, lose students, and lose much-needed revenue? The final section explores the implications of these issues for teaching and learning.

THE NATURE OF TIME IN SEMINARY CULTURE

Becoming a faculty member of a Protestant theological seminary may well be considered hazardous to one's health. Faculty of every denomination complain of being overworked, burned out, stretched to the limits professionally and personally, and unable to handle the multitude of needs that swamp their classrooms, mailboxes, phone-mail, email, and desks each day. While other professionals may experience the same busyness, many seminary faculty feel a sense of holy obligation, a sense of being called and accountable to both the church and the academy, that those in the secular world may not feel. Surrounded by this particular aura of dual obligation, work is never left at the office. The workload of seminary faculty is certainly not all in their heads. Rather, in the last thirty years the nature of that work has radically changed, because of three interrelated factors: a changing student body, increased expectations of faculty members, and financial shortfalls for institutions of theological learning.

DIVERSIFIED STUDENT BODIES

During 1998–99, the first year of The Lexington Seminar, each of the five schools in the program was wrestling with the practical implications of increasingly diverse student bodies on their institution's teaching and learning. The narratives reflected those concerns: Austin Presbyterian Theological Seminary (1999)[1] described the need to find "a more effective and a more efficient delivery system" to serve a student body with a changing student profile and an increasingly complex community ethos. Calvin Theological Seminary (1999) sought to redefine a classical, Reformed theological curriculum to provide more effective professional training for contemporary pastors, having received a letter from four alumni who complained that the seminary was out of step with contemporary needs. Lutheran School of Theology at Chicago (1999) presented the challenges of educating the varied constituencies they serve, including second-career commuters, Ph.D.-bound students, those committed to urban ministry, women, gay and lesbian students, and students of color. Regent College (1999) understood the difficulties of grading well all the various types of degree and non-degree students in their programs as a lens for larger issues of diversity, and Virginia Theological Seminary (1999) focused their narrative on the international students who are so vital to the mission of the campus but whose unique needs require an enormous amount of time and energy from faculty, staff, and administration.

As they describe the challenges precipitated by their diverse student bodies, these five schools are not alone. Rather, they reflect a broader trend that has affected theological student bodies across the United States and Canada. Almost 45 percent of M.Div. students are thirty-five years old or older (Briggs 2002a, 8). Nearly half the students at seminaries and theological schools are married, and 38 percent are women (Preheim 2002, 30). Seminary students also reflect a rich array of cultures, races, sexual preferences, religious backgrounds, and preparation levels. Each year of The Lexington Seminar, participating seminaries have shared both the opportunities and the conundrums presented by an increasingly diverse student body. Dormitories, schedules, programs, and curriculum that were designed for young, single, white males are now stretching and twisting to accommodate diverse students.

ONE SIZE NO LONGER FITS ALL

Seminary students now arrive in a rainbow of diversity. Many are older adults who bring with them families and the accompanying issues of spousal needs, housing, and childcare. Christine, a single mother in the narrative of Lutheran School of Theology at Chicago, complains to her advisor, "I think I bit off more than I can chew. I tried to take three courses this quarter, and the many papers, teaching parish duties, and the kids' illnesses have really driven me crazy" (1999).

Seminarians now also have a wider range of religious training and backgrounds. Students at Gordon-Conwell Theological Seminary (2002) represent sixty-five different denominations. Associated Mennonite Biblical Seminary (2000) focused its narrative on how to "teach the tradition and form students in it when students are at such diverse places with respect to the tradition." The students in the narrative converse about why they do or do not need to take the required course "Mission and Peace," given their varied backgrounds of Mennonite, Methodist, Anglican, and others.

Seminarians arrive with varying levels of proficiency in reading, writing, and speaking English and with various cultural assumptions. At the end of the semester, the character Professor Jones, in Church Divinity School of the Pacific's narrative (2001), is visited in her office by a Japanese student who wants to ask "one small thing": "Could you just tell me what is exegesis?" "I'm not sure what you mean," Professor Jones responds in great surprise. "This whole course has been about exegesis. Part of every chapter has been about using the Greek tools for exegesis. Have you had an introductory scripture course at your school?" "Yes, New Testament," Kiyo replies, "but I didn't agree with professor. I believe it not right to criticize Bible." Multicultural backgrounds that enrich a campus community can also lead to insult and misunderstanding and require time for faculty and students to develop mutual, effective, cross-cultural dialogue.

Students bring outside work to seminary. Fifty years ago, a seminary student might work at a campus job to help support his or her educational costs. Now 40 percent work ten to twenty hours per week while going to seminary, while another 20 percent work more than twenty hours. And 10 percent commute to school more than an hour one way (Preheim 2002, 30). Many students are already involved in parish ministry. One faculty member from Colgate Rochester Crozer Divinity School's narrative (2002) reviewed the church-related reasons that students were missing her class:

> "I can't be in class Monday," one student had e-mailed. "There's been a death in my parish, and the funeral is at 11:00 that day." An older man from a distant Episcopal parish had apologized for missing a lab session, having been unable to get excused from teaching the weekly confirmation class. Another had been so obsessed with pulling off a successful Bible conference at his church that he had completely forgotten the evening class session, until reminded (too late) by his wife. Another, after class, had begged off from the next week's session because of a revival at his church. Finally, a

woman student had pleaded her impending absence due to an unavoidable parish mediation session between her and her recalcitrant board.

The professor mourns, "What am I going to do with these postmodern seminarians? It's hard to argue the live demands of the very ministry in which we want them to excel."

Ralph W. Klein, former dean of the Lutheran School of Theology at Chicago, reflected on the new student diversity and noted wryly in one of The Lexington Seminar's meetings that there were no more Lutherans coming over on boats. In the Lutheran School's narrative (1999), Klein's character remarks: "Thirty-one years ago when I started teaching, all the students were 21, white, male, fresh out of church college. They knew more Hebrew and Greek than the average student today does. I think they read more and wrote better. . . . There were no commuters, no 50-year-olds, no women, almost no part-time students. Teaching today is a lot more exciting—and a lot more work."

WANTED: FACULTY WHO CAN WALK ON WATER

Because of the increased diversity among students, faculty spend more time playing more roles to serve more needs. Barbara, a faculty voice in the narrative of Lutheran School of Theology at Chicago, describes their search for a teacher of Christian Education who will also run the D.Min. program. She jokes, "We want someone who can walk on water, play the guitar, work 60 hours a week, keep up with publishing, and start at a salary in the low 40s." Her statement is not far from the truth. Faculty are expected to stay current with their guilds, publish, teach, serve on multiple committees, lead worship, be multilingual, provide online courses, deliver PowerPoint lectures, be available to students for counseling and formation, grade effectively, tutor, support students through the transitions and crises of seminary life, and keep the scattered community from falling to pieces. At the end of the week, faculty are asking, "How can I offer attention to God and to other people in the midst of days that seem to be shredded into little fragments of time that I cannot control?" (Bass 2000, xii).

Seminary administrators are not immune to the new complications of seminary life. In addition to the duties listed above, one dean described to me the layers of paperwork on his desk produced by more procedural, legal, and state-mandated issues. A president of an urban seminary told me that his school had experienced three attempted suicides in one year.

"What is the procedure for handling that?" I asked.

"We're learning it as we go," he replied.

International students require an enormous amount of time from seminary administrators, even as they bring depth and breadth to the seminary. The appendix to Virginia Theological Seminary's narrative (1999) outlined only some of the administrative duties involved in hosting international students, who make up 6 percent of the student body: "Hospitality to these strangers is no light matter. It is expensive in money. Sorting through the tangles of immigration, visa, taxation, family support, church support, community life, spiritual growth, and physical and emotional wellness call for a good deal of staff and faculty time and creativity."

The diversity of needs, interests, and preparation levels among students have created new markets, precipitating the rise of branch campuses for individual seminaries, leaving administrators juggling the demands of many campuses. Gordon-Conwell Theological Seminary is a multidenominational school of 1,650 students. Its campus in South Hamilton, Massachusetts hosts mostly younger students, mostly bound for pastoral ministry. The Charlotte, North Carolina branch serves mostly older, commuter students who have had much more experience in the church. The Boston branch is the Center for Urban Ministerial Education, serving a Hispanic population. Administrators and faculty at the different campuses spend time keeping the lines of communication open in part through video-conferencing. And all the while they strive to maintain a coherent vision while considering distinct needs.

Another time-consuming and complicating factor in the lives of seminary faculty and administrators is the phenomenon of housing other seminaries on one's campus. The Claremont School of Theology campus hosts other theological institutions, including the Disciples Seminary Foundation, The Episcopal Theological School at Claremont, and San Francisco Theological Seminary/Southern California. These institutions use the facilities of the Claremont School of Theology, including classrooms, office space, chapel, and library. Claremont School of Theology also has a branch campus in Tempe, Arizona, where it offers an M.Div. degree. Faculty who teach on the Claremont campus also teach courses in Arizona.

Time Is Money

In addition to evolving student populations and increased expectations of faculty, the third factor that has so altered the nature of time in seminary culture is the financial picture that permeates and burdens institutions of theological learning. Seminaries are receiving less money from the church. Twenty-five years ago, 60 to 80 percent of a seminary's finances came from its sponsoring churches. The Reverend Dennis Anderson reports in his study of schools in four mainline denominations that that amount has shrunk to between 2 and 25 percent in denominations that offer any support at all (Briggs 2002b, 6).

Not only do mainline churches, with their own membership woes, have less money to give, but they have become increasingly estranged from seminaries. Many no longer believe that seminary graduates have "the practical education needed for sustaining and broadening today's parish ministry" (Briggs 2002b, 6). Some churches have begun to establish their own in-house training programs for ministry.

In addition, many churches no longer have the same respect for the theological endeavors of seminary education. Claremont's narrative describes the predicament of young "Wes," who, in preaching class, is exposed to many perspectives other than his own. Over Christmas break, Wes goes home to preach in the pulpit of the church that raised the money for his scholarship and preaches a sermon that stuns his United Methodist congregation. The pastor calls the associate dean at Claremont School of Theology in a huff.

"What do you think you are doing over there at that school?" he demands.

The best response that seminaries can give is to work more closely with churches so that both institutions can rebuild trust and re-engage in common mission.

Receiving less funding from the church, seminaries are relying more on tuition and endowments to sustain their work, and on extension programs that seek out new markets. Still, Anderson's findings show, "faculties are paid far too little and each year the president must scramble to cover a budget gap that averages about 25 percent of the whole" (Briggs 2002b, 7). Grants also sustain and enrich seminary work, but grants take time. Writing and implementing them along the guidelines provided, attending related conferences, processing results with faculty and staff, and remaining accountable to both the seminary and the granting institution add a load of time pressure undreamt of in earlier decades. Faculty often need assurance that a grant is vital to a previously articulated vision, not simply one more thing to do.

Financial shortfalls have a profound impact on faculty time as well. Modestly paid faculty whose schools do not offer faculty housing often cannot afford to live near campus or must live closer to a spouse's higher-paying job. Faculty who commute for an hour or more have little time for community-building activities such as corporate worship, a rally, or a chapel-choir concert. In addition, cultural expectations about the economic and social situations of families have changed. Increasing consumer demands (in addition to other factors, of course) often place both partners in the workplace. When both partners are employed outside the home, there are new implications for the institution regarding faculty time and availability.

Faculty teaching has also born the impact of a tighter budget. Admission standards at many schools have relaxed as financial needs drive schools to open their gates ever wider. While many deserving students benefit from this trend, faculty are teaching more students who are less prepared for the academic rigors of theological education. Faculty spend more time explaining and tutoring, and redesigning courses, curriculum, and pedagogy to fit the needs of more remedial learners. In addition, most faculty have higher course loads or more students in each course because schools cannot afford to hire more faculty. Otherwise, schools solve the problem by replacing full-time faculty with squads of adjuncts.

At Eastern Baptist Theological Seminary, Interim Dean Elouise Renich Frazer listed what she called "a roll-call of losses," the number of faculty who, in the past two years, had either resigned or endured personal disaster and loss. Because of financial crisis, Eastern Baptist was unable to replace them, leaving existing faculty in an almost impossible situation. Their lack of time was a direct result of the school's lack of money. She explained how this financial crisis has brought them closer together, despite their exhaustion. "We have had to make individual and institutional adjustments," Frazer says, "to accommodate the exhaustion of our colleagues. Yet even when two are down, the others assume a huge burden. They are committed to this, body and soul." But the pressures can be tremendous. Frazer herself took a two-month medical leave (because of exhaustion) in the midst of what faculty called "fire, flood, and the sky falling in." Frazer describes the situation as having taught faculty a life discipline. "We learned that we must live within our means," she says. "We discovered that we have more than enough. It was as if God plunked us down in Eden and said, 'You can have anything you see except that money tree.'"

Ironically, the new part-time commuting students whom seminaries expect to constitute a significant source of revenue are the students who end up taking the most time because they do not match a one-size-fits-all mold or may not mirror the school's founding mission. General Theological Seminary, the oldest seminary of the Episcopal Church, was founded in 1817 and has been a New York landmark since 1826. It has a long history of residential students and residential faculty. Steeped in tradition, the seminary offers twenty-one services a week; the bells ring for chapel three times each day. The community studies, lives, and worships together. Five years ago the school was completely residential. Thus the school still feels monastic, more influenced by Oxford than by the city that surrounds it, and the campus architecture focuses the community inward, not outward, explains Bruce Mullin, sub-dean for academic affairs (Ziegenhals 2002, 1).

Associate Professor of Old Testament Judith H. Newman also spoke of the many legacies embodied in General Theological Seminary. In her closing remarks at the June 2002 Seminar, she described the elaborate rituals at chapel and the ornate architecture, and she noted the days in the not-so-distant past when all faculty were male and ordained, and students wore Oxford-like gowns to class. But the school stands at the threshold of significant changes, she added, some of which are elaborated in General Theological Seminary's narrative (2002).

Entitled "Clashing Perceptions of an Institution," it is a tale of two students (one full-time residential, one part-time commuter) and their insights into their experiences of General Theological Seminary. What the full-timer, Theresa, cherishes is precisely what alienates the part-timer, Ward.

Ward's frustrations are about how "unwelcoming" the institution is for newcomers. He has trouble finding his way around the campus, he never knows what the daily schedule is, where to find his professors, or where to sit in chapel. Part-timers do not receive communications from the seminary, they do not have mailboxes, and they are not on the community email.

Theresa is exasperated with students like Ward. She argues: "That student just doesn't get it. This institution is built on formation. The process starts the very first day. My classmates have been together for every major class for almost three years. We have become a community. We have been arguing, laughing, praying, and hashing over the questions of faith and ministry for three years. Of course we are tightly knit! That is what the seminary process is for . . . communities are built, not bought."

Yet community is being bought. The dean in the narrative worries about the tension epitomized by the two students, which is further complicated by economics: "The budget people always said that the school 'lost' money on full-time students and made money on part-time students. But residential students had been the soul of the institution for well over a century. Where was the answer?" How do we grow without losing what we value: the formative rhythms of work, worship, and rest?[2]

The General Theological Seminary's narrative reflects a school straddling the homogeneous, monastic seminary cultures of the past and the demands of the diverse population of current students. Faculty who could once assume that all their students were young, male, white, Protestant, residential, and well-educated could also make certain assumptions about their time together, and thus while faculty were busy, they enjoyed a set rhythm of time—the bells peal and the group flows forward—a rhythm that most of us teaching today do not have. (Today the bells would more likely remind us of the bitterly contested *Werkglocken*[3] than of any sacred time.) To most of us this kind of homogeneity would seem not only incredibly boring but counter to our theological and personal commitments. Yet we cast furtive, longing glances back at a time when seminaries were less complicated by the dictates of the dollar.

In the future, predicts Daniel Aleshire (2002, 24), executive director of the Association of Theological Schools, the money for sustaining seminaries will need to come from individuals who care about the church or who are loyal to an institution. But identifying and cultivating these relationships will take a little creativity and an enormous amount of time.

SEMINARIES REACTING AT THE LIMITS

Faced with the shortages of time and money that impact the workload and the cultures of so many seminaries, schools are beginning to acknowledge, define, and respond to the situation in a variety of ways. I recently telephoned a seminary dean's office and was greeted by the dean's assistant saying, "Thanks, good-bye!" While I quickly gathered that she was still addressing someone in her office, for a brief moment I thought that the dean had discovered a brilliant way of clearing away the workload.

Some schools, in the spirit of the Protestant work ethic, are working harder and faster, consulting time-management gurus, reshuffling personnel, and recommitting themselves to meeting the many needs required by their constituencies. Other institutions are attempting to see the situation in new ways, seeking blessing in the midst of what seems most days like chaos, accepting their fragmented experiences of time as a reality that cannot be altered. A few seminaries are learning painfully to set limits, to say no, to define new boundaries around faculty time and around what the institution can or cannot do for a given student or group of students. None of these responses are simple, nor are there any right answers. The remarkable thing is that so many faculty are simultaneously raising their heads out of their overwhelming workloads long enough to articulate the issues and attempt a response that is faithful to teaching, learning, and the missions of their schools and yet aimed at self-preservation.

TIME MANAGEMENT APPROACHES

Austin Presbyterian Theological Seminary has experienced significant growth in student and faculty numbers since the 1980s. Hispanic ministries have been a longstanding tradition, and Austin has committed to a cross-cultural focus in all of its courses. More than 25 percent of Austin's students are Methodist, and a large number of Lutherans attend the extension program, the Lutheran Seminary Program in the Southwest. More than 25 percent of degree students live off campus. Among M.Div. students, 10 to 15 percent are minorities, and 40 to 50 percent are women. Presbyterian students are now in the minority, and even the faculty reflect cultural and religious diversity: Austin has hired several Hispanic professors over the years.

Discussions about Austin Presbyterian at the meetings of The Lexington Seminar ranged mostly around the question of how this diversity affects the campus: What are the gifts and challenges of such diversity? But another insight that rose to the surface was the understanding that time was the real issue. In Austin's effort to be family for everyone, to address multiple needs, the time factor was perhaps more challenging than diversity itself. Had Austin Presbyterian Theological Seminary, which is deeply committed to maintaining an ethos of community, created a model in which they had considered every variable but time? Are there parameters to diversity? Can hospitality be stretched too far?

Commenting on the Austin team's experience at The Lexington Seminar's conference in Maine, President Robert Shelton said, "We learned about what is not serving us well—even if it is a good thing: our willingness to be open to students around the clock—no limits or boundaries." He defined their institutional culture as an oral one, Southern style, where nothing is written down, "it's just the way we do things." In such a culture, work knows no limits and service no boundaries.

In an attempt to manage their time and their services more effectively, Austin has done several things. First, they are discussing putting more in writing, being more explicit about responsibilities and the setting of realistic and recognized boundaries. Second, they are reorganizing student services out of the conviction that teaching and learning suffer when they are compartmentalized and separated from the services students may need, such as childcare and support for commuters.

New Ways of Seeing

Seminaries are also asking themselves how they can see their work in light of what Robert Grudin calls the "larger presences" that surround us in time. Grudin (1982, para 1.4) writes:

> People with great projects afoot habitually look further and more clearly into the future than people who are mired in day-to-day concerns. . . . They stake out larger plots and homesteads of time than the rest of us. . . . They have something greater of their own, some sense of their large and coherent motion in time, to compare the present with.

Despite their best intentions, faculty are realizing that the quandaries of serving adult students with a host of needs on multiple campuses cannot be solved solely through better time management techniques. Rather, a transformation is required in the way that seminaries view their work, their ministries, and time itself. As Dorothy C. Bass writes:

Henri Nouwen, a priest and author, was known among his students for his remarkable capacity of attention, an offering he gave to God in prayer and to them in friendship. Yet he could write with conviction about the passions evoked by days gone awry: "Doesn't this unending row of interruptions build in our hearts feelings of anger, frustration and even revenge, so much so that at times we see the real possibility that growing old can become synonymous with growing bitter?" (2000, 40)

Bass continues that Nouwen found "a remedy for the frustrations of interruption" in the comment of another professor who said that he had complained his whole life about interruptions to his work until he discovered that his interruptions were his work. For this professor, Bass notes, "aggravation about the limitations of time found its healing responses in his strengthened sense of vocation," what Grudin might call a "larger presence."

This new way of seeing is reflected in other seminaries as well. Bethel Theological Seminary (2001) spoke of needing "a completely different way of thinking" if they are going to take formation seriously and integrate it holistically. McCormick Theological Seminary (2000) asked, "How can we be both Reformed and ecumenical?" and then began reflecting on ways they are already living in that tension. Luther Seminary (2001) sought to "navigate uncharted waters" of institutional change, by first having a retreat where they honor what they do well, by lifting up their "collective pedagogical imagination" (those ordinary hallway conversations that are so full of extraordinary wisdom) and by "cultivating wonder." Bass reminds us that the Psalmist asks that we learn to count our days, not to increase their number, but rather to "gain a wise heart." Seminaries are learning that to be faithful in educating ministers for the church, we are sometimes required not to seek a way out of our situations but rather to learn to see grace in the midst of those situations.

This new way of seeing includes the way faculty see those students that they often identify as problems—the unprepared, the ungifted for ministry, the "Teflon student" who will not change. Faculty are coming to recognize the importance of liking our students for who they are and accepting them as they are, rather than wishing them to be what they are not. This does not mean that we are no longer responsible for forming our students but that we need to be hospitable to those who do not match our ideal of what they ought to be.

SETTING LIMITS

A third response to issues of time is that seminaries are learning—tentatively, painfully—to set limits on what they can and cannot do. This response is perhaps the most difficult one of all, because there are no models for schools setting the kinds of limits they crave or to the extent to which they need them. Further, setting limits brings with it a certain amount of guilt that we in the church feel when we choose not to meet the needs of someone who asks for help. It can also bring with it financial repercussions.

Despite these concerns and the fact that setting limits runs counter to the prevailing culture in many seminaries today, faculty are recognizing that saying no can be formative as well as life-saving. Creating personal and institutional boundaries in seminary culture not only limits, it defines. It helps us create community; it helps us say, "This is who we are."

Church Divinity School of the Pacific has developed a project through The Lexington Seminar, to "change the ethos of interaction" on campus and to write what President and Dean Donn Morgan calls a *mishnah* of faculty expectations based on the faculty handbook. An ethos subcommittee is helping faculty think through and distinguish between negotiable and nonnegotiable duties and between those that are readily quantifiable (such as teaching two courses a semester) and those that are not (such as speaking and preaching in local parishes). Assistant Professor of Theology Marion Grau, one of the members of the ethos subcommittee, has noted that the *mishnah* will help faculty (and new faculty in particular) get a better sense of what is expected of them.

The seminary also intends to discern appropriate means of communicating with students and staff about their expectations of faculty. For example, says Arthur Holder, former dean of academic affairs, "because of our participation in the GTU doctoral faculty, research and publication expectations for CDSP faculty may need to be somewhat higher than for faculty at other Episcopal seminaries—and yet, our M.Div. students often expect us to be just as accessible and involved in community life as faculty at those other institutions."

Discussion about this "ethos of interaction" continued at the August 2002 faculty retreat in Healdsburg, California. One of the decisions made was to alleviate some of the office-hour crunch by establishing times when faculty are completely available to students. At present, this takes the form of a coffee hour before chapel. Linda Clader, dean of academic affairs and professor of homiletics, states that faculty are determined to take formation as seriously as they expect their students to. Faculty covenanted for the 2002–03 academic year that they would each take one half hour of exercise and one half hour of quiet time a day. They hold each other accountable to this at regular faculty meetings. Grau said a few faculty are starting to cycle to work, and she hopes a few more who are able will walk soon.

Faculty agreed not to worry if certain aspects of their work do not get done as a result of these commitments to health. "We are taking baby steps toward establishing limits," Clader explained. "We are all obsessive-compulsives here, but we don't have to do everything perfectly. We have yet to see how all this will work out!" Clader noted that because over half of the faculty are now women, they may be more receptive to questions of time and self-care.

Clader hopes that finding new ways of handling the overwhelming amounts of information exchanged on campus will also help change the ethos of interaction. She is considering ways to streamline the processes that cross her desk, from phone calls and emails to papers needing to be signed.[4]

Implications for Practice

At the closing session of the June 2002 conference of The Lexington Seminar, Melanie May, academic dean at Colgate Rochester Crozer Divinity School, listed the school's multiple commitments and goals and then said simply, "In light of all this, how do we teach?" May's words cut to the heart of one implication of the busyness in seminary cultures today: Less time for reflection impairs our teaching and learning. Fortunately, schools are recognizing this problem. Associated Mennonite Biblical Seminary faculty made a list of "issues we hope will not get lost," which included, "Gain nonproductive time for the leisure essential to *schola*." Faculty and institutions are recognizing that good teaching takes time—for preparation, for focus, for contemplation, and for conversation.

While faculty cannot go back to the ordered time of the monastery, they also know that time and setting are vital for good teaching. Schools were built with the idea that there would be time for reflection. The task, therefore, is to find a means of reclaiming some sense of sacred time in our fragmented seminary cultures. All of our activity of teaching and learning for the church's ministries is meaningless unless we take the time to contemplate it.

The Benedictines speak of this kind of active reflection as "holy leisure," an essential part of Benedictine spirituality. Entire seminary communities would benefit from this sense of holy leisure. For Benedict, reflecting was as important a task as working. Benedict set aside four hours a day for prayer, six to nine for work, seven to nine for sleep, three hours for eating and rest, and three hours for reading and reflection (Chittister 1990, 98–99). While many of us consider the latter an impossible luxury, Joan Chittister reminds us that we do not have to be monastic or agrarian to find more balance in our lives:

> There is an idea abroad in the land that contemplation is the province of those who live in cloistered communities and that it is out of reach to the rest of us who bear the noonday heat in the midst of the maddening crowds. But if that's the case, then Jesus who was followed by people and surrounded by people and immersed in people was not a contemplative. And Francis of Assisi was not a contemplative. And Teresa of Avila was not a contemplative. And Catherine of Siena was not a contemplative. And Thomas Merton was not a contemplative. And Mohatma Gandhi was not a contemplative.
>
> Obviously, some of our greatest contemplatives have been our most active and most effective people. No, contemplation is not withdrawal from the human race. (Chittister 1990, 102)

Instead, contemplation can be a way of pursuing meaning right where we are, in the midst of the fragments of the day. It does not take us out of reality, but rather, "it puts us in touch with the world around us by giving us the distance we need to see where we are more clearly" (Chittister 1990, 103).

Recapturing the idea of holy leisure is one way of reclaiming the time that has slipped out of our control and left us grappling breathlessly with each crisis pounding on the door. No simple formula exists for attempting this commitment, but attempt it we must. Church Divinity School of the Pacific offers one solution in its "Quiet Days" program, a daylong retreat that occurs once a semester at a Franciscan monastery about forty-five minutes from campus. Occasionally during the program, participants gather for a meditation, but most of the time is spent in quiet—reading or walking on the grounds. Quiet Days are built into the curriculum, and no classes or chapel occur on those days. I have begun a similar practice with my elementary-school-age daughters. Once a semester I let them choose a day to call in "too well" to go to school. It is a way for them to learn, at an early age, how to listen to signals telling them that they need to slow down, to create time to think. Even at their age they feel the pressure not to miss a test, a quiz, or a special activity, but this "well day" teaches them that no one is too invaluable to take time for renewal.

Thus, a second pedagogical implication of the seminary's current relation to time is that, as educators and administrators, we let ourselves get caught up in the doing, implying through our ceaseless motion that we believe we are in control. Kathleen Norris asserts that "workaholism is the opposite of humility" (Norris 1998, 25). A healthy humility would trust God and our colleagues to accomplish what we, lacking time and money, cannot.

Faculty might also find themselves with more time if they would learn to trust administrators to do their share of the work. Could we learn to see a dean as an efficient "heavy lifter," asked one former dean, instead of someone who is "power hungry"? When distrust and suspicion flow freely, members of the community often feel the need to hover over every decision and serve on every committee, a time-consuming and frustrating process. The problem is exacerbated by a small faculty, often equivalent in size to a small department at an undergraduate institution. We've all witnessed the actual stalemate that occurs in these intimate situations in which people are constantly checking up on each other, exerting a kind of destructive control.

The faculty preference for group or consensus decision making, while democratic and honoring of diverse opinions, often eats up hours of time and energy. As we educate students for the church's ministries, perhaps doing less, better—by trusting others to do their work—would help us see the myriad ways in which God moves and works in our history. Our vocation as theological teachers needs to affect the quantity of what we do.

"Everything we do," concludes Walter C. Wright (Wright et al. 1999, 5), executive director of the DuPree Leadership Center at Fuller, "teaches what we actually believe, regardless of what we say in our classrooms. The curriculum of our schools is much more than the classes we teach or the programs we construct. We teach theology and spiritual formation with every action of the day, every policy, and every procedure of the community. Students are watching." He urges us to spend more time thinking not only about our teaching, but about our living together. "Are we workaholics? How do we manage time?" While we try to teach formation in our classes, "around our classes and in our organizational life together, we teach whether or not we really believe what we teach." In the midst of our frantic seminary cultures, perhaps doing less is more because it reflects the very faithfulness in our Maker that we strive to teach. It is not easy to accept the fact that modesty of goals is good. Schools walk an uneasy public ground here: if we lose our programs, will we lose our prestige? Seminaries need to wrestle with this quandary more and more.

Third, if we want to be better theological teachers, we must reclaim a certain mindfulness in the whirlwind, and then model that mindfulness in our classrooms. For instance, do we give students ample time to reflect on and respond to what they read in class, or is more better on our syllabi as well as on our personal calendars? The Reverend Anne Katherine Grieb, associate professor of New Testament at Virginia Theological Seminary, writes:

> I am famous (infamous?) in my New Testament Introduction course for my sense of the urgency of the Gospel, planning everything to the minute and cramming an hour's lecture into 50 minutes. But late one fall, I sensed that the class needed to talk. The students were astonished when I donated most of an hour to inviting their doubts, and listening and responding to their concerns about the Jesus of history in the Gospels. We would have discussed that later, but the students needed that discussion immediately. My actions were simple, but I continued to hear about that day years later. It serves as a reminder to me that teaching the Bible means being taught by the Bible: my students and I are on this journey together. (Wright et al. 1999, 5)

In addition to the kind of flexibility Grieb describes, what else could we do differently in our classrooms to teach students that seminary time is a different sort of time? Could we lecture less and discuss more? Michael Oakeshott writes that conversation provides "a meeting place of various modes of imagining" (Brookfield and Preskill 1999, 6). While we often feel that we have too much material to cover to leave time for discussion, providing a setting and time for conversation is one of the most important ways in which we can help our students make meaning. Could we journal more in class around specific questions in order to teach students how to take the time to reflect on an important issue? Could we tolerate and even welcome and encourage moments of reflective silence in class? Could we teach students the art of active listening to one another, an art that is lost in our frantic culture? Even how we enter the room and our own bearing in class can be instructive. Are we fragmented, forgetful, and rushed? Or are we focused and centered for a thoughtful hour together?

Fourth and finally, an implication of the new and complex demands on our time is that *institutions have to work harder to help faculty feel valued and honored in their vocations as teachers.* This could take several forms, including the kind of leisure time granted to honor the calling of teaching. But a more fundamental daily ritual would be for administrators to take on the crucial task of saying no for faculty, especially young faculty. "It's not good for you," "It's too much," and "It's not productive" have to be phrases that are heard clearly and then supported financially, as young faculty strive to make their mark on an institution, or as older faculty attempt to save the institution yet again. Veteran faculty often believe that they must have a hand in everything because they no longer feel valued in their teaching. A smart institution can help faculty navigate the ebb and flow of a teaching career, because teaching is what suffers when we are too busy with other obligations. At Georgetown College, for example, first-year faculty are not allowed to serve on committees, thus allowing them time to focus on teaching.

CONCLUSION

Before setting these kinds of limits, however, schools need to decide what defines a good faculty. If teaching is to take more time, what will we do less of and what will be the litmus test through which such decisions pass? How do we define what deserves a "no"? What will be our criteria? Seminaries will first need to reexamine their core identities and then locate good teaching within those identities in order to answer these foundational questions.

We have seen a commitment to this process among seminary faculty who have been a part of The Lexington Seminar. These faculties are learning that they must take the time to become faculty together in order to sort through these issues, to go on retreat together in order to know and trust one another outside the settings that besiege and distract them, and to form themselves as individuals with a sense of wholeness and vocation in order to better form their students for the church's ministries. Seminaries must reclaim time as a freely given and abundant gift of God. We must not hoard time nor grieve over it nor count its costs but rather invite it into our pedagogy, share it freely, and celebrate it daily.

NOTES

1. All narratives cited in this book can be found in the Archives section of the Seminar's Web site: http://www.lexingtonseminar.org/.

2. In January 2003, the faculty of General Theological Seminary voted to develop an M.A. program for part-time lay persons, to be implemented in September 2003.

3. *Werkglocken* (Schor 1992, 49) refers to the clocks used by the fourteenth century textile factory owners to wake their workers at precise intervals. The workers came to hate the clocks that did not meld with the traditional and more natural rhythms of time with which they were accustomed to working.

4. Robin Lind (2002, 23) describes a technique that Wilson Yates, president of United Theological Seminary of the Twin Cities, uses to reduce reading unnecessary e-mails: "All e-mail sent to him from within his own school is read first by his assistant and then forwarded to him for action or response as necessary. Given the amount of the e-mail that she could respond to, the messages he had to respond to declined dramatically." Wilson says, "The key to this process's success lies in the fact that a great percentage of the in-house e-mail that comes to me is information she will actually need to treat. Needless to say, anyone needing to convey information directly to me alone can do so by voice mail or by writing 'confidential' in the subject box."

·STEPHEN ELLINGSON·

From Cordiality to Candor

AN ETHNOGRAPHIC STUDY
OF A FACULTY FORMING ITS LIFE TOGETHER

What happens when a long-settled but not especially cohesive faculty agrees to meet regularly for conversation about their vocation as teachers and scholars? Would they be able to reform or reconstitute themselves as a collegial body or would well-established patterns of interaction and argumentation stop conversation and change? Would the faculty be renewed by the process of interaction or would they return to old work habits in guild, church, and classroom? Would weekly conversations inspire them to change the curriculum or their pedagogical practices? These questions arose as I began my work as a participant observer of Pacific Lutheran Theological Seminary's faculty during their Lexington Seminar project.

Originally I had been one of the faculty members involved in the school's leadership team for The Lexington Seminar. And after our participation in the first June meeting of the seminar, Malcolm Warford, seminar director, asked me to conduct an ethnography of our faculty process of reformation. The school's administration and faculty gave their permission for me to study the process and disseminate information about our meetings and conversations, and so I began to observe and record our weekly meetings in August 2001. I found myself occupying the role of participant-observer, which made the task easier in some ways and more challenging in others.[1] As a member of the faculty I was an insider and thus did not experience any problems with gaining entry or the trust of my colleagues as someone from the outside might.

However, I had been in a leadership role during the first phase of the process, and I was institutionally and emotionally invested in the process of faculty reformation and making sure it actually happened. I was also involved in formulating the plan by which the faculty would engage in the process during the early weeks of observation, and I struggled to separate my roles as faculty leader and relatively impersonal and objective recorder of faculty meetings and conversations.

Thus I carried a certain bias with me that potentially could have blinded me to certain questions and comments, patterns of interaction, and ways of seeing the faculty. However, I had only been a faculty member for one year and thus had, in some respects, attributes of an outsider. I had no more than a brief history with the faculty and had only seen them interact, quite cordially, at our regular monthly meetings, so I carried few expectations or foreknowledge of how the process would unfold. I also began to disengage myself from leadership in the school's Lexington Seminar project once the fall semester began. This helped me gain some emotional distance from the process and allowed me to become the "scribe" of our project meetings in which I rarely offered comments and my colleagues rarely asked for my input. The following account is from an insider's perspective but one in which I tried to faithfully record what was said and done in our weekly meetings and answer the questions posed at the beginning of this essay.

PHASE 1: WRITING THE NARRATIVE

In the early weeks of the fall 2000 semester, six of us gathered to begin writing our school's narrative for The Lexington Seminar. The team included the school's president, Tim Lull[2]; its academic dean, Michael Aune; and four faculty members. Marty (Martha Ellen) Stortz, professor of historical theology and ethics, and Tom Rogers, associate professor of homiletics, represented the mid-career senior faculty members who already were providing leadership for the school and were expected to continue to do so in the coming years. Alicia Vargas, assistant professor of contextual and cross-cultural studies, and I (Stephen Ellingson, assistant professor of the sociology of religion) represented the newer faculty and the faculty with a special interest in the contexts of ministry that were a growing concern for the M.Div. curriculum. We came to that first meeting with only a vague sense that our purpose was to begin a process by which the faculty could address questions of collective identity and vision that would shape what and how we teach. We also learned that we would be writing a narrative about the institutional and pedagogical issues facing the school.

In that initial conversation, we identified the issue of scarcity as one that the school has historically faced and that still threatens it: never enough money, too few students, no community, not Lutheran enough. In subsequent team meetings, scarcity became one of the key issues the faculty team identified for the narrative. We spoke about the perennial shortage of money and its effect on programs. We spoke about scarcity of collegiality among the faculty. My older colleagues described a faculty that was "cordial" but minimized interaction and one that was committed to their teaching, research, and service to the church but not necessarily to one another or the school. This scarcity of collegiality was not a product of ill will but of structural constraints. Finally, we spoke of the scarcity of community and the frequent complaints from students that we were not accessible or even visible on campus. All of us seemed a bit chagrined by a comment one of the senior professors made during a recent job interview when the candidate asked about the nature of community on campus. He said, "We teach our classes and then get in our cars and drive home." We were "a community in diaspora," a community that rarely gathered because its members were geographically scattered, intellectually dispersed, and pulled apart by diverse commitments to church, guild, and other local communities. As we met over the course of the first semester, it became evident that we needed to focus first on developing the faculty and a shared commitment and identity as an institution before we could address the teaching and learning issues that faced our students. The result was a narrative that exposed the multifaceted culture of scarcity as well as the opportunities for cutting-edge scholarship and church leadership that Pacific Lutheran's position on the West Coast offered.

PHASE 2: A HOUSE DIVIDED BUT SEEKING UNITY

In June 2001 the Pacific Lutheran team (along with teams from four other schools) attended The Lexington Seminar's weeklong conference in Maine. Each day we spent the morning discussing a different school's narrative with the goal of helping our colleagues develop organizational and pedagogical strategies to address the challenges their school faced. The session set aside to discuss Pacific Lutheran's narrative was not especially helpful, but several other sessions clarified the issues and in some ways steeled the resolve of our president and the team to force Pacific Lutheran's faculty to overcome the inertia fostered by scarcity. My notes from one of our team meetings in Maine discuss this turning point:

> In Maine I saw determination on the part of Tim [Lull], Marty [Stortz] and Michael [Aune] that business as usual was over. As we sat in the screened porch there seemed

to be this moment of collective comprehension when we realized that the school faces serious problems and that the faculty's history of derailing efforts at institutional change could not be repeated. Tim spoke candidly about our financial problems and the arrival of Carol [Jacobson, Assistant Professor of Christian Education], Alicia [Vargas] and myself on campus as the triggers for institutional renewal. Perhaps we are willing to ask questions about why we do things in a particular way; why we don't talk as faculty about our work or what we teach; why we don't hang out together. I think the seminar helped us see the real problems being in diaspora pose for the seminary: Living a significant distance from the seminary prevents us from easily being able to take part in the daily affairs of the seminary; living in different disciplines allows us to avoid talking to one another about how to integrate our different intellectual interests and work in the classroom; living with only one foot in the school allows many of us (some perhaps willingly) to be pulled into other academic, personal, church commitments, and this had led to the team's perception that the seminary is low on the priority list of many faculty—although I bet none will admit it.

In response to the challenges facing us, we developed a strategy to present to the rest of the faculty on our return to Berkeley. Not only did we think we had a plan that would help us begin to deal with our institutional scarcity, but we were also energized by many of the conversations we had had in Maine. Our team was especially helped by conversations about the challenge of integrating the curriculum and managing scarce faculty resources. Raymond Williams, the director of the Wabash Center, gave one of the concluding presentations at the Seminar. In it he identified several critical problems facing theological education. He argued that theological education is experiencing a *kairotic* moment. How seminaries respond to demographic shifts in student bodies, the aging of theological faculties, developments in classroom technologies, and changes within denominations and congregations will determine the future of theological education. We placed Pacific Lutheran's problems within Williams's framework and made that framework an integral part of the action plan we would take back to the faculty.

This initial strategy hinged on the faculty's participation in a project that would require renewed commitment to (1) be available one day a week to one another and the students, (2) engage in weekly conversations with one another about the challenges of the *kairos* moment as well as about what and how we teach, (3) be present for a community coffee hour and chapel each Wednesday, and (4) lead student-formation groups. We hoped this project plan would help us get to know one another more fully, address our problem of being a community in diaspora, and respond to student concerns that faculty were not available to them outside of the classroom.

We met the day after the school's team had returned from Maine. Because some senior colleagues had described how other faculty members had, in the past, used delaying and derailing tactics to thwart potential change, the team entered the meeting feeling somewhat fearful about the reception our ideas would receive, yet hopeful that they would be given a full hearing. Unfortunately, our fears were justified. Delaying and derailing prevailed at the meeting as several faculty members shot down the team's proposed project plan while offering few constructive alternatives. Tom Rogers noted at a debriefing a week later that the rest of the faculty had been relatively unengaged with the drafting of the narrative in the previous months and were suspicious of our work. Clearly the entire faculty had never taken ownership of The Lexington Seminar project.

After the meeting, the team exchanged emails in which we offered our assessment of the meeting and made suggestions about next steps. A few of us were fairly discouraged, but others were less concerned about our colleagues' resistance. One team member noted that, "at least we got beyond being cordial to one another and actually talked about things." In one email I suggested that we had failed to convey the excitement and sense of commitment to theological education that we had experienced in Maine, as well as our sense that now was the time to act upon the *kairos* moment facing theological education. I then suggested that we draft a white paper that presented these thoughts for our annual fall retreat in August. The rest of the team encouraged me to start the process, and from this white paper we developed a new proposal for the work of the school's Lexington Seminar project. It had three main goals: (1) to create and sustain the experience of belonging to and identifying with a particular community in a social context that often makes real community an illusion; (2) to work toward a more integrated curriculum—one in which we help students connect the different disciplines and courses into a more unified understanding of ministry; and (3) to struggle with questions of institutional identity: Are we as a faculty a group of individuals who happen to teach at the same school or are we something more? What kind of faculty do we want to be now in order to address the *kairos* moment within theological education?

In order to achieve these goals, we suggested that the faculty meet together one morning each week for conversation about some issue related to the *kairos* moment and about the specific institutional challenges and opportunities facing us.

With a more modest proposal for faculty involvement and change, we entered this second meeting with some hope but again some trepidation about faculty resistance. And once again the tactics of delay and obstruction dictated the course of our meeting. The new plan, when presented, was met with skepticism or disinterest by several. A couple of older faculty members dismissed our diagnosis of the theological environment as old news and rejected our plan of action with such words as, "doing this won't change anything." Another started by announcing that he really did not want to meet each Wednesday to discuss teaching and learning issues at Pacific Lutheran. Instead, he wanted us to form teams of faculty and students to engage in public conversations about important social issues. This, he argued, would build community and help the faculty get to know one another.

Two team members undercut the new proposal by their comments. One suggested that the current challenges to theological education were neither new nor interesting. Another relayed some comments offered by one of our retired faculty members who had read the project proposal and concluded that trying to answer questions about institutional identity and community at Pacific Lutheran was a "waste of time." "PLTS," argued this emeritus professor, "has always struggled with them. There are no answers to these questions." This team member continued in a similar strain by suggesting that his "thinking about the need to create a community with which we identify and are loyal to is not possible or desirable given our situation [i.e., being in diaspora] . . . maybe the best we can do is to get us all in the same room. We can't be a melting pot, but maybe we're a salad." In my notes on these comments after the meeting, I asked myself the following questions, which were not raised at the August meeting nor asked directly at any subsequent meeting: "Can a theological school continue to operate without being able to say, in a positive way, 'this is who we are'? Can we be satisfied to say we don't know who we are because there is no core?"

As we neared the end of the meeting, I suggested to my colleagues that the Lexington team's modest project proposal was in danger of derailment, and that an alternative plan—to form groups of students and faculty to talk about social issues—was taking shape that would allow us to evade the difficult work of reforming ourselves as a faculty, allow us to avoid addressing the larger issues in theological education that the Maine conference had raised for us, and make it difficult to write the grant proposal for continuing work in the coming year. The dean appointed a new subcommittee to work with the faculty member who had proposed the alternative plan, and we ended our meeting. In my notes following the late August meeting, I wrote the following assessment of the meeting and the faculty's response to the team's work to date:

> There seems to be a continuing leadership vacuum or at least a minimalist approach to leadership—apart from Marty, none of the senior faculty effectively steered the meeting or defended the ideas in the proposal. I was surprised at how quickly we slipped back into the individualist mode in framing the fall schedule [i.e., how will this affect my teaching and work load] and tried to avoid actually talking about many of the questions the proposal raised. No one was willing to address the question: Are we a bunch of individuals who happen to work at the same place? It appears that this faculty would just as soon do their teaching, writing, research with minimal obligations to the collectivity.

Clearly, I was struggling to balance my role as ethnographer with that of faculty member, and my notes reflect that struggle. However, conversations with Jane Strohl and Marty Stortz after the meeting helped me understand the faculty's history and the challenge of creating the space for conversation that might lead to institutional change. During my two years at Pacific Lutheran, I had heard complaints that the faculty had already talked about some of these issues—curriculum revision, inclusive language, sexuality, institutional identity, community building—and that there was little interest in talking about them again. The implicit and sometimes explicit message, as I heard at the August retreat, was that such conversations were pointless; they would not lead anywhere.

Marty noted that "we've been talking about community, integration, and identity since I got here twenty years ago. But we're wrong in thinking we'll ever get these questions 'answered.' Rather the shape of the way we think about them changes dramatically with attendant changes in context, changes in faculty, changes in the student body." Jane and Marty spoke about the faculty's habit of talking without taking action, and we wondered together whether the problem might be that these earlier conversations had taken place without a clear set of goals. Perhaps too many of our faculty conversations were not oriented toward changing our practices, identity, and commitments. We also spoke about the leadership struggle we seemed to face: neither faculty members nor administrators seemed willing to push us toward more focused and outcome-oriented conversations. Throughout these exchanges, I heard my colleagues affirm the value of conversation as part of the faculty's everyday work. The question then became how to make sure that the faculty conversations could happen with less resistance and more engagement.

Concerned that the faculty didn't want to "play" or would seriously undermine the project, Marty Stortz and I asked Tim Lull to intervene more forcefully. Marty asked Tim if we needed to discuss even continuing with the project. In her comments to Tim she said:

> The most dour reading of Friday's meeting leads us to conclude that most faculty are still resistant to what is being proposed. I'm thinking of X citing Z to the effect that, "We've been through all of this before. . . ." When a team member submarines the team's proposal, it's hard to mount opposition . . . and there was a real dearth of positive suggestions. . . . The least dour reading of Friday's meeting is that people are looking for some leadership, some voice of authority on how important Lexington is. Various attempts to steer discussion into the issues of teaching and learning, among them Steve's and my own, were all pretty well shot down, some by the other members of the Lexington team itself. Maybe it is just fine to have conversation together about whatever anyone is interested in—but that misses the sense that this is a *kairos* moment for PLTS, and it loses us the opportunity to have purposeful conversation about issues that are crying for attention.

In a short meeting with Tim following the retreat, we talked about Marty's assessment of the faculty's response. Tim noted that some of our colleagues seemed to be under the impression that the project being proposed would result in a loss of their independence. He then agreed that he and Michael (the dean) needed to be more active, noting that they "couldn't wait for the faculty to police themselves." Tim affirmed that the new proposal we had written was on target and something that this faculty had to address. In a letter a few days later. he wrote to the faculty asking them to "suspend your objections" and follow the post-Maine proposal. He asked us to spend the fall semester talking about how various changes in theological education have influenced our teaching. This would prepare the ground for our follow-up proposal and "have the advantage of having us around campus on Wednesdays—something very important to the life of our school just now." Marty's response to Tim and Michael's memo was telling: "Finally, the administration is saying, here's what we're going to do. End of discussion. Sometimes we just need someone to say that to us, and we'll follow." Our administrators seemingly had stepped into the leadership vacuum the faculty refused to fill.

On September 5 we began our fall meetings somewhat tentatively. Many faculty members were quiet, and several sat with arms folded across their chests or doodled on notepads, their body language denoting their resistance. At this first meeting, about half of the faculty spoke about their teaching in light of one or more of the challenges facing theological education. "Context" emerged as a consistent challenge, whether grappling with the changed context of American Christianity or addressing multiculturalism in our courses. The following Wednesday was the day after the September 11 events, and a somber group gathered to talk about how and what we taught amidst the unfolding tragedy, shock, and uncertainty of 9/11. Faculty members voiced their intention to incorporate these events into the work of their class agendas, again affirming the centrality of context in their teaching. During the next two weeks, we read articles from a recent conference of teaching theologians of the Evangelical Lutheran Church of American (ELCA) regarding Lutheran pedagogy. These sessions became opportunities for the faculty to reflect on the particular *charisms* of PLTS as a Lutheran institution of higher learning, to identify the joys and challenges of teaching Luther in the context of religious pluralism and indifference as well as in the ecumenical setting of the Graduate Theological Union (GTU), and to begin to state positively how Pacific Lutheran is different from its sister seminaries. A second theme for the semester began to emerge around the issue of integration. That is, how can we teach so that our classrooms serve as places in which students can draw on what they learn in Lutheran Confessions or Gospels or Word and Sacrament in a synthetic manner as they learn how to preach and minister?

Integration and contexts became the themes for the remaining sessions of the fall semester. We spent two weeks talking about how we teach contextually. In two and one-half sessions, each of us identified the contexts we try to teach about or address in our courses. These contexts included American Biblicism; sexuality debates; the intersection of race, ethnicity, gender, and class; and the geography and cultural landscapes of Immigrant America and Reformation Europe. At the same time, we spoke about our pedagogical practices—the nuts and bolts of how we teach—sharing with one another strategies and rationales for teaching Luther or for challenging students to think theologically. As we talked, I began to see changes in how the faculty interacted. Our sessions began in September with each person speaking in turn, as if delivering a lecture, each speech unconnected to the others. By October, we had moved to a faculty conversing with one another—listening and responding, finding similarities in how we teach contextually, and learning lessons from one another. We began as a reluctant faculty, somewhat coerced into these Wednesday morning meetings, but we were becoming a faculty that was enjoying our time together, energized by the meetings—a faculty reforming. Halfway through the semester, one faculty member suggested that our goal as a faculty and a school might be to become a "community of argument" (referring to a recent work of Kathryn Tanner)—a community that argues about its tradition and the meaning of discipleship in order to learn from one another and to understand and accept difference.

Two sessions were especially important in the process of formation and identity building for the faculty. In the first, we had read an essay about a distinctly Lutheran pedagogy. We used this article to discuss how PLTS is distinct from the other Lutheran seminaries, a distinctiveness seen in our more open-ended approach to Luther, the Confessions, and the tradition. Our faculty discussed how they treated the tradition as something that is created and re-created in time and space. For us, the tradition is ambiguous and provides a framework with which we can make sense of such things as the World Trade Center attacks or the declining church in the American West. This was the first session in which the language of scarcity was abandoned and the faculty opted for a more positive language about institutional strengths.

The second session occurred near the end of the semester in which we reviewed what we had done in previous weeks in preparation to write the grant proposal for the project. Led by Marty Stortz and Michael Aune, the faculty first identified the goals of the seminary curriculum—forming disciples, fostering the call to ministry, creating lifelong learners—and then started naming how we fulfill those goals. It was a heady discussion in which faculty named the gifts, or in Marty's words "charisms of the community." These include the various ways in which we teach contextually and critically, teach across the disciplines and across traditions, and teach students to live within a complex and ambiguous social world. It was a session in which we once again abandoned the taken-for-granted situation of scarcity and realized that this school and this faculty had important gifts to offer the church.

We finished the semester in a weary but hopeful state. The faculty had moved from "cordiality to candor," in the words of Marty Stortz. We had begun to talk with and listen to one another. We had discovered that we enjoyed our conversations and that perhaps we were more than just a group of individuals who happened to teach at the same school. We had learned new things about each other—what we teach, how we teach, and the underlying passions and commitments behind our teaching. In short, we were becoming a faculty that had not existed in recent years. Our weekly sessions catalyzed this reformation in part because they allowed us to identify shared pedagogies and intellectual interests, shared commitments to understanding the Lutheran tradition in a particular manner, and shared concerns for the intellectual, professional, and spiritual formation of our students.

PHASE 3: THE BAD, THE UGLY, AND THE GOOD

The signs of progress evinced in the fall semester evaporated during much of the spring semester. Our sessions became combative at times and directionless at others. Sometimes the body language of the faculty indicated boredom, indifference, anger, and frustration. Sometimes our words were starkly critical of others' ideas or positions. It was difficult to see that any good was coming of such retrograde meetings. And yet perhaps such turmoil was needed for the faculty to break the bonds of old behavioral habits.

The focus for the spring semester meetings was for us to discuss the courses we taught and examine the ways in which our courses sustained, supported, and built upon one another (or failed to do so). At the first session of the spring semester, Jane Strohl, the seminar director for the semester, described the agenda for weekly meetings. They would be sessions at which the faculty who teach core courses would describe what and how they taught, discuss how to address problems encountered in the classroom, perhaps look to their colleagues for new pedagogical strategies, and examine how each core course connects with other courses. As she introduced our work for the semester, she also provided the underlying rationale of trying to discern the degree to which the core curriculum is integrated and how best to help our students integrate all that they learn in their years at Pacific Lutheran:

> I've noticed how we tend to do our work and teaching rather independently and saw
> a need to look at how our courses are integrated. So where we will start this semester
> is to look at our core courses and pedagogies. I still don't really know what goes on
> in those courses but I learn from my students what some of the connections might be

and I wonder if I can help with integrating the learnings across the courses. . . . The role of the teacher is to take the initiative and be a little bold—to offer an invitation to students to connect the different pieces of their education and that might mean we have to show them those connections at first. To what extent do our core courses not just represent our own intellectual interests but a broader sense of the seminary's identity and its core commitments and as well as the commitments of the ELCA?

We seemed more comfortable speaking about the content of our courses and more reticent discussing how the courses were or were not related to one another. We hoped that talking about the whats, whys, and hows of our courses would be a relatively safe and productive place to deepen our relationships and find some of the intellectual and pedagogical commonalities around which we could reform ourselves as a faculty. By the end of the semester, we realized that while we now had a much clearer understanding of what happened in one another's courses, the weekly meetings had not "reformed the faculty" as ideally envisioned. Instead, the meetings uncovered long simmering tensions, deep-seated interactional patterns, and a powerful culture of faculty autonomy. The meetings were messy. Some faculty members defended their curricular turf even as we tried to shift ownership from "my course" to "our core." Decades-long disagreements about the curriculum, power, and the meaning of multiculturalism gave rise to intense discussion and selective disengagement. At our last session, one professor summarized the semester in the following way: "our worst moments were also our best moments; as we disintegrated, one of us pulled us back together."

Each Wednesday morning a different faculty member presented one of the required M.Div. courses being taught. In general, our collective review of the core courses was considered a helpful exercise to learn what each of us really did in our courses and to begin to identify texts or pedagogical strategies our courses shared (or as Tim Lull said at one meeting, "the unlikely places where our courses connect"). For the most part, we learned more about what and how we taught than about how our courses interrelated.

After a few weeks, Jane Strohl coined the term "curricular capital" to refer to the knowledge, gifts, and skills we each brought to the courses at Pacific Lutheran. She urged us to think about what courses, ideas, and pedagogical strategies should be part of the curriculum and identify which were currently present or absent. She also urged us to move away from thinking about core courses and to think about a core curriculum of which each of us taught a part. Although our walks through each others' syllabi often seemed to be a pedantic exercise, in hindsight, we may have learned more about ourselves and the challenges and possibilities for renewal than were apparent to us at the time.

Within a month, it became clear to several of us that the patterns of this faculty's interaction constituted a critical part of what we were learning. Early on I noticed what I later called our "default interactional pattern," a pattern cultivated over the course of many years and one in which the faculty subverted one another by being confrontational while at the same time evading truly engaged discussion. It was exemplified in one meeting in which our Christian Education professor began to describe her pedagogical approach and was attacked by Professor X for not respecting the learning styles of students who might not learn effectively through her approach. Professor X did not so much ask a question as make a speech that set forth his platform. After he reset the agenda, he never again participated. In fact, he left early and never engaged the other professor in real conversation.

After the first month had passed, Jane, Michael, and I reviewed the meeting process, and Jane announced a few mid-course corrections in order to (1) clarify the purpose of our weekly gatherings, (2) minimize what Jane called the "toxic interactions," and (3) make sure our sessions bore fruit. Jane began our sixth session with the following announcement:

1. We don't have a core curriculum as much as people who teach pieces of the core. We need to move beyond people feeling defensive about what they do and don't do in their courses but to talk about our curricular capital. We need to reflect together about what we have done and what's missing from our core in order to help us during our next curricular review. This is partly about moving from "my course" to "our core."
2. Then we'd like to spend the last fifteen minutes thinking about what are the implications for the core curriculum—how we see others' courses connecting to our own.

Perhaps it shouldn't have come as a surprise that we didn't follow this agenda very closely for the rest of the semester. Nor was the plea to move beyond a rigid defense of our courses in pursuit of dialogue heard. Instead, the faculty continued to present their courses and emphasize whatever they thought was important about them, regardless of the agenda. The passive but confrontational pattern of interaction erupted periodically, usually in one-line zingers that called into question the legitimacy of a particular professor's pedagogy or our collective enterprise. At the last meeting of the seminar, Tim Lull reminded us that our reliance on bombast, resistance, and an unwillingness to listen and converse flattened our individual and collective interest in this project and our willingness to spend time together. These little and not-so-little verbal attacks were subverting the goodwill of the faculty and threatening to derail the process.

For our final meeting of the spring semester, the faculty had read my draft report of the semester's meetings in which I had included substantial verbatim excerpts of our fights over multiculturalism and the core curriculum. I then characterized the faculty's default interactional pattern in the following manner: a confrontational but essentially nonengaging, passive style of behavior that effectively derails conversation and discourages faculty involvement with one another; one makes an attack and then doesn't engage in conversation; hard things are said and then an apology is offered while at the same time maintaining that one's position is the correct one. I continued with a brief discussion of the consequences of this interactional style: We do not defend one another in public and thus undermine trust in one another and in the faculty as a whole; important issues are hijacked or derailed, and we thus avoid addressing the challenges of actually changing how we teach, what we teach, and the environment in which we teach.

Although the report was evenly divided between our conversations about the curriculum and my assessment of our interactions, we spent the majority of the session talking about the interactional pattern. Clearly I had touched a nerve. Gary Pence's[3] opening comments set the tone for the meeting: "This is an exciting, interesting document. It's the most honest, candid, concrete description of the endemic issues for faculties in institutions like ours." He then said that while we could all take issue with some of my comments, in general I had accurately described the faculty and then wryly noted that we would be a unique faculty if we actually talked about how we relate to one another. My other colleagues generally agreed with Gary, thanking me for naming the elephant in our parlor. Tim asked the senior faculty to put my comments in historical perspective, and we heard a number of stories about how prior faculties related. We learned that the faculty had been avoiding nasty confrontations over controversial topics for at least twenty-five years. The senior faculty tempered my more critical assessment by arguing that the faculty's history of conflict avoidance had also been one of the reasons that the faculty had functioned as well as it had over time. Michael Aune noted that there had always been a deep loyalty to one another and a genuine interest in one another's work, which had mitigated conflict.

A few affirmed the culture of autonomy they had experienced at Pacific Lutheran and acknowledged that this autonomy (that is, doing our own thing with minimal engagement in institutional governance) had also encouraged a conflict-avoiding pattern. Gary suggested that most faculties have an ethos of individual independence. "We like to do our own thing, and we see the administration as existing to assure our autonomy." He continued to describe some work he had done earlier in his career on group dynamics that led him to the conclusion that faculties foster an ethos of narcissism, a sort of intellectual and collegial self-centeredness that masks our fears and encourages us to pretend we do not care about one another's opinions or ideas. Jane, with tongue firmly in cheek, suggested that we had "faculty of origin" problems, but then turned serious, noting that many of us came from different faculties and their imprint on us as young professors had cast a long shadow.

LESSONS LEARNED

We left for the summer unsure that we could become a reformed faculty with a redefined curriculum. There was still resistance to more intentional collaboration within the required course of study in the M.Div. program. Some voiced resistance to interference with "their courses," displaying the persistence of a culture of autonomy and a commitment to individual disciplines rather than collective pedagogical goals. We also recognized significant structural resistance to addressing curricular integration. Intentional collaboration would require us to (1) plan our courses in consultation with one another; (2) develop readings, assignments, or discussion topics that build on the work done in other courses and that address the same or similar issues but from different perspectives; and (3) perhaps even team teach more of the core courses. The scatteredness of the faculty, the strong culture of faculty autonomy, sabbatical schedules, and a certain amount of incommensurability among courses would make this a difficult challenge.

Several questioned the purpose and direction of the spring seminar. At times the seminar seemed to have no endgame, nor did the process seem to be uniting us or forming us as a faculty. We also saw a disconnect between the work of The Lexington Seminar project and the work of the academic committee on curriculum review and faculty hiring. Once again we lacked strong faculty leadership.

Yet there were more positive notes on which we ended. The cantankerous sessions about multiculturalism led to several sessions in which we talked about the courses that intentionally addressed the issue and how other courses could do the same. This development was seen as a sign that we were moving toward a more active engagement with one another. By the end of the semester, we had actually begun to listen and learn from one another, and a few faculty members spoke of working more collaboratively. The dean encouraged us to propose modest pedagogical experiments through which we might bridge our courses and disciplines in new ways.

PHASE 4: A FACULTY REFORMED?

A funny thing happened on the way to the fall 2002 semester: The faculty of Pacific Lutheran Theological Seminary decided to be engaged and work together. The reasons for this still elude me. Perhaps it was the need to meet an institutional crisis that had arisen because of financial strains and a third straight year of small entering classes. Perhaps it was the goodwill that had emerged during the course of the school's fiftieth anniversary celebration. Perhaps it was the senior faculty's greater involvement with and ownership of The Lexington Seminar project. Perhaps the difficult and honest self-examination of the previous semester had borne fruit.

We began the semester in August with an extended faculty retreat at which we first heard from the president about the financial strains we faced and spent much of the time reading and discussing one another's teaching auto-biographies. The conversations were remarkably honest. Faculty members seemed willing to risk speaking about their own misgivings about teaching and the challenges faced in the classroom. Pleasant surprise was the common response afterwards as we chatted informally about the retreat. Another uni-fying feature, I believe, was the time we spent with Tim at the opening, dur-ing which he spoke with us about the financial stress on the school.

We began the fall semester's weekly meetings with a presentation by one of the senior faculty members, who had previously been less engaged and a bit difficult. He and the dean had examined the curricular plan recently developed by the Washington Theological Union and adapted it to Pacific Lutheran. The plan was divided into thirds on an eleven-by-seventeen sheet of paper. In the right-hand column was a list of competencies a graduate of the Pacific Lutheran's M.Div. program would possess. The left-hand column contained a list of leadership, formation, and intellectual goals attached to each year of the program. The middle column was blank with the intention that it would eventually be filled in with specific courses that would help students fulfill the curricular goals and accrue the general competencies for ministry.

We spent the first two weeks of the semester talking about and revising this document. Everyone agreed with the document and saw it as a major step for-ward. For the first time, many pieces of the faculty's work during the past four years began to fall into place. We were in the final year of a board-mandated curricular revision, and the work of The Lexington Seminar project began to feed directly into this. The academic committee and the original Lexington Seminar team came together in a spirit of collaboration, thus engaging most of the faculty. No longer could some of us view the weekly Wednesday morn-ing meetings as an additional task, unconnected to our other work. Instead, The Lexington Seminar project became integral to the life of the faculty.

We revisited conversations at various faculty retreats in which we examined the curriculum and the kind of leaders we hoped we were training. We came back to old conversations about the ways in which we teach content and con-text and affirmed the need for Pacific Lutheran to start with the content of the

Christian and Lutheran traditions. Marty Stortz spoke for many when she affirmed this approach:

> Starting with the contents of our tradition is more seeker-sensitive or friendly given the larger number of converts and seekers we have in comparison to Luther. Starting with content also serves our students well as we are part of the ecumenical GTU and our students need to be able rather quickly to speak about what it means to be Lutheran in this environment.

Throughout the semester, we asked key constituencies (such as bishops of the eleven western synods, students, and teaching parish pastors) to help us determine better ways to train students for leadership in the church. Some reviewed our curricular document and spoke with us about it. We spent time debriefing after these conversations and then revising our curriculum guide. The listening sessions were extremely helpful, because different groups pointed out gaps and confusions in our guide. Imaginations seemed to be released, and the possibilities for the revised curriculum began to look exciting. We began to identify possible "mission emphases" (or areas of concentration) that would make Pacific Lutheran's program even more distinct among the eight Lutheran seminaries. These mission emphases included: Latino/Hispanic ministry, congregational redevelopment, global missions, and youth and family ministry. One faculty member proposed that we commit ourselves as a faculty to becoming fluent in Spanish within five years, and faculty members (especially the president) spoke repeatedly about our need to collectively own multiculturalism. We began to talk about a greater faculty role in the contextual education process (which was generally run by the staff with little involvement or leadership from the faculty) and explicitly integrating classroom work and parish work. Finally, we picked up a frequent conversation, really a lament, about the failure of the fourth-year curriculum and began imagining a year-long integrative seminar.

IMPLICATIONS OF THE PROCESS

The curriculum remains unfinished, but the faculty is moving forward. Incremental change and proceeding with caution remain the *modus operandi*, but there is a sense that the faculty is more united, more than cordial, more than a group of people who happen to teach at the same place. Two years of weekly meetings have begun to form us into a community and, indirectly, have infused new life into the community as a whole, as students and staff now regularly see us meeting, talking in hallways, and leading public events on campus. Have we reformed? Yes, at least provisionally. Perhaps the comments from someone who was, at the start of the process, among the less engaged senior faculty members indicates the progress this faculty has made toward reformation:

> I've been thinking about team teaching and even if I'm not in class with another faculty member, I think we function as a team in our teaching. Because of last year's conversations I know a lot more about what everyone else does in their classes. There is a sense in which I'm fascinated with the ways we are team teaching. Students go from class to class and they're not hearing a different gospel or a different culture. There is some coherence here. We have different accents but there is a lot of common stuff.

The most important lesson learned from Pacific Lutheran's experience is that regular and focused conversation about the vocation of teachers at theological schools is critical for any work of institutional change or curriculum renewal. Although in the early phases of the project, the faculty seemed merely to be following familiar patterns of interaction and rehashing the same old problems, we were really doing a deeper and more radical thing. Old relationships and institutional commitments to one another were reactivated; new connections between courses and pedagogies were made; genuine listening was taking place; and the sense that we had too little time to do too many tasks was slowly being replaced by a sense that we were in this thing together. The turning point was connecting The Lexington Seminar project with the academic committee's board-mandated curriculum review. This adjustment gave the project a sharper focus, included more senior colleagues who had not been part of the original Lexington team, and created an environment in which it was increasingly safe to speak honestly about the struggles and joys of teaching and working at Pacific Lutheran Theological Seminary.

The weekly conversations forced the faculty to confront their own history and strong culture of autonomy and recognize that their shared commitment to training students for ministry was stronger than old grievances and the desire to "get in our cars and drive home." The dean's strategy of rotating mid-career faculty members into positions of leadership and minimizing the leadership roles of most of the original team helped increase faculty involvement and ownership in the process. However, more widespread faculty involvement from the very beginning of the seminar, especially if more members had been given a hand in writing the school's narrative, may have prompted a greater sense of faculty ownership early on or at least eased some of the initial resistance.

In the end, The Lexington Seminar project has changed the faculty of Pacific Lutheran Theological Seminary. While the faculty remember our history of autonomy and the ways in which being in diaspora strengthens that autonomy, such autonomy may not be as important as our renewed sense of collegiality. We are energized by the current curricular review process and plan to continue the regular conversations in the coming academic year even after the Seminar project is officially over. Perhaps we have learned that a theological school faculty, especially one that is in diaspora, cannot operate effectively or faithfully without creating the time and space to talk about the common task and the vision that animates them.

Although this ethnography examined only one school, it suggests several practical implications for processes of institutional change, faculty development, and leadership at theological schools.

First, any effort at deep-seated institutional change will generate resistance because it requires a significant investment in the time and energies of the faculty and may threaten to disrupt the longstanding culture and practices of a school. One should expect resistance to be especially strong at schools with a largely tenured (and hence senior) faculty, those whose faculty have an entrenched culture of autonomy, and those whose faculty are very involved in governance and tend to resist top-down initiatives. Overcoming the initial resistance to change requires creative leadership to push or pull a faculty toward participation. Inviting resisting faculty members into leadership positions or releasing some faculty from teaching or administrative loads may be necessary to induce more willing or engaged participation.

Second, the general structure of conversation and reflection that Pacific Lutheran used invites participation and can lead to change. The structure is organized around the where, who, why, and what questions facing a school and its faculty. Starting with the question of where—that is, the context of theological education—is a relatively safe topic, and by defining context broadly to include the context of ministry and mission for the church and the social, cultural, and political context of the United States and the world forces a faculty to look beyond themselves and their school. Clearly the faculty of Pacific Lutheran Theological Seminary had to address the events of September 11 and its aftermath because they have fundamentally changed the context for preparing church leaders. Moving to the question of who—that is, the identity of faculty members as teachers, scholars, persons of faith—can build new relationships and deepen trust among colleagues as faculty members publicly share their teaching autobiographies, syllabi, and pedagogical approaches. For the Pacific Lutheran faculty, the who question placed on the table many of the faculty members' positions on race and multiculturalism, the curriculum and curricular change, faculty autonomy, and governance and forced us to talk with one another about them.

Like the where question, the question of why—that is, the purpose of a seminary education—can encourage a faculty to look beyond itself. In the case of Pacific Lutheran, we became energized by the vision of ministry we heard from the ELCA bishops and clergy of the western states during the school's fiftieth anniversary. During this stage, a faculty would be well-served to listen to key stakeholders of the school and the church in order to make sure the school's mission and programs are aligned with the mission needs of the congregations their students will serve. The question of what—that is, the courses and cocurricular activities of a school—cannot be addressed properly without engaging the first three questions.

Third, Pacific Lutheran Theological Seminary learned several practical lessons about navigating through these conversations. Regular meetings, weekly if possible, occurring for several semesters are needed to (1) build trust; (2) place all concerns, histories, and hopes on the table; and (3) create a new culture of collegiality. Clear ground rules for the conversations may help keep the conversations productive, although in our case, the toxic conversations pushed us along toward greater collegiality and a willingness to keep talking. Having a recorder of the conversations, whether a disinterested third party or a trusted faculty member, is important because the written record makes evanescent conversation concrete, can remind the faculty of commitments made, and keeps the participants honest. The faculty made several breakthroughs after reading the ethnographic accounts of our weekly meetings.

Finally, Pacific Lutheran learned that junior and senior faculty have different expectations and needs for development and involvement during the process of institutional change. It is easy for some to dismiss senior faculty, especially those nearing retirement, as irrelevant to the process, because they appear to have few reasons to be vested in the process of change. Yet senior faculty members possess the wisdom of experience and hold a school's memory. Both should be tapped, and a school can encourage its senior faculty members to understand the outcomes of fundamental institutional change as one of the legacies they may leave behind. At the other extreme, junior faculty can be groomed for future leadership by providing them with modest leadership positions at different phases of the process and by encouraging more senior colleagues to model leadership for them.

In the end, this study suggests that the process of faculty formation must precede curricular revision, or at least go hand-in-hand. The temptation may be to jump immediately into curricular change because of the enormous time pressures faculty face along with demands from students for a more efficient and relevant curriculum that will better prepare them for ministry. Yet without the long and difficult process of faculty formation, real curricular or institutional change is less likely to occur. The case of Pacific Lutheran Theological Seminary shows how a process in which faculty publicly speak together about their identities as teachers and scholars, share their pedagogies, and try to learn how one another's courses work and relate to those of their colleagues prepares the ground for true reformation.

Notes

1. On the challenges of the participant-observer role, see Emerson (2001) and Orsi (1994).
2. Tim Lull's death in 2003 was a great loss for theological education. In many ways, he embodied the ideals of the theological teacher we affirm in this text.
3. Gary Pence, professor of pastoral theology, pastoral care, and counseling, and academic dean.

Understanding the Context of Change

·JANE SHAW·

The Seminary Dispersed

THEOLOGICAL TEACHING IN A CHANGING WORLD

Once upon a time, in seminaries all over the United States and Britain, students were extremely well-prepared. In fact, some of them even knew Hebrew and Greek before they arrived. They always went to class. They turned their assignments in on time. They never grumbled, and they completed their seminary studies in three years with no problems. The faculty members were never overworked, and after a good day of teaching, community worship, leisurely office hours, and supper with students in the refectory, they would go home to an evening of research while someone else put the children to bed.

I do not know whether this golden age of seminary education ever existed. I rather doubt it, but I do detect that we tend to operate as if it did, as we worry and ponder about how to make things better in the face of overworked faculty and administrators; commuting, part-time, and older students with various levels of education; and a diverse student body. Even if that golden age did exist in some places and at some times, we should always ask: For whom was it golden? Not, I think, for those of the "wrong" gender or ethnicity or class or age whose vocations went unanswered, ignored by the churches, and whose gifts of intellect and teaching were discounted by the academy.

We find ourselves today in the midst of some confusion, some messiness, and much diversity of expectation and experience. We also find ourselves with a great opportunity to educate ministers who might truly represent all God's people in a new and invigorating way. This exciting development presents us with a number of challenges to which many of the narratives for The Lexington Seminar give witness.

In this essay, I look at two issues. First, I draw an analogy between the student bodies in today's seminaries and the reality of today's congregations and their churchgoing patterns. Second, I examine the diverse nature of seminaries' student bodies. Following these discussions, I then make some suggestions—grounded in a thoroughly incarnational theology—for new possibilities in teaching, learning, and community formation to break through the stalemate situations in which we often seem to find ourselves.

Before beginning, though, I wish to sound a note of caution. We are often hard on ourselves as teachers and learners, imagining that if we can find just the right magic formula, then we will get everything absolutely right in theological education. At the same time, we might think we can build the kingdom of heaven on earth overnight. As Christians, we operate with a vision of something better, which sustains and motivates us. It is part of our theology. It is part of our practice. We operate with a vision of God's kingdom, and that vision is vital, but just as vital is the recognition that the vision will not be fully achieved in this lifetime. In that space of tension between the "not yet" and the "could be," we operate as Christians, and that includes what we do in theological schools.

THE SEMINARY DISPERSED, THE CHURCH DISPERSED

Seminary student bodies are changing, and this affects the nature of seminary community life, as illustrated by many of the narratives developed for the Lexington Seminar. The Church Divinity School of the Pacific's narrative (2001)[1] illustrates the pressures on both students and faculty. For Priscilla, the part-time commuting student, life in her placement church is rather more exciting than seminary commitments, and family and church commitments mean that she can only come to seminary one day a week, for one course a semester. Consequently, she feels that she will need more than the six years allotted for a part-time student to complete her training and theological education in the M.Div. program. Furthermore, she is not showing up for her duties on the chapel rota and does not seem to understand the importance of her involvement in a central part of community life: worship. It is, at first glance, easy to blame Priscilla for not grasping the commitments required of those engaged in a seminary education. At second glance, it is easy to blame the seminary for opening its doors to part-time students, for offering such students the opportunity to train for ordained ministry, for thinking (in all likelihood) of its own financial benefit, without necessarily anticipating the repercussions of its new strategy. The reality is that the institution, the students, and the professors each have different expectations that are not necessarily being met, which lead to clashes, built-up resentment, and considerable pressures on all parties.

A similar pattern is echoed in the narrative of Colgate Rochester Crozer Divinity School (2002). The dean expresses the faculty's frustration when she wonders to herself how the seminary can even consider goals such as formation when its students "seem barely able to keep up with basic class work, while the faculty is envisioning moving to a curriculum beyond basics: values and outcomes, aptitudes and attitudes, sequencing, evaluation . . . Dare we continue this cloistered, visionary discussion? Or should we problem-solve around students living in a 'reality' world?" All along the corridor, faculty members listen to the explanations (and rationalizations) students give for not attending classes or completing assignments—"I had to facilitate Bible discussion groups," "I had to teach a confirmation class," "I had to attend a revival"—all of which are put before time in the classroom. Again, the clash is between students who want to do ministry in the real world and have many commitments outside the seminary, and faculty who are, as the narratives indicate, overwhelmed by obligations that leave them little time for scholarly pursuits or spiritual contemplation and frustrated by the burdens of trying to teach a seemingly resistant or ungrateful student body.

In Austin Presbyterian Theological Seminary's narrative (1999), a part-time student and single mother named Jean expresses her frustration both with the content of her courses—why, for example, does she have to take two classes in systematic theology when her own denomination emphasizes practical theology?—and with the feeling that "everything is structured for a certain type of person, and I'm not that person." In Lexington Theological Seminary's narrative (2002), Wayne, a twenty-eight-year-old student, expresses his frustration at being made to write papers on theology. "No one really cares about theology," he explains to, of all people, his theology professor, "or any of the other 'ologies' we spend so much time on at seminary. What relevance for today is there in wading through Tillich, Barth and Schleiermacher?" As another student in the same narrative says, "I came here to prepare for ministry and for me that's more about spiritual formation than it is about abstract intellectual stuff. If I wanted that, I would have gone to a graduate program in religious studies."

General Theological Seminary's narrative (2002) shifts the focus from the clash between the expectations of the students and those of the faculty to the clash between resident and nonresident students in the seminary. The narrative describes a seminary coming to grips for the first time with a serious volume of commuter students that threatens to change its well-established, indeed famed, ethos as a residential community. A new commuting student complains to the academic dean that he can't find anything, that he doesn't know anyone, and that he can't make sense of the seemingly arcane chapel worship (even though it is basic Anglican evensong in an Episcopal chapel). In contrast, a residential student complains that the commuting students show no respect for the ethos of the seminary, an ethos that involves growing commitment and a dedication to community life. "Communities are built, not bought," says the residential student. "The problem with . . . some of the part-time students is that they think theological education is something you purchase. They've got a consumer mentality."

Two major themes emerge from these four narratives. First, as a result of the demographic shifts in the student body, formation—so long a staple of residential seminary life, occurring by osmosis over meals together in the refectory, corporate worship, and late-night chats in the dorms—does not now occur in the same way. Perhaps it does not occur at all for some seminary students. Second, many students perceive little or no connection between the "real" ministry they are doing and what they are required to learn in seminary. A clash between student and faculty expectations for ministerial training and theological education therefore ensues. As the theology professor in Lexington Theological Seminary's narrative says, "How do we help students integrate questions of theology and practice in ministry?" With a gracious hermeneutics of generosity—given that her subject has been declared irrelevant by student Wayne—and a keen desire to learn how to be a more effective teacher, the theology professor puts the responsibility back onto the faculty and asks, "What do we in the faculty have to learn to do if we are to teach in a way that helps students become thoughtful and theologically reflective pastors?"

In addressing these two themes, it is helpful, I think, to make an analogy with models of the church. A church is traditionally thought of as the church gathered, especially by the ordained minister who is around the church for much of the week, whose mental, spiritual, and emotional focus is necessarily church life as it revolves around a particular place. But as Vincent Strudwick has pointed out, for most members of a church, the church is only gathered once or twice a week. The rest of the time those members form the church dispersed. Strudwick (2001) writes, "The church exists in two modes: gathered and dispersed. The clergy often spend most of their time in the 'gathered' mode and this means that they can easily forget that the laity spend 98% of their time in the 'dispersed mode'. Yet how much time when we are 'gathered' do we spend preparing people spiritually, theologically and psychologically for being Christians in the secular world?" What we have to recognize is that the seminary today is, in many cases, much more the seminary dispersed than the seminary gathered. Even for the residential students and the full-time faculty, the reality of a significant proportion of the student body being almost constantly dispersed affects their own formation because it affects the nature of community life.

In the church dispersed, the sensible minister recognizes that the church's mission is not simply to get people into church but to guide the spiritual proclivities of people outside of church. Similarly, seminary professors should be considering ways to harness those student activities that are apparently not about seminary classes and worship—work, church placements, relationships, families, shopping for groceries, getting the car fixed—and incorporating them into the process of formation and learning theology. Shouldn't seminaries and professors be trying to develop a truly incarnational model of theological education?

William Temple, the mid-twentieth-century archbishop of Canterbury, articulated a thoroughly incarnational model of theology. Through his work in education, especially through his role as president of the Workers Educational Association (WEA), Temple came to see that all human experience was "religious" or could be interpreted religiously. God so loved the world that he gave his only begotten son, as John's Gospel tells us, which means that Christ does not need to be brought into the world; Christ was, is, and will be already in the world. For Temple, then, one cannot go straight to scripture or doctrine to find answers to any social or ethical situation; one must rather acquire and assess the evidence, listen to people's stories and experiences, and use the work of experts in their own fields outside the discipline of theology as an essential part of theological work. Temple reminded us, too, that the ongoing activity of most people in their families, jobs, and civil life is where their Christian discipleship and principles need to be applied. He wrote, in his best-selling book *Christianity and Social Order* (1976, 39), "Nine-tenths of the work of the Church in the world is done by Christian people fulfilling responsibilities and performing tasks which in themselves are not part of the official system of the Church at all."

This serves as an important reminder to all clergy, to all seminary professors, and to all those training for ordination that "church"—and, by analogy, "seminary"—is not just a building or set of buildings where people gather but is also the people dispersed in the world.[2] So, if seminary teachers develop a truly incarnational model of theological education, and if they do that well, then they will be modeling something extremely important for seminarians when those students go on to become ministers of the church dispersed. They will be giving them the tools to help the members of their congregations *be* church wherever they are: in the workplace, in family and friendship circles, and in community activities.

Some seminaries that have strong formational patterns in place—such as General Theological Seminary—struggle to maintain them, while others who cannot approximate anything like a residential model—as illustrated in the narrative of Bethel Theological Seminary (2001)—struggle to integrate issues of personal and community formation into the classroom. However, all seminaries, whatever their denomination and demographic composition, face the fact that mixed modes of learning are here to stay, and each school must find a way to address its own distinctive issues.

In the United States, the current model is usually one of a seminary, formerly composed entirely of residential, full-time students, gradually acquiring a number of commuting and part-time students, often to the point that such commuting and part-time students become the statistical norm (as at Church Divinity School of the Pacific), while the norm of seminary training, education, and formation remains that which was designed for a fully residential, full-time community. In Britain, this pattern sometimes occurs, but in the last two or three decades, the Church of England in particular has developed a number of part-time ordination training courses. These usually entail attendance at several lectures and a worship service one evening a week during term time and a number of study weekends throughout the year, plus a week of summer school. These courses are increasingly popular. They cost less than residential training, and they enable older students and students with families to train for ordination without uprooting themselves or their families, often without leaving their full-time employment.

While the attractions of such courses are considerable, they also create the troubling likelihood of a two-tier level of theological training. The type of student attracted to such courses, and often placed in them by bishops and ministry committees (who, in the Church of England, have the power to determine where and how someone will be trained for ordained ministry because the Church of England funds all such training), tends to be older and female. By contrast, the type of student more regularly accepted for full-time, residential training in the several theological colleges that still exist around the country tend to be younger, free of family responsibilities, and male. There are, then, issues of power at play in who gets educated and how, and these issues must be carefully monitored so as not to disadvantage the so-called unconventional students. We need to be careful not to welcome them with one hand (smugly proud of ourselves for opening our doors to them) while relegating them to an education that is often perceived and even experienced as second-class, one that is seen as less rigorous than that received by full-time residential students.

Such perceptions and experiences occur when part-time courses are modeled on full-time courses, usually by simply stretching the full-time course over a greater period of time. The challenge is to build courses of study and notions of formation out of a new understanding of the seminary, an understanding in which the seminary is perceived as the seminary dispersed as well as the seminary gathered. What students experience when they are not in the seminary buildings can then be newly understood as part of their seminary education when they are given the right tools of analysis and the appropriate support systems. Such tools and support systems are explored in the final section of the essay.

IDENTITY AND DIVERSITY IN THEOLOGICAL EDUCATION

Another reality of the changing demography of our seminary populations is that issues of diversity and pluralism—having to do with gender, ethnicity, age, and sexual orientation—are prominent in many of our seminary communities. The articulation of that diversity and how people experience it is often highly charged, simmering with all sorts of resentments and half-understandings and then emerging in explosive moments of crisis.

Austin Presbyterian's narrative (1999) ends with a letter to the dean from an African American student saying that he has been a victim of racism on the seminary campus: "I know you pride yourself on openness, but things only seem to be 'open' when we manage to fit in. Once again, I was left out of a study group because I am black and don't 'act' white enough." United Theological Seminary's narrative (2000) explores—in the form of a letter from Julie, a white, lesbian evangelical student—the repercussions of both living and learning together as a diverse community and the pedagogical minefields this can open up. Julie's letter to her advisor demonstrates that she has not succeeded in integrating her experiences with her academic study (nor her sometimes conflicting experiences of being both evangelical and lesbian), nor has she opened herself to learning from others. Through this letter, the narrative suggests the range of perspectives and backgrounds amongst the other students: from Sara, the white, heterosexual, divorced woman who is learning how to use her experiences as a starting point and not as the primary criterion for her ministry and study; to Clarice, the only African American woman in the class who does not know how to be herself in the seminary as she can be in her own community; to Mark, the middle-aged, married, liberal white man who has learned *about* others' experiences but not *from* them. He has not challenged himself in that process of learning and has therefore not stretched himself through his experience in seminary.

The question at play here is how students might relate theology to their own context while also attempting to understand the other, such that their own presuppositions are challenged and their ministry becomes more effective. In my experience as a teacher, the two are related; the inner and the outer, so to speak, are utterly connected. Too often, contextual theology is thought of as something that people who "have a context" do. Thus, contextual theology is Latin American liberation theology, feminist theology, black theology, and urban theology, rather than, for example, Tillich's systematic theology, which, as I discuss later, is equally contextual. I am always amused when the students at the theological colleges in and around the leafy green suburbs of Oxford—who will mostly go on to pastor in leafy green suburbs around Britain—tell me that they have been reading urban theology as contextual theology, as if their own situation at present (and in the future) were not a context!

We all have a context, and encouraging students and, indeed, teachers to reflect on that is the first step toward any real possibility of engagement with the other. Once we see our own situatedness, our own context, our own pre-suppositions, then—the hope is—we can begin to shed our own parochial and universalizing tendencies and our paternalistic tendencies as pastors and pastors-in-training. We can understand by means of both compassion—or perhaps a better expression is "sympathetic understanding"—and analogy, as I suggested earlier, but also by standing alongside others and grasping that difference *is* difference. This is only possible when "whiteness" or heterosexuality or being male or, for that matter, being a full-time residential student is no longer perceived as the norm and is seen as one contextual position amongst many, albeit often carrying with it particular privileges and considerable power.

PRACTICAL IMPLICATIONS

Once we begin to perceive diversity and the seminary dispersed as the normal condition in which we operate rather than the exception, we can begin to establish strategies that make our work not only more effective but more fulfilling, both for ourselves and our students. We can begin to link the "real world" to the study of theology in all its facets. Applied to questions of teaching and learning in theological education, the insights of an incarnational theology, as expressed by someone like Temple, and the model of the seminary as dispersed, would suggest a breaking down of the barrier between theology and the real world (between seminary and not-seminary, between church and not-church) as perceived by faculty and students, so that all activity is seen as theological and students are given the proper tools to analyze that activity in theological terms. As The Lexington Seminar narratives suggest, increasingly diverse student bodies call teachers to question their assumptions about the process of teaching and learning, for those diverse student bodies bring a wide range of gifts and experiences but do not necessarily come with traditional educational preparation for seminary learning.

FINDING QUESTIONS FOR THE TEXT

How do teachers present seemingly alien material so that students might understand it? As is well-known—though, in my own experience, often forgotten by teachers and students alike—for a text to have any meaning, the reader has to have some questions to put to it, so the text can come alive. Simply put, I don't understand a physics textbook because I have no questions to put to the text. I stopped doing physics when I was sixteen. I hated every minute of studying physics. Consequently, two and a half decades later, I have no questions to put to a physics textbook and I don't understand it. Sometimes I have to remind myself, as a teacher, that for many seminary students, especially in their first term and their first year, their experience of theological education is like my experience of reading a physics textbook. They have no questions to put to the texts they are reading. And we teachers do not necessarily offer them any questions to put to those texts. Or, rather, we fail to discover what questions they do have which would help them make sense of the material with which they are faced. When learning about the scriptures, church history, systematic theology, and all those seemingly abstract things they learn about in a classroom, what questions do both students and faculty have which would enable the students to understand that what seems so abstract and disconnected from the real world has always, in fact, emerged out of real, live, dynamic, bubbling contexts?

Some excellent suggestions have arisen in the meetings of The Lexington Seminar, and I offer some of those now. As a historian, I am attracted by the idea of presenting apparently abstract systematic theologies in their historical context so they can be shown to be vital theological responses to the questions and cutting-edge issues of their day. By demonstrating this link between theory and the day-to-day world, we might avoid the situation in which a student named Wayne dismisses Tillich, Barth, and Schleiermacher.

I was fortunate to be taught twentieth-century systematic theology by Sharon Welch at Harvard in the mid-1980s, and she brought those thinkers to life by teaching their ideas in the context of their lives and times. In her lectures, Tillich was no longer an abstract thinker but the beatnik of the theological world who, just like those beatnik poets and writers of the 1950s, had an existential crisis—but he formulated a theological response to that crisis. Presented that way, we were all longing to know what Tillich's response to that crisis was, and what God had to do with it. This sort of approach may involve reorganizing the curriculum to combine the teaching of systematic theology and church history; Church Divinity School of the Pacific has done this in recent years, and to excellent effect.

How do we bring alive the debates of the past and the contexts in which theology was discussed? Fourth-century discussions of the Trinity may seem dry to many a seminary student, but Gregory of Nyssa sketches a picture in his *On the Divinity of the Son and the Holy Spirit* in which every part of his city was filled with talk of the Trinity—alleys, squares, crossroads, and avenues. Everyone was talking about the nature of God. If you asked a baker about the quality and price of bread, he would give you an answer about the nature of the Father and the Son. Ask a money changer for the going rate on the drachma, and he would tell you about the begotten and unbegotten. And the manager of the baths, instead of telling you whether the water was ready, would give you a discourse upon the Holy Spirit. Surely we can bring to life the theological debates of the past in two ways: first, by putting them in context rather than teaching them as a set of abstract ideas, and second, by making analogies with the debates of our own day.

How, too, might we link the classroom with students' experiences with field education placements, church work, and family life? One suggestion is to have students retell biblical stories in their own words. Through this they learn the tradition of *midrash* and a good deal about the storytelling methods and oral traditions of the ancient world that forged the written scriptures we have today, while also connecting the insights of scripture to their own experiences and the experiences of those whom they encounter in daily life. This is also good preparation for preaching and can be combined with the scholarly study of the meaning of words in their context—putting the oft-hated Greek and Hebrew to immediate, practical use in group work—so that parallels can be made between different cultures and a range of meanings and theological responses to any given situation explored. In church traditions that follow a lectionary, seminaries might have a weekly informal lunch for students and faculty to discuss the lectionary texts for the coming Sunday, combining personal storytelling in response to the scripture with the scholarly study of the text, as outlined above. In this way, students can begin to prepare for sermons in dialogue with other students and their teachers, bringing seminary learning together with the real world and generating a practical outcome for their church life and field education placement.

These sorts of methods also address the lament, often heard from older students who arrive at seminary with much experience in their fields, that they are being de-skilled or infantilized in their theological education. Such complaints reflect the fact that the old model of preparing students for the ministry by stripping them of all they know still lingers, implicitly if not by design. The challenge for seminary teachers is to use the students' existing skills and experience—upon which we place so much emphasis in assessing their fitness for ordination and then too often forget the minute they walk into the classroom—as the starting point for their academic and practical study of theology and the ordering of community worship. Such skills and experience should be a starting point but not the primary criterion for theological work, for leaving a student's skills and experiences unchallenged can lead to uncritical and self-centered study, which is the opposite of what I am advocating. By forming the starting points for study, life experiences are the key—via compassion and analogy—to understanding other cultural and social circumstances and, thereby, to grasping in a fresh way what appears to be alien academic material. Life experiences provide us with the questions we need to put to the text.

Avoiding a Two-Tiered System

To prevent a two-tiered system of theological education from developing, we need to think carefully about how the seminary dispersed can be a starting point for the education of all students, part-time commuting and full-time residential, rather than a default position for the commuters who struggle and end up in the dean's office three times a month with problems. All students come with skills and life experiences which can be used as jumping-off points for professors' teaching and students' learning—or, from time to time, students' teaching and professors' learning—thus contributing to a new model of formation that models for students ways in which they can enable the members of their future churches to build on their skills and life experiences in *being* church out in the world. This is not to undermine what goes on in the seminary or church buildings. The seminary gathered and the church gathered will always remain vital moments of community life, corporate worship, sustained teaching and learning, and shared reflection. However, such a new balance encourages people to understand that they can be in church or are engaged in theological education even when they are dispersed.

Discovering Common Ground through Our Own Ethnicity

For many of us who teach or have taught in primarily white seminaries and theological colleges, our experience is that there are usually five or six black people in the community—students, administrative staff, domestic staff, and teachers. In those circumstances, we tend to see race or ethnicity as being about those five or six black people in the community. But we all have ethnic identities with histories and consequences, and we who are white reflect on these far too little. (Similarly, the point needs to be reinforced that gender is not just about women, and sexuality is not just about gay and lesbian people, though they are often the ones who highlight the issues precisely because they have been defined as "not the norm"). Getting students and teachers to examine their own "whiteness" is vital for tackling the unexamined issues of power and privilege that are inherent in all our communities—at faculty, staff, and student levels. This is something that Robert Beckford, the most prominent black theologian in Britain, consistently points out to those of us in the profession who are white (though we do not always take much notice).[3]

Patricia Williams, in the first of her 1997 Reith lectures, broadcast on BBC radio in Britain, put it like this: "This is a dilemma—being coloured, so to speak, in a world of normative whiteness—whiteness being defined as the absence of colour." She continues:

> Perhaps one reason that conversations about race are so often doomed to frustration is that the notion of whiteness as "race" is almost never implicated. One of the more difficult legacies of slavery and colonialism is the degree to which racism's tenacious hold is manifested not merely in the divided demographies of neighbourhood or education or class but also in the process of what media expert John Fiske calls the "exnomination" of whiteness as racial identity. Whiteness is unnamed, suppressed, beyond the realm of race. Exnomination permits whites to entertain the notion that "race" lives over there on the other side of the tracks, in black bodies and inner-city neighbourhoods, in a dark netherworld where whites are not involved. (1997, 4–5)

The work of the historian Matthew Frye Jacobson is also instructive here. First, race, as a concept, is a product of the nineteenth century; it is not something natural but was constructed within the politics of immigration patterns and empire building. As Jacobson puts it, "race resides not in nature but in politics and culture." Jacobson shows the ways in which, during the great waves of immigration to the United States in the nineteenth and early twentieth centuries, who counted as white was not at all straightforward. In short, whiteness also has its own particularities, though often perceived and presented as universal or the norm. Racial categories are often shifting and contested. Second, Jacobson also points to the fact that power was (and is) an important part of those shifting racial categories and of the ways in which they are constructed. He demonstrates the "historic legacies of white privilege," suggesting that "recognising how that privilege is constituted depends upon our first understanding how whiteness itself has been built and maintained" (1998, 9, 12).

Mary Foulke has suggested that the process of coming to terms with our own whiteness is a spiritual journey and, in a helpful article, has mapped out the three stages of "unlearning racism" which are to be followed by the three stages of building a positive, antiracist, white identity. She suggests that this work goes on both at a personal, individual level and in dialogue with others. Community is the result of struggle and hard work, and so, Foulke suggests, is identity—as it is forged in communities. Both identity and community are, for Foulke, journeys—journeys to come into our own, journeys toward God, with God, and with one another. As she points out, "in the scriptures, journeying implies movement and change, peril, discovery, loss, gains, repeated departures, uprooting and adventure" (1996, 35–36).

How do these journeys of transformation occur in seminary life? Talking about all of this, embarking on this journey of exploration and change with one another, is difficult and requires sensitivity. "Creating community, in other words, involves this most difficult work of negotiating real divisions, of considering boundaries before we go crashing through, and of pondering our differences before we can ever agree on the terms of our sameness" (P. Williams 1997, 4). Real conversations are required for the creation of true community, but they only occur when each one of us is willing to be vulnerable in examining our own situatedness in careful and boundaried ways. The danger otherwise is that there will always be an explicit feeling that those "others" in the community have somehow ruined its golden age. Such conversations are not easy. They require patience; they take a long time. People make mistakes and they don't always have the right language, but all of the conversation and all of the mistakes can be seen and experienced, in the right environment, as a part of growth and formation by students and teachers.

If we believe in the Incarnation, then those conversations are and must be a vital part of community building, formation, and theological teaching and learning. Seminary professors are explicitly engaged in teaching the whole person. Other teachers may feel they are engaged in this too (others may not), but seminary professors take on as a part of their role a commitment to teach the whole person. And the whole person is always situated in particular communities and has identity markers of gender, sexuality, ethnicity, age, and so forth. Not only do students experience their own situatedness, but so do faculty, as has been noted in a number of the conversations at The Lexington Seminar.

Professors face many of the same pressures of overwork and family commitments as the students, and as faculties become more diverse, they also reflect more of the tensions felt by students who feel they are not perceived as the norm. As we face these exciting challenges in seminary education, it is important that the teachers take care of themselves. This is not always easy in understaffed and financially struggling communities, a hallmark of many seminaries in the United States and theological colleges in the Britain. When I was teaching in another college in Oxford, one that trains ministers and educates undergraduate and graduate students in various disciplines, I was once asked to preach a sermon on work. To comply, I preached on the importance of observing the Sabbath, of taking at least one day a week off from work. During my time at that college, I preached many sermons that I thought might upset people, but this sermon caused the greatest stir, especially amongst some of my colleagues who felt chastised. But in that sermon I felt that I was saying something important about pedagogy.

As seminary teachers, we should not model for students the Protestant work ethic gone mad. Offering such an example does not help them survive as healthy ministers. It is vital that we model good practice for them, both in work and in rest. By showing them the importance of taking essential time with family and friends, we model for them a means by which they can recharge themselves for ministry. But such modeling is not simply for the students' benefit. As faculties of seminaries and theological colleges become more diverse and engage a wider range of external commitments—both of which are healthy developments—former patterns of working cannot be sustained if professors are to give of their best in their teaching.

CONCLUSION

These remarks on diversity within seminary communities bring me, in concluding, to the question of vulnerability and thus back to some of my opening comments. We operate, in our expectations and in our vision, in the tension between the "not yet" and the "could be." In doing so, we—both students and teachers—will not get it right all the time, and we should not expect to do so. Our faith, rooted in a loving and forgiving God, does not expect it of us. Theological education at its best has the possibility of *exploration* in it. All of us who have taught in seminaries and theological colleges have encountered the students who go through seminary with no doubts about their faith, their current endeavors, or their future vocations, learning little or nothing because they have no questions. We all know that they are disasters waiting to happen in the parish. Healthy seminaries give students the space to ask questions, make mistakes, and be forgiven in the context of a loving and compassionate community. Teachers have a particular responsibility to stand alongside these ministers-in-training as they ask their questions and make their mistakes, just as those students when they become ministers will stand alongside the people of their congregations in the future, helping them to grow in their relationship with God through the rubble and the joys of their lives.

NOTES

1. All narratives cited in this book can be found in the Archives section of the Seminar's Web site: http://www.lexingtonseminar.org/.

2. On William Temple, see Spencer (2001); of Temple's works, see especially, *Christianity and Social Order* (1976).

3. For an example of such an analysis of "whiteness," see Ware (1992) and Ware and Back (2002).

· G L E N N   T.   M I L L E R ·

Historical Influences on Seminary Culture

The narratives prepared by theological schools participating in The Lexington Seminar indicate that, despite the considerable interest in teaching and learning over the last decade, seminary faculty members are struggling with day-by-day professional tasks. Of the many insights to be gained from the Seminar's narratives, two seem most dramatic to me. On the one hand, the narratives reflect a general malaise in American higher education. After a half century of unprecedented expansion and public confidence, Americans are actively questioning their educators and demanding that formal criteria of effectiveness be established and proof offered that these standards are attained. These same questions are asked of theological educators, and people are again asking, even demanding, that churches investigate alternative means to ministry. Also, as in other branches of American education, the advent of increased racial and ethnic diversity has created a demand for cultural and linguistic diversity as well. When one adds the haunting questions raised by postmodernist philosophy about cultural learning, embattled theologians are forced to wrestle with the question: Whose faith should be studied and transmitted? The *Tradition* has become the many *traditions*.

These concerns are magnified by the fact that seminaries, as primarily small institutions, require consensus in order to function effectively. Unlike the mega-university or even the large college where one can teach, do research, and go home, the size of the seminary enterprise demands that everyone be "on board" for every major decision. Consensus is demanded even when consensus is not present. And perhaps because of the nature of religion or at least of American Christianity, people are quick to read moral and even apocalyptic significance into seminary business. Seminaries are also comparatively expensive to maintain, and they are facing, as are all American institutions of higher education, continuing rising costs and expectations. Many problems that might be alleviated in larger institutions by hiring new faculty or establishing new departments or appointing new administrators cannot be so solved in the seminary, because few surplus funds are available to invest in innovation or compromise.

Much of this discussion revolves around the word "change." The word is repeated in schools' narratives over and over again almost as if it were a mantra that might open the gates to a higher consciousness. People resist change, they do not want to change, they resent change, they welcome change. In part, this is simply the human condition. Each new generation must remake the world after its own likeness, and each departing generation struggles to leave a legacy that subsequent generations "ought" to respect. But the narratives indicate more than this. Change is like the magic bullet that the medical sciences sought so earnestly in the last century, the one medicine that would cure all diseases. If only we change, then everything will be okay.

The narratives, however, do not indicate that we are on the verge of the millennium. Just as seminaries participate in academia and have their problems, so they participate in the churches and share their problems. And these problems are acute. Since the 1960s, Protestant churches have steadily declined in influence, membership, and funds. Many of the problems with students, teaching and learning, and curriculum are related to a very simple sociological fact: Socially weak institutions attract weak candidates for their leadership. Far fewer volunteers can be found for a position that pays poorly and has declining status and little influence. Further, many of the leadership candidates who enter the institution will have less academic and social ability than those who wish to serve in more prosperous professions. In other simple terms, those professional schools that offer high rewards will tend to get, if not all, then the bulk of the more able and committed candidates. American Catholics, although not yet in the same numerical situation as American Protestants, have likewise faced a vocational crisis that has extended over decades. Seminaries educate the students who come, but those students are increasingly seeking a position that is on the margins, not at the center of society.

There is also the haunting question, often whispered between the lines of the narratives, as to whether the seminaries themselves have not contributed to the current crisis. For almost two centuries, seminaries have claimed that they could produce better and more able ministers, and the current church leadership has the highest number of seminary graduates of any cohort of American clergy. While we must not be too quick to draw a causal relationship between decline and ministry, we must not ignore any connections that might be there.

At the risk of reading more into the narratives than is there, I would also suggest that part of the malaise that we see is the result of a continuing intellectual crisis. Despite all the glitz of postmodernism and the discovery of various kinds and theories of cultural learning, religious organizations continue to face a crisis of credibility in the present world. Exactly what truth, if any, is involved in religious talk? For example, it is interesting to examine what African Americans believe about God as a matter of historical or cultural information. But that knowledge becomes vital only if the God of African American theology exists as more than a social construct. It does no good to tell the oppressed of the world that God will deliver them if there is no god to do so.

Having outlined the issues that seem most crucial to me, I then must ask, what can an historian contribute to this discussion? As Hegel noted, historians tend to do their work best in the twilight of a movement or discussion. What history provides is a perspective on the present that comes from seeing our current situation in the light of the succession of spiritual worlds that served as its temporal forebears. The ultimate goal is that we gain an understanding of ourselves that has depth as well as height and width.

This essay, therefore, is written from a clear thesis: American theological education did not develop independently. Seminaries and divinity schools are comparatively small, underfinanced institutions that have served limited publics.[1] While small institutions have their own ethos, they are also easily influenced by larger cultural and institutional trends. Although a handful of theological educators formulated a rationale for the seminary, particularly its curriculum, based on criteria internal to theology,[2] American seminaries have lived in the shadows of two important cultural phenomena: the university and religious awakenings.

In any walk through the woods, the larger trees cast shadows that cover the understory trees that grow beneath them. Such shadows are not constant. As the sun moves, the shadows change their shapes and density. Two large trees may shadow the same space. On cloudy and rainy days, both the larger and the small trees experience the larger shadow cast by the clouds. At other times, the understory trees receive the full light of day. Likewise, the effects of university and revival vary. At times, the seminaries are so colored by one or the other of these larger movements as to appear completely dominated by them; at other times, the effects of the larger movements may be almost invisible.

My purpose, therefore, is to describe the evolution of these two influences and their effect on seminaries from colonial times to the present, after which I offer some thoughts about the direction that I think seminaries could and should take in response to the current state of these two overshadowing influences.

THE SHADOW OF THE UNIVERSITY

In colonial America, early eighteenth-century colleges, such as Harvard, Yale, and William and Mary, had teachers specifically assigned to theological subjects, but the most common eighteenth-century pattern of theological education was for prospective candidates—usually after receiving some instruction in the liberal arts or at least a modicum of Latin and Greek—to study with a senior minister. While some recent interpreters have seen this as a period of apprenticeship, it was much closer to the tutorial system used in English universities. The supervising minister assigned reading to the candidate and required the candidate to prepare a commentary on it. Successful theological teachers, such as Nathaniel Emmons, pastor in Franklin, Massachusetts, from 1773 until 1827, had more than one student resident at a time and, hence, assigned the same academic work to several students at once. As in the English colleges, the student worked with the tutor until he felt prepared. This period might be as short as three months or as long as three years, and some intellectually precocious scholars, like Jedidiah Morse, studied with more than one instructor. As in England, the tutor determined the curriculum and customized it to fit the needs of the student and, usually, his own theological proclivities.

THE ENGLISH TUTORIAL INFLUENCE

Nevertheless, important differences existed between the English tutorial and the colonial reading of divinity. In England, the tutor was often a young man, fresh from his own studies, waiting for ordination or for a full appointment. Part of the purpose of a "fellowship" was to provide the tutor with time to pursue his own studies, theoretically, in preparation for the master of arts or for his own ordination examination (though such examinations were usually perfunctory). In contrast, his American counterpart was a fully ordained clergyman with his own parish or an officer of the college.[3] Whatever instruction he could impart was given in the time not devoted to other duties. In England and America, the tutorial was made to order for the factionalism that has often characterized the religious life of the mother country and her daughter. After all, students only had to find a tutor who agreed with their own theological perspective, and tutors were more than willing to impart their own theology to students who held no prior opinions. The colonial form may have been even more given to partisanship. Isolated with his teacher in a rural parish, miles from the nearest competition, the student rarely had the advantage of other teachers or students whose thought differed from his own.

By 1800, the American tutorial system was ripe for change. Had American society been more homogeneous, the natural road might have been for the colleges gradually to expand their own tutorial programs until theological instruction became a department or faculty in its own right. Something like this, in fact, happened at Yale. Unlike either the religiously pluralistic middle colonies or theologically fragmented Massachusetts, Connecticut Congregationalists were more or less religiously homogeneous, although Baptists and Episcopalians were rapidly growing there. Massachusetts was otherwise. In addition to the challenges provided by other denominations, Congregationalists were deeply divided among themselves: some were Unitarian, some were traditional Calvinists, and some were New Divinity. Profoundly aware that one size would not fit all, the traditional Calvinists and New Divinity men joined forces in 1808 to establish a new institution for theological study in conjunction with Phillips Academy in Andover, Massachusetts, that pointedly excluded Unitarians.

While Andover had many distinctive elements, the one most significant for this essay was the new understanding of the theological teacher. From the beginning, Andover's founders envisioned a school that assigned different fields of knowledge to different teachers. Moses Stuart, Andover's Bible teacher, became a highly educated specialist in biblical language and authority on biblical interpretation. Called to Andover from New Haven's Center Church in New Haven, Stuart learned Hebrew and several cognate languages, established a press with the fonts needed to publish research in linguistics, established a postgraduate program of study, and inhaled all the German scholarship that he could find, carefully noting the most important works in the seminary's own journal. Despite suspicion that he had violated the school's already arcane creed, Stuart retained his job. Other seminaries employed his students in their biblical departments.

THE GERMAN UNIVERSITY INFLUENCE

Almost from the beginning, a European shadow fell on the small American seminary that consciously or unconsciously recapitulated German developments in theological education. Like Andover, the contemporary University of Berlin, founded by the Prussian government in the wake of the French seizure of Halle, had four professors in its theological faculty. German theologians had always written, perhaps to excess, but much of their intellectual effort had primarily been directed toward the representation of the timeless truths of the various confessions. In contrast, Berlin embraced the new enlightenment scholarship that stressed the independent examination of a subject and, hopefully, the discovery of new truth. Although the various German states certified the competence of professionals, including ministers, through a rigorous program of state examinations, university teaching followed another course. While various German *Land* (state) governments continued to make university appointments on political grounds, as time passed, they increasingly relied on published research, especially the doctorate and the habilitation, as the criteria for promotion and retention.[4] The meaning of an advanced education changed. Whereas learning had previously been measured by the mastery of traditional texts, it was now measured by a professor's research and its place in the complex pedigree of the current "state of the question." In turn, the research standard encouraged academic specialization; the field in which anyone might hope to break new ground was, almost by definition, narrow. As in the United States, the Old Testament was the first area of theological specialization, and the New Testament, believed to be the common study of all theologians, was the last.

American theological professors began pouring into German universities in the 1840s and continued to make the trip, almost ritualistically, until after the First World War. Like Mark Twain's "innocents abroad," they were impressed by everything they saw and heard. And those who did not make the trip often learned German a verb at a time as they strained to decipher the latest book from the Continent. Like their German teachers, American professors compiled bibliographies; published dictionaries, handbooks, and encyclopedias; and put their most original work in scholarly journals and monographs. Beginning at Yale in 1860, American universities established their own doctoral programs to train people in the newer methods. William Rainey Harper, who opened the reborn University of Chicago in 1892, was among the first Americans to receive a Ph.D. from an American institution, specializing in Semitic language. He was proud to state in his inaugural that he proposed to "make the work of investigation primary" and "the work of instruction secondary" (Lucas 1992, 173).

Care should be taken not to see the German educational paradigm as implying a Teutonic monopoly on American thought. Despite the widespread American fascination with things German, many theologians looked to the British Isles, particularly Scotland, for inspiration. In part, this was because Great Britain and the United States shared a common language, making the work of scholars readily available to each other. But the affinity went deeper than that. In the early nineteenth century, Common Sense Realism was the dominant academic philosophy in Scotland and the new United States, and intellectual leaders on both sides of the Atlantic distrusted speculative theories. By century's end, many American moderate thinkers saw British biblical scholarship as an important counterweight to what they believed were the unwarranted conclusions of more radical continental scholars.[5]

The desire of seminary professors to understand themselves as independent professionals and researchers was similar to the passion of collegiate teachers for the same status. Well before the beginning of the twentieth century, seminary faculty members had established their own guild structure, complete with professional organizations, including the Society for Biblical Literature and the American Society of Church History. The guild structure provided many services for the professors, including the publication of important papers in their journals and annual opportunities to discuss the latest developments with other specialists. The annual meetings of the guilds were also places where seasoned teachers might sing the praises of their most able graduate students and help place them in professional positions at other schools. At first in the better schools and progressively in others, the Ph.D., the Th.D., or their equivalents were required for appointment, and even such gifted and well-connected new appointments as Union's William Adams Brown were expected to jump through this hoop. Although he had spent two years of close work with Harnack in Berlin, Brown still had to complete a Ph.D. (from Yale) during his first years as a Union professor. The system was never completely airtight. Many seminaries preferred seasoned practitioners for their appointments in the practical field, and room was found for such uncredentialed geniuses as Reinhold Niebuhr. Nonetheless, the road to academic success in theology was well-marked.

The most significant difference between Stuart's Andover and Berlin was that Andover was a new type of organization: a nonprofit corporation (Hall 1982). Like classical government corporations, such as cities, towns, and counties, these new bodies were organizations tied to the achievement of public goals; however, unlike governmental organizations, a private board of trustees, not accountable to any public agency, governed them. This type of foundation ideally suited the post-Revolutionary American churches. Like other charitable organizations, denominations had public purposes and public visibility, but they were also private organizations, owned by their members and governed by their own sect's rules and procedures. Interestingly, such corporations could, at least in theory, "own" another institution, if that institution's charter gave that group the right to appoint its board. Among the most important duties of the new boards was the hiring (often after recommendation of the faculty) of new faculty members.

THE SCHOLARLY COMMUNITY AND THE INCORPORATED INSTITUTION IN CONFLICT

From the beginning, then, the American theological professor belonged to two worlds. As scholars and intellectuals, professors belonged to the emerging scholarly (*wissenschaftlich*) community and were responsible to it for their research and its results. But, as employees of a private corporation, teachers were expected to conform to the aims and purposes of those who controlled the schools where the scholars worked. Combined, these two tall oaks of scholarly community and incorporated institution shadowed the life of the average faculty member and influenced faculty self-understanding in myriad ways.

Ideally, the scholarly pursuit of public truth and the sponsors' desire to have their own perspective taught did not conflict. Nineteenth-century Princeton professors, such as the prolific Charles Hodge, felt no distance between their obligations as researchers and their role as representatives of the Presbyterian Church. Hodge parsed Hebrew verbs with the speed and accuracy of Moses Stuart, and his students continued the tradition of mastering philology as part of the learning of theology. But the harmony between ecclesiastical teaching and research that the Princeton theologians prized was ultimately eroded by the inherent tension between the seminary and its public. In the twentieth century, the descendants of Hodge battled other Presbyterians over whose understanding of their seminary ought to prevail. Interestingly, in this titanic struggle, the usual positions were reversed: The faculty struggled for more accountability, while their denominational opponents pled for greater freedom in research and teaching.

As Machen put it, "In the sphere of religion, as in other spheres, the things about which men are agreed are apt to be the things that are least worth holding; the really important things are the things about which men will fight" (Machen 1923, 1–2). Perhaps this is a partial explanation of why seminary battles have been so intense. In most battles over academic freedom, the issue is usually the right of this or that professor to take a position. Many of these struggles, particularly in state universities, involve political issues. In contrast, what is at stake in seminary battles is the mission of the institution itself, especially as it influences the private or ecclesiastical ends for which the school was founded. Seminary teachers have had a dual identity. On the one hand, they are academic instructors who live and work in the same world as other people employed in the knowledge industry. Yet, on the other, they are also the unique bearers of an institution's identity and mission. No seminary battle, consequently, is only about what is taught or the academic quality of the scholarly work of the faculty. The issue always involves the school's very soul.

The great battles in the history of American theological education—the 1840s battle over Tractarianism at New York's General Seminary, the 1920s Fundamentalist-Modernist controversy, the 1970s Missouri Synod battle over Concordia, and the 1980s Southern Baptist civil war—shared common characteristics. In each of these, conservatives believed and believed passionately that the seminaries had deserted their role as ecclesiastical advocates, and they were able to point to the exact wording of seminary charters and denominational confessions to support their point. The schools were, in their view, scholarly means to ecclesiastical goals, and they were determined to hold institutions accountable to the covenants the institutions had made with their founders. In contrast, the faculties often stumbled into the fray. Few seminary teachers sought a battle[6] and often expressed surprise when hostilities broke out. More often than not, the teachers had reached their conclusions after long hours of study, criticism, and publication. Because their work had public warrant, the instructors believed that should satisfy the private wishes of the churches as well. In other words, they believed that the public approval of their work had priority over the private and partial goals of an institution's founders or sponsors. The accused had only been doing their jobs.

The irony was that both faculty and their critics were right about the vocation of the seminary professor. Each side understood the vocation of the theological teacher from its own vantage point and assumed that they held the winning cards whenever someone called for a showdown. But neither side could turn the other loose. The faculties depended on the churches for contributors, students, and ecclesiastic legitimacy, in short, for their lifeblood; the churches depended on the faculties to help their leaders establish their place in the American social constellation.

The Declining Prestige of Seminaries in the Academic World

Before 1960, most seminaries were part of an informal network that united denominational colleges with specific theological schools. Collegiate campus ministers directed students who participated in the religious activities that they sponsored to the "right" school, and professors of Bible (sometimes called religion) often served as recruiters for their own alma mater. In addition, popular religion teachers, like Yale's Charles Foster Kent and his companions in the National Association of Bible Teachers, understood themselves as the enlighteners of the churches, raising up an educated class of laymen who would influence public and ecclesiastical opinion. Following the conclusion of the Second World War, many university and collegiate educators renewed their interest in the liberal arts as part of effective training for citizenship. College teachers of religion were ready to respond to this emphasis. Many schools added new religion departments, and many existing departments added new members. America's new leadership role in world affairs also indirectly contributed to the popularity of religion departments whose teachers often had personal knowledge of the far-flung places that TV news was making familiar.

Strangely enough, at least in retrospect, seminary leaders were not pleased with this arrangement. The American Association of Theological Schools repeatedly reaffirmed its position that religious studies was not a proper major for those preparing for seminary. In part, this was because of the seminary's desire to establish the pattern of four years of college and three years of seminary as a norm. If they gave too much credit to the collegiate departments, some reasoned, then the churches might question the larger paradigm.[7] Others seemed to believe that the seminaries could offer more thorough introductions to such central theological disciplines as Bible or systematic theology. But such issues were not central to the debates. The seminaries wanted a monopoly in the training of ministers and were determined to secure it at any cost. Of all the proposed "preseminary" prerequisites, religion was only assigned three hours and that almost as an afterthought. Charles Taylor, executive director of the Association of Theological Schools (ATS), added salt to the wound when he said, "courses in religion are not offered according to the best academic standards. Even in some of our universities they are not on a par with studies in other fields" (Beardslee 1966, 100).

In Greek mythology, pride always precedes a fall, and it was so in this case. Almost without anyone noticing, the teaching of religion in colleges and universities received a boost from the Supreme Court. In the highly controversial *School District v. Schempp* (374US203 1963), the court noted explicitly:

> Nothing we have said here indicates that such study of the Bible or of religion, when presented objectively as part of a secular program of education, may not be effected consistent with the First Amendment.

These simple words provided legitimacy for the study of religion apart from theology. While this was important to the newer state university departments, their collegiate cousins also welcomed it. The teaching of religion could and ought to be separated from the teaching of theology.

Theorists in the new field of religious studies moved quickly to claim the more public academic ground for themselves. The new "religionists" were determined to establish their discipline as quickly as possible. Following a by-now familiar pattern among academics, they commissioned such leaders in the field as Clyde Holbrook to study the new discipline. Moreover, they transformed the National Association of Bible Instructors (NABI) into the far more imposing American Academy of Religion (AAR) (Holbrook 1991). Each word in the title was significant, but the term "Academy" may have said more than the others. The leaders of the new association were determined to be scholars in their own right and to develop their own guild along classic lines. Significantly, perhaps, the NABI traditionally had met on seminary campuses during the Christmas break when space was available; the new AAR met in convention centers and major hotels.

The separation of the teaching of religious studies from the teaching of theology was never total. As late as 1991, most college teachers of Bible and church history continued to identify with their seminary counterparts, partially because the practitioners in those fields believed that they shared a common historical method that was part and parcel of modern academic life (Hart 1991). But this should not hide the substantial success of the new AAR in establishing itself and its discipline. Scholarship, even in traditional theological fields, had migrated from the theological seminaries and had found its primary home in the university divinity schools and in the larger state universities.

The increasing visibility of the college and university departments of religious studies was not the only reason for the spread of such symbols of university professionalism as tenure and standards of promotion to the seminaries. The handful of university-related divinity schools, which continued to train the majority of theological teachers, had as much, if not more, influence. But such cautions should not obscure the fact that the new understanding of religious studies raised the academic standards of both seminary and college faculties.

The darker shadows cast by the university on seminary life, however, more than offset these gains in academic standards. Seminary faculties and college religion teachers traded places in the academic hierarchy. In the first half of the century, the seminaries were the most prestigious appointments, and all but a handful of college and seminary teachers were ordained; by the end of the century, the most prestigious appointments were in the university departments or divinity schools, and fewer college or university faculty members felt a need to be ordained to legitimate their position. Professorial status was determined by a professor's standing in the guild and not by ecclesiastical recognition. Seminary faculty members enjoyed the improved secular recognition of their scholarship, but they were now clearly in institutions that did not have the prestige of the institutions that employed their former underlings.

THE SHADOW OF THE REVIVAL

Historians have long recognized the centrality of movements of renewal and revival in American Protestant history, and many American religious historians still conventionally count four or five "great awakenings" in our history. Like many other historical heuristics, such conventions are useful if they are not used too woodenly or literally. Seen from a distance, American Protestant life appears to be marked by periods of surge, followed by periods of comparative calmness, which is in turn followed by a new period of growth and expansion. In some respects, the various cycles in American religious life are very similar to the business cycles of rapid economic growth, followed by comparative contraction, that are so common in economic history. The United States is a vast free market in religion in which people select faith for a variety of purposes that satisfy their own internal criteria. Periods of revival and renewal represent times when many people invest more of their emotional and financial resources in religious life and institutions than at other times.[8]

Language about business and religious cycles must be qualified by similar cautions about both. In the greatest periods of prosperity, some lose everything due to a poorly chosen investment, and some people prosper in the darkest of depressions. Likewise, religious revivals do not affect all aspects of the religious marketplace equally. During most periods of religious awakening, some churches lose members, while others gain, and sometimes a revival may be more influential in some regions than others.[9]

THE NATURE OF RELIGIOUS MOVEMENTS

In addition to the terms "revival" and "awakening," American Protestants have used the term "movement" to describe groups involved in a drive for a particular goal or end. Thus, the antislavery movement directed the energy of its adherents toward the abolition of slavery, the student volunteer movement directed the energy of college students toward the "evangelization of the world in this generation," and the peace movement directed the energy of its adherents toward the outlawing of war. Periods of revival and renewal are times when religious life generates a significant number of movements that direct the religious energies of the newly converted or renewed, although movements can exist apart from such periods of excitement.

Those involved in a revival or a movement often establish schools to continue or promote their revitalized faith. Thus, the early nineteenth-century evangelical surge encouraged believers to establish Newton, Lane, Oberlin, Boston, and Southern Baptist, while the missionary revival of the late nineteenth century inspired the founding of Moody Bible Institute, The Divinity School of the University of Chicago, and the Bible Institute of Los Angeles. In turn, the post–World War II revival encouraged the founding of Southeastern Baptist Seminary, Midwestern Baptist Seminary, Fuller Theological Seminary, the Methodist Seminary in Ohio, and the Saint Paul School of Theology (Kansas City).

Seminaries are deeply influenced by revival and renewal movements, for they provide seminaries with emotional and intellectual energy. In times when religious interest is strong, awakened individuals are willing to invest their spiritual and earthly capital in the future of their particular faith. Religious revivals are often millenarian in their vision, pointing to the coming victory of faith in the life of the nation and of individuals. The seminary or the Bible school is a natural place for enthusiastic believers to invest in this future. The seminary and its faculty are, thus, seedbeds of more than academic learning. They are the churches' down payment on the coming consummation of their religious vision.

Seminaries have traditionally been part of the ecology of religious movements, and seminary faculties have served as important public spokespeople for these movements. In the early nineteenth century, such theologically diverse seminary teachers as Leonard Wood of Andover, Bernas Sears of Newton, and Charles Hodge of Princeton were aggressive supporters of the missionary movement. Students listened to speakers, prepared papers on faraway places and their people, and prayed for divine guidance regarding the claim of the foreign field on their lives. Every graduation was marked by a harvest of new missionaries, determined to minister overseas or on the American frontier.

THE MISSIONARY MOVEMENT

In turn, missionary leaders became avid supporters of the seminaries. After improvements in transportation made "furloughing" missionaries a common practice, the returnees would often stay at a seminary. By 1900, the leading schools had their own missionary residences, often homes on or adjacent to the campus, that provided missionaries with a base for their fundraising activities. In addition, visiting missionaries indoctrinated the current student body with the ideas of the missionary movement and made new recruits to the cause.

Initially, the missionary movement influenced the work of seminary faculties indirectly. The missionary was an anomaly. On the one hand, missionaries were among the most specialized of ministers; on the other, the very nature of their work made them generalists. As late as 1939, Professor John Baillie, a noted philosopher of religion who served both at Union (NY) and Edinburgh, argued that the seminary course was the best preparation for missionaries because "the advantage which the trained theologian has over the saint is not unlike the advantage which the trained anatomist has over the athlete. The anatomist cannot use his body any better than the athlete but he understands it better. The theological student is not a better Christian than the unschooled and unlettered saint but his understanding is better" (539). Although there were periodic calls for the seminaries to provide more specialized education for missionary work,[10] the schools tended to leave that training to the denominations. An important exception to this observation was the establishment of the Kennedy School of Missions as part of the Hartford Seminary Foundation. Hartford's adventuresome president, W. Douglas Mackenzie, established a school of missions as well as a school of education to provide specialized training in comparative religion, languages, and sociology for further missionaries (Mackenzie, Jacobus, and Mitchell 1911). Ironically, the liberal Mackenzie's idea of a "theological university" that would teach all the skills needed for Christian leadership later provided Southern Baptists and other religious conservatives with a conceptual model for their own institutions.

The missionary enterprise influenced theological education directly through the ecumenical movement, both at home and abroad. With a few exceptions, such as New York's Union Theological Seminary and the Yale Divinity School, from 1820 to 1920 most theological schools were denominational institutions. In concrete terms that meant that the faculties of the schools were exclusively drawn from the clergy of the sponsoring denomination and often that the school had a denominationally based confession of faith for faculty and occasionally for members of the governing board. But these were the formal marks of denominational control. The actual influence of the denominations was far more extensive. Seminary faculties and boards were deeply involved in ecclesiastical politics, and the seminary often served almost as a talent pool for the churches. While some good scholarship was produced under this system, much of it was primarily directed toward denominational needs. In times of controversy, seminaries could become prizes of war that were conquered and held by one side or the other. Seminary faculties were acutely aware of their exposed place in ecclesiastical controversy, and while many professors primarily wanted to be left alone with their students and books, they knew that their every action was watched by the champions of this side or that. The Fundamentalist-Modernist battles of the 1920s, the Missouri Lutheran battle over Concordia in the 1970s, and the extended Southern Baptist battles of the 1980s saw faculties caught in a maelstrom of seemingly indeterminable debate.

There were two primary ways out of the morass. The university divinity school offered one model. Ultimately reaching back to the very influential German theologian, Friedrich Schleiermacher, this interpretation saw the seminary as primarily a professional school, similar to the schools of medicine, law, and social service.[11] Because the churches were important parts of American culture, the provision of a well-trained, efficient, and professional ministry was an important public task. Particularly during the 1960s and 1970s, the American Association of Theological Schools promoted this understanding. This model had a positive impact on many theological faculties and their thought about their own work.

But the university professional model had two serious problems. First, no Protestant church was large enough or held sufficient influence to claim to be the "American national church." Even the wealthiest and most influential of the churches had comparatively small memberships and had comparatively few representatives in national government. On a purely statistical basis, it would be difficult to argue that providing leadership for these organizations was important. Second, the university and professional model lacked religious power. At best, professionalism commanded the allegiance of the mind, never the heart.[12]

THE ECUMENICAL MOVEMENT

The ecumenical movement was the emotional bridge that provided the needed impetus for change. Like all significant religious and theological movements, ecumenism had many roots that reached deep into the collective psyche. In its modern Protestant form, the ecumenical movement was the convergence of four different movements of renewal and revival. First, the new big-city revivalism associated with Dwight L. Moody and later Billy Sunday was remarkably free of denominational identification. The revivalists believed that they represented all Protestant churches and that their message was a simple distillation of biblical truth, similar to Bill Bright's later Four Spiritual Laws. More liberal American Christians had a similar understanding of theology. What humanity needed, they believed, were not creeds but the message of Jesus that one should love God and neighbor. At the same time, American Protestants were becoming more concerned with various forms of social service and social action. The number of organizations devoted to doing good in the average American city skyrocketed. As liberal theologian Walter Rauschenbusch noted, the social gospel was a fact of Christian life. What the church needed, he argued, was a theology adequate to Christian practice. The formation of the Federal Council of Churches was a natural outgrowth of the success of these interdenominational organizations. Historians of gender (Cairns 1990) have noted that the new emphasis on the social gospel produced a mini-awakening among American males who saw it as a more masculine approach to Christianity than the emotion-laden sentimentality of the average pulpit. Ecclesiastical bureaucracies exploded as the churches struggled to put the new wine of this awakening into the old wineskins of traditional ecclesiastical organizations.

At the heart of this awakening was a revived interest in foreign and home missions. From 1890 to 1914, American Protestants witnessed a major expansion of interest in missionary activity of all sorts. Beginning in 1886 at a meeting at Mt. Hermon called by Dwight L. Moody, the Student Volunteer Movement rapidly expanded on college campuses. Usually identified simply by its initials, the SVM generated deep support on the nation's campuses and inspired both denominational and ecumenical agencies to increase their giving to the cause. The Layman's Missionary Movement, the last of the prewar Protestant financial crusades, illustrated the interest and the financial power that the movement had. Between 1907 and 1924, Protestant giving to missions increased from $8,980,000 to $45,272,000. The new money was needed to enable the churches to use the vast human resources pouring from college campuses. Because missionary work enlisted large numbers of women as well as men, the question of how these talented women should be educated was an acute one.

Meanwhile, missionaries abroad and missiologists at home began to advocate cooperation in the missionary enterprise. The great missionary conferences, beginning with Edinburgh in 1910, made it clear that the churches could attain their common goals only by common action.

The contemporary tendency to identify mainstream Christianity with the ecumenical movement should not obscure the fact that contemporary evangelicalism has many of its roots in this same missionary revival. After 1890, few, if any, evangelical organizations were denominationally centered, and most were explicitly interdenominational, and the handful that were so organized, such as Baptist Gordon, moved quickly away from their denominational moorings.

The 1963 opening of the Second Vatican Council by Pope John XXIII seemed an answer to many prayers. Many Protestant observers believed that it marked a new openness on the part of Roman leaders to ecumenical cooperation and perhaps even eventual unity. One of the deepest fissures in Christian history seemed about to be spanned.

Many seminary teachers and administrators were involved at every level of the ecumenical movement, and their participation made them familiar with its larger goals. However, what was more interesting was the way in which the ecumenical movements reshaped the understanding of the seminary faculty. John A. Mackay, president of Princeton, the most successful of the denominational schools, enthused that the denominational school with the greatest contribution to make was one "where confessional boundaries are transcended" (Mackay 1956, 7). This was most evident in the reading lists of the various schools which often contained the same texts.

ECUMENISM AND THE DECLINE OF DENOMINATIONALISM

The application of the ecumenical ideal to the task of faculty building was obvious: an ecumenical faculty, blessed by a healthy diversity, might provide a more substantial theological education than a purely denominational school could provide. The process of mixing faculties was under way before 1965, but it changed in character after that date. In addition to representatives from other Protestant churches, Roman Catholics joined Protestant faculties, and Protestants, although in smaller numbers, joined Catholic faculties. The new hope was that the theological faculty might represent in its membership some of the richness and diversity of the Christian tradition.

Although the ecumenical movement peaked in the 1960s, the ecumenical ideal suggested that the seminary needed to be as broad as possible in order to accomplish its basic task of training pastors. In effect, ecumenical experience suggested that seminaries needed to reflect, as much as possible, the theological and ecclesiastical diversity of the broader Christian movement. This understanding stood seminary faculties in good stead as they responded to the movements for greater equality in American social and political life. Gradually, seminary faculties came to include more women and more people of color. Some adventuresome schools also began to include gay and lesbian persons on their faculties. Schools were best, it was assumed in this ecumenical spirit, when they represented the full range of Christian diversity.

The decline of denominationalism as an organizing principle for theological faculties had a very important corollary: the identity of seminary teachers was no longer directly connected to their ordination or ecclesiastical standing. In effect, seminary teachers had become "theological educators" who drew their identity from their service to the church. This post-1960 understanding of the seminary faculty member's role came at the same time that the American Academy of Religion was reshaping the understanding of college and university teaching in the United States, and the ecumenical understanding of the role of the seminary teacher was always in danger of becoming theological camouflage for an essentially secular understanding.

The ecumenical origins of the ideal of theological education served, at least partially, to offset this problem. Roman Catholic, Greek Orthodox, and many Protestant evangelicals had seen education for ministry in terms of the spiritual formation of the person.[13] While none of these traditions downplayed the role of a well-trained mind, they believed that the minister was in some real sense a person of God whose spiritual life was indivisible from his or her professional activities.

Advocates of the role of the faculty in the spiritual formation of the clergy had important allies in the Association of Theological Schools. The association had been formed by the older and often more liberal theological seminaries as a way of maintaining the academic standards of the institutions. In the 1950s, due in part to a large grant from the Rockefeller-controlled Sealtantic Fund (Weber 1997, 164), the ATS became the think tank of American theological education in addition to its early role as the government-recognized accreditor of theological schools. After Vatican II, the ATS changed character, as Catholic, Eastern Orthodox, evangelical, and charismatic schools applied for and were granted membership. As the dialogue in the ATS developed, theological educators became aware that a good school must "provide opportunities for formational experiences . . . essential for the practice of ministry, namely, emotional maturity, personal faith, moral integrity, and social concern" (Association of Theological Schools, *General Standards* 4.2.1.1).

Ecumenical diversity had changed the way that theological faculties understood themselves.

The Mid-Century Expansion and Its Aftermath

From the late 1930s to the 1950s, American religious organizations experienced a period of rapid expansion. This revival was marked by increased church membership, an increase in church contributions, the expansion of state and local church bureaucracies, and increasing financial support for nondenominational Christian organizations.[14] Seminaries, whose enrollments swelled as a result of the GI Bill, shared in this general prosperity. Enrollments grew, new buildings were constructed (including expensive housing for married students), and the ideal of both college and seminary for pastors became more widely accepted. Naturally, faculty size also grew as schools were able to add personnel. Much of this growth was in the newer, practical fields, especially counseling, that had been pioneered in the 1920s and 1930s but whose growth had been stymied economically by the Great Depression.

Part of the religious excitement of this period found its source in the "theological revival." Not only did Reinhold Niebuhr and Paul Tillich appear on the cover of *Time* magazine, but there was substantial popular and intellectual interest in religious and theological questions. Among evangelicals, a similar renaissance occurred, although on a small scale, as such noted theologians as E. J. Carnell and Carl F. Henry published significant works.

The Rockefeller Brothers' Fund hoped to utilize this excitement by financing a year in theological school for promising undergraduates. The fund's managers believed that this would expose some of America's brightest and best to the issues that mattered and, hopefully, to lead some into the ministry. While it is difficult to gauge the intellectual level of the teaching and discussion on the average theological campus, the level of theological instruction appears to have been high.

In short, this revival gave theological educators much to crow about. To the less cautious, the future that lay before schools and churches appeared very bright. However, by 1957, some able ecclesiastical and seminary leaders were beginning to warn of dangers ahead. In his last address to the Andover-Newton community in 1965, Herbert Gezork foretold:

> At the beginning of my ministry one of three persons on earth was a Christian, at least nominally. At the end of yours only one in six will be a Christian. . . . Accept then, as ministers of the gospel, the fact that you live in a world which presents to the people of our day numerous options from which to choose a philosophy and a way of life, that the Christian faith is only one of these, and that only a minority choose it. (10)

Although Gezork's words fell on unperceiving ears, he was right that the period of renewal and new energy was coming to an end. The passionate debate among younger theologians over who would be the successors of Niebuhr came to a disappointing conclusion: no one.

Much of the turmoil and malaise experienced by mainstream theological faculty since the 1960s has arisen from their failure to recognize that the revival that had treated them so well had ended. This was not, of course, an apocalyptic fate, for church membership has continued at about the level that it was in the 1920s. But despite the pressure on church bureaucracies to downsize, their staffs appear to be as large today (and in many cases larger) as they were in the 1920s and 1930s. The same might be said of the mainstream seminaries. Few of them have reduced faculties to the levels of the 1920s, and most still support essentially the same number of faculty as they supported at the high-water mark of the revival.

In response to financial pressures, almost all schools have had to diversify their curricular offerings to appeal to new constituencies, develop new degrees, and demand more from their faculties. At many places, faculty secretaries and other such support staff have been reduced. More institutional energy has had to go into fundraising. This has drawn the attention of seminary presidents away from their institutions and turned it outwards. Deans and faculties naturally have had to take up the slack. Committee work, the bane of the researching class, has increased, and scholarly production has decreased.

In contrast, the evangelical and charismatic seminaries have benefited from a smaller awakening. For reasons not completely clear, conservative churches have undergone a significant rebirth in the 1970s and 1980s. In part this rebirth was related to the renaissance of conservative politics, and the old adage that people pray as they vote may be applicable. But, like most dynamic religious movements, the evangelical mini-revival has roots that are primarily religious and cultural. The promise of rebirth, very much a part of many non-Christian religious movements in the same period,[15] has deep appeal in periods of uncertainty and indirection. In addition, evangelical theological faculties have not only provided courses in church growth and evangelism, they have played a major role in providing evangelicalism with coherence and direction.

For good or ill, seminaries continue to live in the shadow of the revival. When the nation or a part of it is gripped by religious excitement, seminary faculties do well, their numbers increase, and new fields of study open. The converse, unfortunately, is also true. Seminaries and their faculties are affected deeply by the ebbs of the American religious tide.

RENEWAL ON THE ROAD LESS TRAVELED

Operating in the shadow of the university and movements of religious renew-al, some theological professors are more influenced by their academic guilds than by the churches; others see themselves as the spearheads of religious and political movements of renewal and revival. Certainly the excitement on present-day campuses comes primarily from those teachers who have pledged themselves passionately to a larger cause, whether it is gay rights, feminism, or the recovery of the Bible. Yet I wonder, both as a seminary teacher and a his-torian, whether either of these alternatives is satisfactory or satisfying. Cautiously, and aware of the various shadows that tincture our path, I would like to suggest another understanding of the theological professor's vocation, one that follows a historical road less traveled.

In 1956, H. Richard Niebuhr, assisted by Daniel Day Williams and James M. Gustafson, published a short volume, *The Purpose of the Church and Its Ministry: Reflections on the Aims of Theological Education*. Despite the gener-ous attribution of authorship to Williams and Gustafson, the essay bears the marks of Niebuhr's wisdom and guidance. The text is somewhat deceptive. On first reading, one is tempted to treat the volume as a period piece, a gold mine of quotations that can be used to illustrate the ideas about theological schools in the 1940s and 1950s. This perspective is not by the point. Like its compan-ion volume, the *Advancement of Theological Education* (Niebuhr, Williams, and Gustafson 1957), *The Purpose of the Church* contains many commonplace observations that reflect the time in which it was written. Yet, even when all of these qualifications are carefully noted, the book still has contemporary applicability.

Niebuhr began with the insistence that the work of theological education must be understood from a theological standpoint.[16] Although Niebuhr rec-ognized the shadows cast by the universities and the revivals, he did not want to define theological schools or their faculties in those terms. Instead, he believed that seminary faculties need to find their purpose in the deeper aim of the church: the increase of the love of God and neighbor (Niebuhr, Williams, and Gustafson 1956, 27). To use the language of Jonathan Edwards, one of Niebuhr's theological exemplars, the seminary and its faculty must align them-selves with the intrinsic good that is implicit in their work and not with the var-ious extrinsic goods that lie too ready at hand. By aligning ourselves, thus, with God's ultimate end, we theological educators might set a course into God's future that is greater than any revival or any triumph of university influence. Such a theological focus may allow us, as Niebuhr suggested, to assert ourselves as Christian intellectuals and use our minds to reflect God's glory and thus lead our students beyond a narrow comprehension of our scholarly disciplines and into a realm of wisdom from which they can go forth and minister to the saints.

IMPLICATIONS FOR SEMINARY EDUCATION

In light of this understanding of the purposes of theological education, we need to admit that there are limits to how many different programs schools can sustain and still retain a focus on being an intellectual center of the church's life. The question is at what point do institutions resolve to get off the treadmill of program marketing in order to consider what they are actually doing and how well they are doing it. I would even hope that schools might engage in a kind of zero programming of their academic work to see what is essential in light of the purpose of theological education I have argued for. This will mean saying no to some commitments in order to honor the ones they deem most important. For some schools, it might even mean recognizing that they need to reconceive their mission in order to strengthen the quality of what they are able to do.

Seminaries need to keep in mind what is central to their practices of teaching and learning. The objective is not simply to improve certain techniques of teaching or even to better understand student learning; instead, the goal of our efforts to improve theological education is formed by our hope to equip students to join the conversation about faith and to learn how to call others into this conversation. As Christian intellectuals, church pastors and leaders are shaped by the gospel's insistence that we engage the issues of the Christian life and the church's witness in the public community through this continuing conversation.

The challenge for theological faculties is learning how to assist students in making up their academic deficiencies and developing the kinds of skills needed to acquire knowledge and understanding that make it possible for them to participate in theological conversations and teach others how to do this themselves in congregational life and in their vocation as Christians.

The intellectual conversation about faith and public issues that I have been discussing is not synonymous with scholarly discussion. The goal is not to make seminary students like seminary faculties, but to support them in becoming Christian intellectuals in the practice of ministry. The claim for "Christian intellectual" as an image of ministry is the fundamental recognition that pastoral ministry requires us to think about and engage the issues of our life in the church and our practice of the Christian life in the public square. The purpose of theological education is to equip men and women to join this conversation and help others engage the conversation as well. Our efforts to strengthen theological teaching and learning must be grounded in this aim.

NOTES

1.   There were some exceptions, of course. When it was founded in 1808, Andover was among the best-financed American institutions, and Union Theological Seminary (New York) was similarly well endowed at the beginning of the twentieth century. Even in today's world of mega-endowments, Presbyterian Princeton Seminary ranks high, and the Cooperative program of the Southern Baptist Convention has given that denomination's seminaries more financial security than most of their siblings.

2.   See Kelsey (1992, 1993), Wood (1985), and Farley (1983).

3.   The divinity professors at Harvard and Yale conducted reading programs similar to those maintained by parish clergy.

4.   The various German states had the right of appointment to many university positions, and political pressures could affect the process. During the height of the various controversies over the Bible, the governments often required theology faculties to appoint representatives of all factions.

5.   The *International Critical Commentary*, published by T & T Clark, was the product of cooperation between American and British scholars. The Brown-Driver-Briggs *Hebrew Lexicon*, various editions since 1907, was another example of American and British biblical scholarship. Although most American Lutherans were very aware of the importance of German neo-confessionalism (often called neo-orthodoxy in German historical writings), other American Christians tended to see German theology in terms of a straight line from the enlightenment and Schleiermacher to Ritschl or Harnack. British thinkers also shared this picture of nineteenth-century German theology.

6.   Union (NY) Seminary's Charles A. Briggs was an exception to this generalization. Briggs delighted in goading the conservatives in his denomination and welcomed the battle, at least in its earliest stages. He thought it inconceivable that the Presbyterian Church would reject his scholarship, highly prized on the public stage. He was, of course, wrong. He was convicted of heresy.

7.   Ironically, the collegiate departments may have been the best recruiters that the seminaries had.

8.   The implications of rational choice sociology for the study of American religion are explored in Stark and Finke (2000) and Finke and Stark (1992).

9.   This qualification is particularly important when considering the effects of revivals on theological education. Southern evangelical religion, for example, received a decisive push in the camp revivals in the Confederate Army of Northern Virginia. Northern evangelicals, however, experienced a decline in the same period. In a similar vein, the surge of religious excitement and energy in the charismatic movement has not had a proportional impact on all American denominations.

10. The 1910 Edinburgh Conference called for all prospective missionaries to receive training in five areas: the science and history of missions, the religions of the world, sociology, pedagogy, and the science of language.

11. Friedrich Schleiermacher (1988) offers the classic expression of this professional model. In the United States, William Adams Brown (1920, 1938) was perhaps the most intellectually acute advocate of this understanding.

12. Shailer Mathews, dean of the University of Chicago in the 1920s and 1930s, was noted for his use of the term "ministerial efficiency." He used the term precisely and sought to show

that seminary education improved the on-the-job performance of Baptist ministers. While his arguments were convincing, they do not appear to have attracted as much attention as they deserved at the time, partly because they were often presented in an uninspiring manner.

13. The term "formation" has come to be used by a variety of people with little attention to its Catholic origins. I have followed that usage, using "formation" as an inclusive term for the spiritual dimension of the ministry.

14. As in the case of other periods of awakening, some thoughtful people believed that this was not a period of religious health for American churches. These included such leaders as Henry Pitt van Dusen and the young Martin E. Marty. Robert D. Putnam, in *Bowling Alone* (2000), notes the various ways in which Americans were involved in community building activities in this period. The church was part and parcel of this American search for meaningful places for personal interaction.

15. Religious movements that stressed individual spirituality and personal religious creativity have characterized the last thirty years. Evangelicalism may be more like the New Age than many evangelicals would want to admit.

16. A similar point was made during the discussion in the 1980s and early 1990s around the work of David Kelsey and Edward Farley. As Kelsey (1993, 2) noted, "Most striking of all, perhaps, is the fact that it has been a theological debate. Its central focus has been on the question of what is theological about theological education." My turn to Niebuhr is partially a matter of personal preference, but it also reflects my own sense that it is easier to evaluate a book almost fifty years old than a more current volume.

· J E R R Y L . S U M N E Y ·

Do Not Be Conformed to This Age

BIBLICAL UNDERSTANDINGS
OF MINISTERIAL LEADERSHIP

The narratives from the various seminaries that participated in The Lexington Seminar contain many similarities, one of which is that they describe the ways in which seminaries do not meet student expectations. In the narrative of the Austin Presbyterian Theological Seminary (1999),[1] for example, a commuter student feels left out and unimportant, at least in part because of the ways in which various responsibilities beyond seminary make her work at the seminary more difficult. Similarly, Professor Jones at Church Divinity School of the Pacific (2001) struggles through multiple interruptions to give proper attention to a commuter student who feels the institution makes unreasonable demands on her. (Yet the student shows an unwillingness to do the simple thing—check her campus mailbox—that might alleviate some of her conflicts with the school.)

Such dissatisfactions are further complicated when students do not meet faculty expectations. For example, one of the students who interrupts Professor Jones at CDSP cannot write English proficiently enough to complete a paper for class and does not seem willing to be available when the professor can work with him. In the narrative of United Theological Seminary of the Twin Cities (2001), students seem to evaluate their experience of seminary by the extent to which their life story is affirmed. Finally, many students perceive no connection between their seminary education and their work as ministers. The students in the Lexington Theological Seminary narrative (2002) find little use for theology, and those recent graduates of Calvin Theological Seminary (1999) who send a critical letter to its president find no connection between academic work and pastoral ministry. There is, it seems to them, too much emphasis on church history, biblical languages, and theology and too little on the practical skills needed for pastoral ministry. Eastern Baptist Theological Seminary (2000) hears similar concerns and considers "agenda-setting" courses to show students the relevance of what they are learning. And though the students at Claremont School of Theology (2000) are more accepting of critical scholarship, they still have a difficult time knowing what to do with it.

I think these concerns (institutions not meeting student expectations, students not meeting faculty expectations, the need to have one's experience heard and affirmed, and the perceived gulf between academics and pastoral work) are related to one another and to understandings of ministry.

THE PROBLEM OF PERSONAL EXPERIENCE

Most students coming to seminary at this time put an extremely high value on personal experience, which means that their personal stories, whether we think about them as autobiography or as faith journey, contribute in extraordinarily powerful ways to their understanding of Christian faith and ministry. Indeed, their personal experience often seems to have more genuine authority for them than the Christian community's communal experience in the present, in the tradition, or in Scripture. That is, of the Wesleyan Quadrilateral's four sources of revelation, they privilege experience, particularly private experience, to such an extent that the other sources are largely irrelevant. Placing such a high value on their individual, personal, and private experience also means that meeting their own needs is a high priority. Thus, they come with high expectations for what institutions should do for them and find it an institutional failure when things do not conform to their specific needs or expectations.

Such an outlook is hardly unique. Rather, this looking to one's own experience and evaluating other things primarily by whether they meet one's own individual needs is a broad cultural trend that reflects our culture's narcissism and extreme individualism. In the culture of the United States, the wants of an individual are often privileged above the needs of the community. While this began with concerns about the disadvantaged, it has become a cultural outlook that has many less helpful consequences.

One of the important consequences for those of us involved with seminary education is that it has led to a broad relativism, particularly where religious beliefs are concerned. The authority of one's conscience, an important element in much Protestant thought, including the tradition of my denomination, has become the arbiter of all things to the extent that rational argumentation about important religious issues is nearly impossible. When there is disagreement about important matters, those who rely heavily on unexamined personal experience and individual conscience simply resort to comments about truth being different for each person or about their opinion being as good as the other person's because it is theirs. It is not unusual in such company to hear much talk about the importance of not judging. Such a retreat from rational argumentation renders much of seminary education meaningless. It is easy to see why theology and biblical exegesis are not important once we note that they are outside the person's individual experience. What students who place such value on personal experience want, what they *feel* they need, are tools with which to "be with people" who are suffering or celebrating. They do not think these tools need to be rooted in any theology beyond that of personal experience, which they assume to be self-interpreting. These students want to help people by simply sharing their own experiences with them. The altruism of this outlook is commendable, but it is not sufficient for faithful, effective Christian ministry.

Such unreflective reliance on personal experience also runs counter to the desire of seminaries to be institutions that engage in formation. Formation implies change; it means that students are being led to conform to particular ways of being. Because they are being asked to change, it may well be that students will sometimes feel that their needs are not being met. Perhaps this is a necessary part of formation. Those being led to a more reflective faith will sometimes yearn for that simple faith they once experienced and relied on, that sense of certainty and security (and I can confess this from personal experience). But seminaries are not intended to be havens for unscrutinized experience, but rather communities that enable examination of one's faith and help one find ways to be in God's presence while undertaking the intellectual task that leads to the work of ministry. Seminary faculties, therefore, need to be clearer about their expectations and the reasons for those expectations.

These comments are not meant to denigrate our students' intellects or motivations. Our students are people of our culture, not so unlike those who enter many educational institutions (Klimoski 2003). As teachers and institutions we need to accept that this is the starting point with many of our students. Therefore, we must find ways to reach them. This does not mean that we should be satisfied with their overly personal way of perceiving and making meaning in the world. We must help them become more reflective about their experiences. In some way, we must help them use their experience as an entrance into the breadth and richness of the Christian tradition rather than as the only basis for their faith and ministry. We need to find a way, in the words of Paul, to "transform [their] minds"—and perhaps our own as well. If seminaries wish to prepare leaders in ways that are consistent with the gospel, they must provide their students with a broader base than personal experience for the foundation of their ministry. An important part of this task is coming to a clear understanding of the nature of ministry. Recapturing something of a biblical understanding of ministry may help us integrate theological curriculum and help make it important for our students.

A corollary of the unexamined emphasis on one's own experience is the belief that one is called to the ministry because one's experience of God is superior to that of others. Thus, the pastor, by virtue of this experience of God, deserves deference and expects parishioners to do as she says and acknowledge that she is the one who knows the will of God. But such understandings of ministry are not consistent with the ways ministry is envisioned in the New Testament. To help students become the leaders the church needs, we must give careful thought to what it means to be a pastor. The New Testament is an important starting point for this renewed reflection on the nature of Christian leadership.

The early church needed to find ways of ordering its communities that were consistent with the Christian faith. Therefore, most of the New Testament's explicit discussions of leadership appear in the Pauline letters, in contexts in which there were active debates about the sort of leadership the church should adopt. The church explicitly rejected some models of leadership and affirmed others. Of course, practices of ordination have developed in differing ways in various confessional traditions, but all seek to be compatible with what the Gospels give us as the teaching of Jesus and with the interpretations of leadership found throughout the New Testament. Thus, it is important to root our understandings of ministry in Scripture.

LEADERSHIP IN PAUL

Paul's churches existed in a cultural environment in which the dominant model of leadership placed leaders above others in a hierarchical order in which those above exercised dominance over those below. Those above expected privilege, deference, and honor from those below them. Leaders were expected to possess a powerful demeanor and thereby embody the image of success and be able to impose their will on others.[2] Because this was the culturally accepted manner of leadership, Paul's converts looked for these traits in their leaders as well. Paul, however, repeatedly rejects such leadership.

The Corinthian church, in particular, fell victim to oppressive forms of leadership. They accepted their culture's understanding of leadership without recognizing that it was incompatible with the gospel. The Corinthians were drawn to accept leadership from those who looked impressive and successful and those who possessed powerful personalities. In 1 Corinthians 1–4, Paul rejects this understanding of leadership, arguing that a Christian understanding of leadership does not include exercising dominance or control over others. Paul calls himself and other leaders servants rather than superiors.

In 1 Corinthians 12–14, Paul celebrates the diversity of the gifts with which God had blessed the church, calling all gifts of the Spirit ministries (12:5).[3] Every Christian has a gift by virtue of possessing the Spirit, so every Christian has a ministry and needs to participate in the church's ministry. Having a gift and exercising it in the context of the church is a constituent part of being a Christian for Paul, so being gifted by God does not set one apart from other Christians. Paul demands that every gift be honored and every gift be exercised for the good of the church.

First Corinthians failed to change its recipients' view of leadership and ministry enough to enable them to reject teachers who arrived in Corinth soon after it. In the letters of 2 Corinthians, Paul opposes these traveling preachers who legitimate their claims to leadership by pointing to their powerful personalities and presence, along with their superior experiences of the presence of God. They claim that God's Spirit dwells in them in a way that sets them apart from others and so requires others to defer to them, even acquiesce to their demanding demeanor. They argue that their air of superiority and success is a demonstration of God's power.

Such understandings of ministry bring into the church models of ministry that are incompatible with the gospel. Paul draws a stark contrast between his theology of ministry and that of those he will call "super-apostles" (2 Cor. 11:5) by saying, "we do not preach ourselves, but Jesus Christ as Lord and ourselves as your slaves for the sake of Jesus" (4:5). When he says his competitors "preach themselves," he is referring to their assertion that the Spirit enables their impressive demeanor and gives them the trappings of success. After all, this is the Spirit of the God who raised Jesus from the dead. Of course, God continues to work in God's ministers in this powerful manner. But Paul rejects this train of thought. He makes his point dramatically in 4:7: "we have this treasure in clay jars, so that it may be clear that this extraordinary power belongs to God and does not come from us." When Paul compares ministers to "clay jars," he compares them to the styrofoam cups of the day. Such "clay jars" were the cheap, expendable containers of the first century. This is how the lives of ministers compare with the precious gospel they proclaim.

Far from appearing to bask in the power of the resurrection, the lives of ministers are manifestations of the death of Jesus. In bearing troubles with faith they bring life to the congregation. The task of representing the death of Jesus for the good of the congregation is not unique to ministers. It is part of the life of all Christians (see 1 Thess. 2:14). The distinction between ministers and others is that the hardships of ministers are more public. Paul argues that ministers accept this role for the good of the church, so that praise to God will increase as people see them endure such difficulties and yet retain their faith.

Paul makes a startling statement about his relationship with his church in 2 Corinthians 4:5; he speaks of himself as "your slave." Paul often calls himself a servant of Christ. When referring to himself in this way he usually uses the word *diakonos*, the word from which we get "deacon." The basic meaning of *diakonos* is "servant." However, it identifies the person neither as a slave nor as servile. Paul uses this word throughout 2 Corinthians to speak of ministry, that of apostles, other leaders, and of the whole church (8:4; 9:1, 12).

But Paul does not use *diakonos* in 4:5; rather he calls himself the Corinthians' *doulos*. The basic meaning of *doulos* is "slave," and it usually does connote servility and hard labor, especially in comparison with *diakonos*. Among the many times Paul refers to himself as a servant of Christ, he uses *doulos* only three times to do so (Rom. 1:1; Gal. 1:10; Phil. 1:1). So it is rather astonishing that he calls himself a *doulos*, slave, of the Corinthian church. While the "super-apostles" assert authority over the congregation, Paul adopts the opposite position: He is their slave. This is the demeanor and the relationship between leaders and the rest of the church that Paul's understanding of the gospel requires.[4] Paul can think of himself and speak of himself as a slave because he does not confuse the status or importance of the minister with the importance of the message. In practice this distinction is sometimes difficult to maintain, but it is essential.

Writing in the midst of a fierce debate, Paul makes some exaggerated statements about ministry and suffering. He has no desire to suffer and does not think ministers should seek it out. On the other hand, ministers should be willing to suffer for the good of the church. Furthermore, they must not set themselves apart from others as superior in their experience of God. Such voluntary humility violated the first century's standards for leadership, much as it conflicts with ours. But Paul argues that this type of ministry is consistent with the gospel of the crucified Christ. Were Paul to address the topic of ministry in a less polemical context, mutual subordination would probably be a significant theme, as it is in his discussion of relationships within the church throughout 1 Corinthians. This would be the case because he expects all Christians, not just leaders, to reflect the crucified Christ in their lives. His churches' willingness to accept their culture's view of leadership required Paul to place the emphasis where he does. This polemical setting, however, demonstrates that some understandings of leadership are incompatible with the gospel.

JESUS ON LEADERSHIP

The Gospels relate the stories about and sayings of Jesus as they do to lead their readers to adopt a particular outlook on a given question. Given that all four Gospels have Jesus address the nature of leadership within the Christian community, it is probable that there were discussions in their communities about appropriate forms of Christian leadership. So these texts offer some guidance as we formulate a theology of ministry.

Leadership is among the many things the Twelve misunderstand in the Gospel of Mark. When Jesus asks who the disciples believe he is, Peter replies that Jesus is the Christ. Jesus acknowledges this identity and then tells them that when they get to Jerusalem he will be killed but then rise. When Peter rejects this understanding of Jesus' ministry, Jesus calls him Satan. In 9:30–32 Jesus again tells them that when they arrive in Jerusalem he will be arrested, killed, and then raised on the third day. Mark says the disciples do not understand but are, understandably, afraid to ask for clarification. Perhaps to demonstrate just how little they understand the meaning of Jesus' mission and ministry, Mark immediately has the disciples argue about who would be greatest in the kingdom of God. So when Jesus proclaims his rejection and death, they respond by arguing about status and privilege. Jesus responds to their dispute by asserting that anyone who wants to be great in his kingdom must become a servant to all, even to those with no status (that is, children; 9:35–37). But the disciples' desire for status will not be rebuffed so easily. John now tells Jesus that they had seen someone they did not know exorcising demons in the name of Jesus, and because he was not in their group, they commanded him to stop. Essentially, John responds to Jesus' rejection of claims to status within the apostolic company by suggesting that even if they cannot claim status over one another, they as a group are at least superior to those not in their group. But Jesus says no. Rather, God will reward anyone who does good in Jesus' name (9:38–41).

The next time Jesus predicts his suffering, death, and resurrection, Mark has James and John surreptitiously ask Jesus for the highest positions in the kingdom (10:32–45). The juxtaposition of these attempts to attain status with Jesus' explication of the end of his ministry implies that the desire to claim authority is diametrically opposed to the meaning of the life and ministry of Jesus; claiming status and privilege have no part in the kind of leadership that follows the example of Jesus or understands his ministry. On this occasion Mark has Jesus contrast the way authority is exercised in their culture with what Jesus expects of leaders. In their culture, leaders impose their will on those below them and exercise lordship. Jesus says it must be radically different in God's kingdom. In this realm, those who want to be great must act as servants (*diakonos*) to others, and the one who wants the highest position is to be the slave (*doulos*) of everyone. The use of *doulos* is again arresting. Jesus commands anyone who wants to be the recognized leader, even among the leaders, to act as and to understand himself as the most lowly. This is the only acceptable understanding of leadership in the Christian community because it follows the example of Jesus, the one who came to serve others and to give his life for them.

The account of this story in Matthew 20:20–28 makes the same point with the same shift from *diakonos* to *doulos*. Luke's account of the dispute about who would be the greatest, which immediately follows the institution of the Lord's Supper (22:24–30), makes the point by contrasting cultural models of leadership with Christian leadership.

John's account of Jesus washing the disciples' feet also includes a lesson on leadership. John begins this story by saying that Jesus now knows that God has given him all things, that he had come from God, and was about to return to God (13:2–3). When Jesus recognizes this fully, he performs the most menial of tasks. Washing feet was a servile task, one often performed by a slave. John connects Jesus' confidence in his relationship with God and the coming crucifixion to this task. Such service to others is the symbolic enactment of the ministry of Jesus.

In this act Jesus sets an example for all, but most directly this is an example for leaders to follow. As leaders they are to imitate Jesus by performing menial tasks for others. Jesus washing the disciples' feet is a symbolic enactment of the type of leadership Jesus expects within the church.

In the Gospels, Jesus consistently rejected understandings of leadership that claim privilege and status. By example and explicit teaching, he denounced the ways authority was exercised in their world; he advocated a theology of leadership, of ministry, that disallowed claims of power and demands of deference. He called for a theology of leadership that rests on his example and the values of the kingdom of God. Leaders who adopt this outlook will accept menial tasks, knowing that being a servant imitates Christ more than being served.

LEADERSHIP IN THE LATER PAULINE LETTERS

The letters of 2 Thessalonians and Ephesians also contribute to our understanding of ministry in important ways. But before we turn to those texts, a comment on the Pastoral Epistles is in order.

The Pastoral Epistles are often understood to represent a shift within Christianity toward hierarchy and the kinds of ministry and leadership that the Gospels and Paul seem to reject. But in some ways this contrast has been overdrawn. The Pastorals expect Christians to respect and honor those who are elders and deacons, but the Pastorals do not give these leaders power or authority. Indeed, there is little description of their duties or responsibilities. Instead, there is a rather extensive list of qualifications, perhaps suggesting that their primary duty is to be an example of the way the gospel forms a person's life. Thus, a primary way that elders and deacons lead in the Pastorals is by example.

Whether written after Paul's death or by Paul soon after 1 Thessalonians, 2 Thessalonians addresses issues relevant to our development of a theology of ministry. The primary purpose of 2 Thessalonians is to reject the teaching of some who hold an overrealized eschatology. As 2 Thessalonians characterizes it, they claim that "the Day of the Lord has already come" (2:2). A group in the church that 2 Thessalonians addresses has redefined the Second Coming so that it is not a cosmic event witnessed by all, but rather a personal experience of the Lord that only some have received. Those with this experience claim spiritual superiority because they have a more intimate relationship with God. Who could be more qualified to minister to the needs of others than Christians with such experiences of God? Because of this experience, some among the Thessalonians have appointed themselves the spiritual leaders of the congregation and have left their former occupations to devote themselves fully to work within the church.[5]

The writer of 2 Thessalonians refuses to grant such people positions of leadership because they base their claim to leadership on their superior spiritual experiences, their participation in the Day of the Lord. He commands this church to repudiate them as leaders and even to refuse to include them in their circle of fellowship until they relinquish those claims to superiority, a repentance that must be accompanied by returning to their jobs.

The dispute that 2 Thessalonians joins, then, is in part about leadership. More particularly, it includes a discussion of what qualifies a person for positions of leadership. This letter rejects the idea that superior spiritual experiences qualify a person for a position of leadership in the church.

Ephesians celebrates the unity Christians possess in Christ as a unity that overcomes ethnic differences, one of the most basic differences in their existence. At the same time, it encourages its readers to live out this unity in their lives as the church because this unity manifests the multifaceted wisdom of God. Chapter 4 begins a series of discourses on the ways they are to live out this unity. Verses 1–16, the first in this series, explicate how the readers are to live in the Lord in a manner that is worthy of their calling (4:1). After affirming the unity of the church and enumerating the many things that create this unity, the writer asserts that Christ has given each member of the church a gift. Verse 11 contains a partial accounting of the gifts Christ brings to the church. The writer mentions apostles, prophets, evangelists, pastors, and teachers.

As we saw in 1 Corinthians 12–14, the church recognized from its earliest days that God gifted people in different ways, enabling each to perform particular tasks. Ephesians speaks within that tradition. Ephesians 4 emphasizes unity and identifies a common source for the variety of gifts in a way that is similar to the discussion in 1 Corinthians. Thus, even though its list of gifts is limited to those that entail leadership, this passage does not suggest that the people with these gifts should rule or dominate those with other gifts nor that a variety of other gifts does not exist. This is particularly clear when we remember that "pastors" probably refers to the elders of the congregation. Given the usage of this language elsewhere in the New Testament, that is the most probable meaning of "pastor" during this early period.[6]

For the present discussion, perhaps the most important point we may draw from Ephesians 4 is the purpose it gives for Christ's distribution of these gifts. Christ gives these gifts of leadership so that the leaders may equip the saints for the work of ministry (v. 12), which assumes that all Christians have a ministry and are engaged in the work of ministry. This ministry of all the saints builds up the body of Christ, moving it toward its maturity in the likeness of Christ (vv. 12–13). Here the task of the leaders is preparatory to the basic ministries of the church. The leaders are to be engaged in work that enables the other members of the church to carry out their ministries.

Envisioning leadership as equipping directs attention to the tasks of teaching, encouraging, supporting, enabling, directing, convincing, and modeling. Such tasks are often more difficult, time-consuming, and frustrating than simply taking charge and completing the task at hand. But Ephesians calls for leadership that helps all claim their gifts from God and use them in the service of God, the church, and the world. This kind of leadership, in the words of Ephesians, "builds up the body of Christ."

This is a very different model of leadership than the original readers of Ephesians (or we have usually) envisioned. In the model of Ephesians, *preparing others* to fulfill their ministries, including taking charge of ministry efforts or leading in the public roles or visible ministries, is the task of leaders. This kind of leading involves working behind the scenes to help others begin to carry out types of leadership and service that may have been heretofore the prerogative of the leader. Perhaps they became the prerogative of the pastor because no one else had been taught how to do them. This means that the ministry of the church has been diminished. When parts of the body of Christ wither from disuse or are never strengthened to perform the service that God has gifted them for, the church has been damaged. The immediate task may have been completed, but the church has not moved forward in its living out of the faith when the pastor simply does the task rather than equipping others to do it.

Seeing leadership, and particularly pastoral leadership, as equipping the rest of the church to fulfill its ministry entails a particular ecclesiology. Often, when churches do not own their own ministries, they begin to see the pastor as someone they hire to be religious for them. Then their church becomes just another charity and their faith has no power to help them interpret their lives and the world. Equipping members for ministry will help faith maintain its place in or move it to the center of the person's life where it can be a formative element in her construction of a worldview and meaning for herself within that world. Such "equipping [of] the saints" is the formidable and foundationally important task Ephesians sets before leaders.

SEMINARY AND MINISTRY

Having thus established a biblical foundation for a proper understanding of ministry, the question remains, What does seminary have to do with ministry? It is a question asked in many of the narratives. The Methodist student at Austin Presbyterian Theological Seminary, the Episcopal student at Church Divinity School of the Pacific, those disengaged Baptist students at Eastern Baptist Theological Seminary, and the soccer-playing Disciples at Lexington Theological Seminary all want to know what the things they learn at seminary have to do with the work of ministry. The ways the New Testament addresses issues surrounding leadership have, I think, much to say to us about the nature of ministry and what seminary education needs to accomplish if it is to prepare students for faithful work in ministry.

As we have seen, much in the New Testament runs counter to the tendency to emphasize the special nature of the minister's relationship with God. The individual's experience of God is not, by itself, a sufficient basis for the ministry that the New Testament envisions. Believing that their call to ministry is based on an especially intimate experience of God will almost inevitably lead pastors to see themselves as superior to other Christians, and Paul certainly fought such understandings of leadership in 1 Corinthians.

Paul also saw undesirable connections between dwelling on one's own gifts, including claiming them as evidence of spirituality, and the egotism that claims superiority and demands recognition of status. To have a ministry that effectively represents the church and its ministry of Jesus Christ, pastors must have more than a claim that they are closer to God than others and so can mediate the presence of God to others who are less fortunate. Pastors must be vigilant to avoid falling prey to the alluring notion that they are spiritually superior. Avoiding this snare is almost impossible if pastors believe their decision to be ordained and their work as pastors to be the manifestation of a more special experience of God. Those who think they are superior will find it difficult to sustain a ministry of being a servant of the church.

Perhaps the closest analogy to the current tendency to legitimate ministry on the basis of personal experience is the problem addressed in 2 Thessalonians. The writer of that letter rejects the Thessalonian leaders because they have legitimated their ministry by claiming a fuller experience of the presence of Christ in their lives. I think he would respond in similar ways to those who now rely on their personal experience as their primary basis for ministry. Such an understanding of ministry is not consistent with the gospel and its call to servanthood, because it includes, by definition, a claim to superiority. Therefore, we who teach in seminaries must help those training for the pastorate to understand that personal experience alone is not a sufficient basis for ministry. We must show them how the disciplines of seminary education will help them and their churches discern the voice of God. We must not simply take away what they thought was their reason for entering the ministry; we must help them think of ministry in new and richer ways, ways that are consistent with Scripture and meaningful for them and the church.

Students want and deserve to have their experiences honored, so seminary faculties must find ways to value their students' experiences while not allowing unexamined experiences to retain the central place they have previously held in students' thoughts. We need to help students like Julie at United Theological Seminary of the Twin Cities (2001) learn how to integrate their personal experience with what they are learning about other sources of revelation.

According to Ephesians, the work of leaders is to help others recognize their gifts and then to enable those people to use their gifts for the good of the church and the expansion of the borders of God's kingdom. This is demanding work! It is also work that requires the leader to be thoughtful enough that he can articulate reasons for what he does and thoughtful enough that he will be able to teach others how to engage in the meaningful work of ministry.

If preparing the saints to carry out their ministry is a primary task of the pastor, then teaching is a central element of pastoral ministry and Christian leadership. I think this understanding of pastoral ministry and leadership is not only coherent with the gospel and Scripture, it is also crucial in our cultural context, which has important parallels with the situation in which the church of the New Testament found itself. Now as then (perhaps always) there are competing interpretations of the world. Some of these interpretations are explicitly articulated and advocated by philosophers and religious propagandists; some are expressed in the culture's manner of life. After some time of not recognizing the ways that American culture was built on values that sometimes conflict with those of Christianity, the church has begun the work of critiquing the culture's outlook, seeking where we can participate in it and remain faithful to the gospel and where we must oppose it, or at least stand apart from it. This is profoundly spiritual and intensely intellectual work.

The church today exists in a world that offers many constructions of meaning. As it was in the ancient world, so now, some of these constructs are explicit. Philosophical schools develop different understandings of existence and advocate their view as the one that brings meaning to life, or perhaps exposes life as not being meaningful. Whichever they claim, they articulate a way to view the world that they claim is true. Postmodern relativists claim there is no single truth about the world (though they seem to hold that statement itself to be just such a truth), thus implying no meaning for existence is any more or less authentic than another and that all personal or cultural perspectives are equally valid. Various religious groups also offer different understandings of the events of the day, of history, of our existence. If Christians are to have a credible voice that has integrity, leaders must be able to help churches think through these options. Pastors need to be able, in an informed and articulate manner, to converse with competing ways of making meaning in the world. When so many options confront them, thinking Christians need to have reasons for being Christians. Those who would be pastors need to be expert analysts and interpreters of the world in which they exist. Such work is both intellectual and deeply spiritual.

If teaching, because it offers a means to understand the world and conduct one's ministry, occupies a place near the heart of pastoral ministry, seminary education is invaluable. Seminaries should be places that challenge students to engage those competing understandings of the world and come to understand the gospel and appropriate ways in which the gospel message should be expressed in the ministries of the church. To be the community's teacher, the pastor must not only know how to perform certain functions (whether liturgical or pastoral) but must be able to teach others to do them. Ninety hours of seminary education seems to offer far too few opportunities to accomplish all of this. But the first step is to demonstrate to our students that intellectual work is in fact spiritual work and that it is central to being a pastor. The letter to the president of Calvin Theological Seminary and the students who expected something very different at Austin Presbyterian and Lexington Theological Seminary saw academic and intellectual endeavors as distinct from, if not opposed to, spiritual growth. We need to demonstrate that these endeavors are not opposed but are indeed entwined. Perhaps the place to start is with an understanding of ministry such as that articulated in the New Testament. The understanding of leadership we have discovered there brings together the intellectual and spiritual; it identifies preparing others for their ministries as the spiritual task to which leaders are called. This could be a starting point for helping our students see the connections between the more theoretical parts of seminary education and ministry. The narratives of Church Divinity School of the Pacific and Eastern Baptist Theological Seminary illustrate that this coherence of formation must be evident to both faculty and students if such an understanding of ministry is to shape our students.

Those of us who teach at seminaries, therefore, must reinvigorate the understanding of our vocation as a ministry. We do not simply perpetuate our discipline or increase knowledge of the world. Our primary task is that of preparing leaders for Christ's church. Thus, as seminary teachers we must regain sight of the fact that we are engaged in the task of equipping those who are to equip the saints for the work of ministry.

PRACTICAL IMPLICATIONS

We may begin helping our students find value in their theological education by having them first articulate and reflect critically on their own experience. Parts of Thomas Groome's (1980, 184–232) five-step process for religious education can be helpful to us at this point. Using a praxis-reflection model, he asserts that the first two steps in this process are clear articulation of present practice and critical reflection on that practice. A subsequent step is engaging Scripture and tradition with the understanding of oneself gained through critical reflection. Groome's method requires people to reflect on their current practices and setting.[7]

Entering seminary students often want to "tell their story," perhaps as a way to validate their decision to come to seminary. Rather than deny this impulse or encourage it uncritically, teachers can use the impulse to begin their students' engagement with the tradition. Students should be invited to tell their stories but also, following Groome's lead, to reflect on the social, personal, religious, and political influences that led them to accord their stories the meaning they now hold for them. While encouraging such analysis, teachers will probably need to reassure the students that the analysis does not invalidate their experience but helps them recognize that the experience itself and the meaning they have given it are produced, in part, by factors they may not have considered. Such analysis simply acknowledges that God's revelation to us always comes in a historical context.

If we think of Scripture and tradition as conscious and careful articulations of their writers' experiences of God in their own historical, social, and ecclesial contexts, the exercise of reflecting critically on their own experience may help students engage these foundations of seminary education. Scripture, theology, and church history can be presented as the struggle of God's people to understand and explicate their experience of God in their own cultural settings.

The vocabulary and critical methods of these disciplines may appear foreign to the students, but the struggle to clarify and articulate an understanding of God is one that can be made familiar. Furthermore, students can be led to see how a particular writer's understanding of God draws on previous writers to gain insight and clarity, even if that clarity is achieved by rejecting the previous writers' views. Thus, we show our students that knowing their predecessors may help them clarify and articulate their own experience as they recognize those writers as sources from which they have drawn ideas (even if unconsciously) and as conversation partners who can help them reject ideas with unacceptable consequences and sharpen good ideas. If the students can see the framers of the church engaged in the same tasks in which they are engaged, they may be moved to take them more seriously. Moreover, the students, in the process of their genuine engagement with these texts and ideas, will begin to grant them some authority.

In many ways, these will be lessons in humility and in counterculturalism. It is humbling to acknowledge that some authority stands over our personal experience. Many are not pleased to hear this message. To assert such a proposition runs counter to much we hear in our culture today, and convincing students (and ourselves) to submit to other authorities will not be accomplished in a single session. This work will entail redefining many things, even things as basic as spirituality. Such lessons will need to be repeated in many settings and disciplines if we expect formation to occur.

One way to decrease the difficulty of acknowledging other authorities is to raise examples that students will reject and then ask them to give reasons for their rejection. (I have in mind issues that energize students, such as social justice issues.) For example, few of our students are willing to accept that racism accords with the will and character of God. But as soon as they assert that one position is right for all, they have begun drawing on sources other than personal experience, and we must ask them to identify their sources of authority and think about how they are functioning. Then we must expect consistency from them. That is, we must push them to adopt a theological method (a way to use the elements of the Wesleyan Quadrilateral or some other paradigm) that they can use when approaching theological and ethical questions. Such encounters with how they actually use other sources when there are competing personal experiences will not automatically guarantee that students will be consistent in their thinking and begin to value other sources of revelation and theological reflection. But with the right help, they may begin to see the importance these sources of the faith have as they discern what it means to be Christian in their time and place.

Finally, some of the Seminar narratives speak of students who remain focused on their own experiences, particularly upon their own healing. The narrative of United Theological Seminary of the Twin Cities (2001) exemplifies this as Julie and her colleagues think of their education in terms of what it has done for them as they recover from personal traumas or difficulties. As seminary teachers, we must seek ways to refocus the attention of those who are to be pastors. Clarity about the centrality of the good of the church, about a spirituality that often privileges the group over the individual, may help us talk to our students about the relative importance of their personal struggles. Such clarity might be modeled in the way we allow the content of our classes to be determined in part by the whole of the faculty, by the goals of the current curriculum, and by the needs of the students.

Internalizing the idea that the good of the group, the church, is a compelling truth of the Christian life was a difficult task for the Corinthians. Certainly it will be a difficult task for our students—and for some of us—but necessary nonetheless.

NOTES

1. All narratives cited in this book can be found in the Archives section of the Seminar's Web site: http://www.lexingtonseminar.org/.

2. See the summary of the cultural models of leadership in Clarke (2000, 1–141).

3. The NRSV renders the word, "services," but the noun is *diakonia*, a cognate of *diakonos*. This is the word Paul uses most often to refer to ministry.

4. Compare Paul's use of the cognate verb, *douloo*, in 1 Cor 9, in which he gives himself as an example of someone who voluntarily surrenders his own rights, makes himself a slave, for the good of others (9:19).

5. The Thessalonian Christians would not be the first to leave their trade to become teachers of a new faith. This sometimes happened when a person accepted the teaching of the Cynics. While the other philosophical schools criticized them for this, it was still a well-known Cynic practice. For more detailed argument for this understanding of those opposed in 2 Thessalonians, see Sumney (1999, 229–252) and Malherbe (2000).

6. See 1 Pet 5:1–2 in which elders (*presbuteroi*) are told to "pastor" (NRSV: "tend") the flock over which they have been appointed. The verb in 1 Pet 5 is the cognate of the noun "pastor." Acts 17:28 uses the same verb to speak of the work of elders.

7. I thank my colleague Sharon Warner for her conversations about pedagogy and for directing me to Groome's work.

·SAMUEL ESCOBAR·

What Is the Ministry toward Which We Teach?

Are seminaries educating students for Christian ministry in the world as it is or the world as it once was? Such is the pedagogical problem repeatedly identified in the narratives of The Lexington Seminar. As we examine the role of seminaries in preparing students for ministry, this problem should be recognized not only as pedagogical but as theological and missional as well. It is a problem that has taken on dramatic urgency because of the sociological and cultural transitions that the United States and its churches are experiencing at this point in history. These transitions can be identified in four related yet independent developments in international culture.

First, a fairly homogeneous society dominated by Western European cultural patterns is transitioning into a society significantly changed by the cultural patterns of ethnic minorities. Second, a Protestant era defined by denominational traditions is transitioning into a postdenominational era in which many different independent churches and movements are flourishing. Third, a society shaped by the culture of modernity is transitioning into one shaped by postmodern cultural trends. Fourth, a religious establishment that was once segmented into Protestant-Catholic-Jewish is transitioning into a pluralistic, post-Christendom society in which the Judeo-Christian tradition is losing power and relevance. As I revisit the nature and content of Christian ministry, I will refer to these transitions as the new context for ministry.

MINISTRY REVISITED

The American church scene has been the center of an ongoing discussion about the nature and form of Christian ministry, and the questions formulated in the past show some of the same sense of puzzlement and will to change found in the narratives of The Lexington Seminar. A helpful example is the situation described by James Smart in his book *The Rebirth of Ministry*. Although published more than forty years ago, Smart's book maintains a remarkable cogency for the contemporary scene. Smart summarizes the study of theological education led by H. Richard Niebuhr during a decade in the 1950s (Niebuhr and Williams 1956; Niebuhr, Williams, and Gustafson 1956; Niebuhr, Williams, and Gustafson 1957) by writing, "From their sifting of evidence from ministers and laymen and from our theological seminaries, they assert unequivocally that at the heart of the problem is an inability from our churches to say what a minister is intended to be" (Smart 1960, 17). Smart reminds his readers that the medieval church had a clear-cut picture of the minister as the director of souls, the Reformation church saw the minister as a preacher of the Word, and for Pietism the minister was an evangelist. By contrast, he says, "in twentieth century Protestantism no such unitary and unifying principle exists" (18).

Smart offers a long list of expected roles that show the confusion of perceptions among churches in the 1960s. "What is a minister?" he asked, and he offered the following possible answers: an evangelist, a preacher, a priest, a religious administrator, a social reformer, a species of amateur psychiatrist, an educator (17). Some of these perceptions remain in our present discussions, but each of them can be qualified within the context of current social conditions. A minister is an evangelist, yes, but now we have specialists, such as television preachers and campus crusade workers; a minister is a preacher, yes, but nowadays people seem to ask for storytellers; a minister is a priest, but who wants to be a priest after so many scandals? And how will a minister compete with those who have specialized MBAs in church administration or with social reformers who are opposed to explicit religious involvement in social reform? Several decades of social analysis have made us aware that other institutions are now providing many of the services that the church was once expected to provide.

THE MINISTRY OF JESUS CHRIST

Theological education was established to produce a certain type of result according to a well-established tradition that was based on the well-defined roles that ministers once played in society. At present we face a new situation which is partially the result of the sociocultural transitions I mentioned earlier. The challenges we face now give us a unique opportunity to perceive anew the *mission* of the church and the vision of *ministry* by returning to the sources of our faith. Smart's proposal still makes sense, but we must contextualize it within the frame of the twenty-first century: "The ministry into which we enter is the ministry of Jesus Christ. We are not free to determine its nature as we will; its nature has already been determined for us by his life, death and resurrection and by the work of the Spirit in the shaping of the Apostolic ministry. That is in part the significance of the line that the second-century church drew around the canonical books of Scripture" (20).

A helpful schema to explore the ministry of Jesus Christ comes from the Reformed tradition that arranged the biblical material around the vision of Jesus as prophet, priest, and king (more recently understood as pastor). This schema allows us to see the ministry of Jesus, as we find it in the Gospels, within the context of its roots in the Old Testament. Smart follows it by exploring those roots but showing at the same time the uniqueness of Jesus' ministry (22–28). It was a ministry in which there was no separation between his teaching, his actions, and his being as a person. It was an itinerant ministry going out to those to whom he ministered, looking for his lost sheep. It was a proclamation of God's reign (or kingdom), and he himself moved by the Spirit of God was the king. Central to his ministry was his forgiveness of sins, which accomplished his purpose of restoring human beings to the true life in God. His ministry took the form of service, and he interpreted his ministry with Old Testament images of servanthood. Summing up, "All aspects of Jesus' ministry come to their climactic expression in the cross. Strangely, it was in his dying that his ministry was fulfilled with the profoundest power. Again we meet the oneness of gospel, ministry and person" (28).

Jesus' ministry in the training of his disciples also throws light on the nature of the apostolic ministry. Smart explores in depth the relationship between Jesus and the disciples that establishes the continuity between his ministry and theirs:

> When Jesus trained the twelve it was not for some secondary ministry different in kind from his own; it was for participation with him in the only ministry he knew. But before they could share his ministry with him there had to be a sharing on a yet deeper and more decisive level (29).

There are key moments in the synoptic Gospels in which this training process is evident, and especially in the Fourth Gospel the teaching and prayers of Jesus are explicit about the continuity between his ministry and the ministry to which he called the disciples. As Smart says, "John's Gospel dwells on this again and again, that the life of God, which was incarnate in Jesus Christ, became the life also of his disciples, and that the Spirit of God, which dwelt in all his fullness in Jesus Christ, took up his dwelling place in the disciples and created Christ afresh in them" (29). More recently, Justo González, a scholar who has modeled how to place scholarship at the service of ministry, has offered us a rich meditation on the spiritual life of the minister that dwells in the teaching of the Gospels. It is the kind of book that one would categorize as spirituality, but it is a theologically based spirituality, forged in the experience of a theological educator. In the introduction to his book, González proposes to show how Jesus' "ministry calls our ministry into being and how his ministry shapes ours." But he emphasizes his intention to go beyond mere intellectual exploration when he says that "we are not seeking merely to learn how to imitate Jesus. It is much more a matter of probing the depths of what it means to be in Christ, to be transformed by Christ and to have Christ formed in us and living in us" (González 1995, 8).

The persistent effort to establish continuity with the ministry of Jesus Christ as it was developed in the life of the apostolic church has been the source of a formulation of ministry that uses a set of Greek words—*martyria, koinonia, leitourgia, kerygma, didache, diakonia,* and *propheteia*—that have become familiar to those who reflect upon the mission of the church in the world.[1]

As a community of believers in Jesus Christ, the very presence of the church in the world is a reminder of the coming of Christ that was history, marked history, and gives meaning to history; in that sense the church is a living testimony—*martyria*. The way of being the church in the world is to be a gathered fellowship, a cohesive community bound by love in Christ—*koinonia*. A unique and distinctive activity of this gathered fellowship is worship—*leitourgia*—a response to God's revelation as Creator, Savior, and empowering Spirit. The gathering of the community is made possible by the proclamation of God's word in Christ—*kerygma*—followed by instruction in the Word—*didache*. The gathered fellowship is marked by the same vocation of service—*diakonia*—to the needs of human beings in the church and outside the church, the kind of service that was the way of life and death for Jesus Christ. More recently, as the ministry of Jesus himself was rediscovered, the centrality of God's reign in his self-understanding, preaching, teaching, and healing has been recovered and with it the relevance of the courageous denunciation of evil when God's reign is proclaimed—*propheteia*.

Each one of these words points to attitudes and activities that constitute the why, what, and how of ministry. A helpful summary from Groome (1991, 331–332) serves well here by way of synthesis:

> The *modus operandi* of Christian ministry should be appropriate to the overarching purpose of God's reign and effective in the tasks of evangelizing, preaching and teaching Christian Story/Vision; in building up inclusive and witnessing communities of Jesus' disciples, of enabling communities to worship God and to celebrate the sacraments of

encounter with the Risen Christ; and of rendering personal and social/political service for the welfare of all and the integrity of creation.

Such is the ministry toward which we teach, which must now be formulated and developed within the context of the cultural and ecclesiastical transitions of our time. These transitions are the setting within which our reflection takes place, and they are already affecting the daily life of faculty and students in seminaries. It is evident from the narratives of The Lexington Seminar that the characteristics of the new context for ministry are now shaping the social landscape and the pace of life of theological seminaries. The way these communities respond to the new situations will model future ministerial praxis.

I now explore in more detail and with due regard for society's current transitional context the components of ministry I have just outlined, placing particular emphasis on *koinonia, kerygma, martyria, leitourgia,* and *diakonia.*[2]

KOINONIA IN THE GLOBAL VILLAGE

The presence of minorities and international students is one of the ways in which seminaries experience the reality of the global village. The Two-Thirds World has come to the United States, and it resides not just in the heart of our cities but amid the green lawns of suburbia and on the shaded streets of small-town America. The two-thirds church is no longer a distant reality described by foreign missionaries. It is right here, down the street, in the seminary: multicultural, multiethnic, multilingual realities from the global village. The narratives of The Lexington Seminar dramatize some of the disconcerting characteristics of diversity in seminary communities: Japanese students who do not understand English adequately, African students who find critical approaches to the biblical text intolerable, single mothers who feel marginalized because their needs are not taken into account. Add to that the presence of students from Pentecostal and independent churches that until a few years ago were at the margins of Protestant theological education but may now be becoming the new mainline denominations. How is *koinonia* fostered in such a diverse company?

When the current student generation graduates, a growing number of ministry situations will have the characteristics of the global village. In the late nineteenth and early twentieth centuries when massive immigration brought people from diverse cultures to the United States, ministry in many American mainline churches made a conscious effort to "Americanize" the newcomers, to assimilate them into middle-class Anglo-Saxon life and values. Today, however, the scenario is different. Several references to contextualization in the narratives are evidence that seminary communities are grappling now with the issues that in the past were associated with global mission, with the work of the church in missionary territories where it was not so easy to impose a dominant cultural pattern. A ministry committed to *koinonia* will have to deal with cultural diversity. Such a ministry will require its practitioners to scrutinize their own cultural presuppositions, be open to the cultural differences of others, and yet still be willing and able to strengthen the fundamental commitments of the church.

A missiologist who has done much work on diversity, from a church growth perspective, is George Hunter III, who says that the cultural barrier between churches and unchurched people is the largest single cause of the decline of European Christianity and a bigger problem for mainline American Christianity. Hunter poses a dramatic question, "The U.S.A. is a vast secular mission field with many cultures and subcultures. Are we imaginative enough and compassionate enough to sponsor and unleash many forms of indigenous Christianity in this land?" (Hunter 2001, 105). He thinks that the so-called apostolic congregations that are proliferating in North America are responding to this missionary challenge. His choice of some well-known mega-churches may not be the answer I would choose, but I think his question is the right one to ask. A church that claims to be an embodiment of the new, a sign of the kingdom, must come to terms with this new global reality, and its ministers, whose responsibility is to cooperate with God's Spirit as he fashions a new church, must be educated to fulfill their task in this new situation.

THE TEXT OF *KERYGMA* IN THE CONTEXT OF POSTMODERNITY

Preaching and teaching are key elements of the Protestant concept of ministry. The Reformation brought back the conviction that the very existence and life of the church came from the creative power of the Word. It was not the church that gave birth to Scripture; it was God's Word in the apostolic preaching, recorded later in Scripture, that gave birth to the church. If the church lived by the Word, then the ministry of the Word was at the heart of Christian ministry. Thus, Protestantism revolutionized theological education, placing the study of Scripture at the heart of the curriculum. This explains why, as Protestantism developed within the setting of modern culture, Protestants came to emphasize *true doctrine* or *reasonable belief* as a mark of the church (although important sectors among them have not fully perceived the value of *ritual and symbol* in human life and communication). Nevertheless, within the structures of the culture of modernity, rigorous seminary training enabled theological students to take a parable of Jesus, one of those masterpieces of narrative, and generate from it a sermon that had the structure of a philosophical essay. One could say that the curriculum in traditional theological education reflects this bias toward preaching and teaching as the most fundamental activities of ministry, which address especially the mind and the rational abilities of the hearers.

The attention we now pay to narrative as a form of communication is evidence that something is happening to the predominance of rationality that was characteristic of modernity. The term "postmodernity" describes a cultural atmosphere in which we can identify an open or veiled rejection of the ideologies, worldviews, and values that were shaped by the Enlightenment and which constituted our concept of modernity. We might describe a postmodern culture as one in which there is a predominance of feeling and a revolt against reason as seen in such phenomena as the search for ever more sophisticated forms of pleasure. Sports and popular artistic shows take the shape of religious celebration and replace church services as a way to provide relief from the drudgery of routine work and duty.

Ministry within the context of a postmodern culture will have to pay attention to new elements of content and style. The whole process of communication that includes preaching and teaching in church will need to address not only the reasoning ability of people but also their imagination, their feelings, their ability to grasp symbols, and their need for belonging. Postmodernity motivates us to revise our view of the human and the minister in a more holistic way by being ourselves whole persons. In the past, being familiar with people's various learning patterns was almost solely within the professional purview of educational specialists. Today, theological educators must prepare ministers who are aware of the various learning patterns in postmodern culture and who can conduct their ministry accordingly.

As to the question of content, take for instance an important aspect of postmodernity, such as the exaltation of the body. Postmodern culture depicts the body in all forms and shapes and offers thousands of products to beautify, perfume, modify, improve, and perfect the body, even to the point of promising ways to overcome the inroads of natural decay. There are products, methods, and stimuli for enhancing physical pleasure in all its forms. This search for pleasure has become a mark of contemporary life that, coupled with the hopelessness brought by the collapse of ideologies, becomes pure and simple hedonism. Ministry in this situation requires a rediscovery of references and perspectives on human materiality and pleasure in the sources of our faith. The text of Scripture may have surprising angles as we read it within this new context.

MARTYRIA IN A POST-CHRISTENDOM SITUATION

Although the United States has never had a nationally established church, most churchgoing Americans have, until recently, assumed that they lived in a nation with a Christian social order, a social order in dramatic contrast with that of faraway mission territories. Within a Christian social order—call it Christendom—the church is a privileged entity because it fills a recognized role, and ministers enjoy social acceptance and privileges. Christendom developed after the marriage of church and state that came with the conversion of emperor Constantine. "The church was blended into a half-civil, half-religious society, *Christendom*. It has covered a whole civilization with its authority, inspired a politic, and has become an essentially Western reality" (Mehl 1970, 67). Christendom presupposed the predominance of Christianity in Western societies and a certain degree of influence of Christian ideas and principles on the social life of nations. However, the West is moving into a new situation that can be described as post-Christendom, one in which Christianity is losing its privileged status because of secularization, numerical decline of mainline churches, loss of spiritual vigor, privatization of religious commitment, and the growing presence of other religious traditions. This phenomenon has not affected Christianity in the United States to the same degree that it has in Europe, but it is certainly at work in American society.

In this new situation, Christians cannot expect society to facilitate through social mechanisms the kind of life that reflects the qualities of Christian character and ethics, nor can ministers expect as much as formerly in terms of recognition and status. The Christian stance in the West today has to become a missionary stance in which the quality of Christian life goes "against the stream." Two Methodist ministers and scholars, Stanley Hauerwas and William H. Willimon (1989) have studied this situation and outlined the kind of response it requires from churches and ministers. The title of their book, *Resident Aliens*, describes well the response required from Christians who want to live their faith in American society. The same qualities that were required of the pioneers who planted Christianity in mission fields are now required from the Christians who stay at home and want to be faithful witnesses of Jesus Christ. Coming from a life of missionary experience in Asia, Rosemary Dowsett (2001, 449) has said it forcefully, "Neither the Lord Jesus himself nor the early church regarded minority status as abnormal. It was only with the advent of Christendom that the church was seduced into believing that she should exercise majority control by force, not faith (in parts of Europe we are still paying the price for that wrong turning)." Missionaries have learned and have been inspired by the way in which Christians live their lives in a hostile environment when they are a tiny minority. Christians living in the West can learn much from Christians who every day must practice their faith in traditional missionary fields.

During worship at Eastern Baptist Theological Seminary in Philadelphia I am often reminded of the environment in which we teach when I hear and am touched by the realities of intercessory prayer. While mainline, middle-class students have asked us to pray for their grades and their sick aunts, students from poorer backgrounds have asked us to pray for the lady who directs Sunday school in their church, because her grandson has gone into prison for drug-pushing. Such moments are today an important part of the formative process of ministers as disciple-makers in years to come.

LEITOURGIA IN THE CONTEXT OF THE NEW RELIGIOSITY

One of the tenets of "enlightened" modernity was the idea that religion was in the process of waning away. Christian thinkers were confronted in cultural circles by a hostile rationalism nourished by the three "fathers of suspicion"— Marx, Nietzsche, and Freud—who announced the end of religion. Some theologians wrote in praise of the advent of secularity, and in many quarters ministry did indeed become secularized, losing the spiritual source of the divine call. But now, at the beginning of the twenty-first century, we live in a world in which religions have multiplied to the point that sociologists are now describing the desecularization of the world (Berger 1999).

From the perspective of Christian ministry, the return of an attitude of openness to the sacred and the mysterious could be interpreted as a sign of improvement. In many cases this new attitude has allowed Christians to demonstrate through prayer, song, and drama a freer and less inhibited expression of Christian faith. But Christians are also confronted with a new and more subtle challenge. Ministers find themselves engaged in dialogue with people whose language is strangely similar to church language—"joy in the heart," a feeling of "self-realization," a sense of "peace and harmony," a feeling of "goodwill toward all human beings." However, if a Christian minister wants to deal with specific issues such as suffering, death, compassion, final hope, failure, and sin, the hollowness of this new religious mood often becomes apparent. Furthermore, when such traditional themes are expressed, hostility sometimes develops against what is considered Christian exclusivism and intolerance.

The new attitude toward religion and the proliferation of religious practices has to be understood as part of the revolt against modernity. The modern ideologies of indefinite progress and social utopia were actually myths that attracted and mobilized the masses to action. Their failure to materialize for large portions of the world's population have brought awareness of a vacuum and disillusionment about the ability of human reason to give meaning to life and provide answers to deep existential questions. This awareness is at the root of the search for spiritual alternatives, for a contact with the occult, for an ability to handle mystery, for a connection with extrarational forces that may influence the course of human events, both in individual lives as well as in communities and nations. The new uninhibited forms of religiosity in American life run the gamut from Afro-Caribbean "santería" to self-destructive messianic sects, from elegant New Age types of spirituality to racist fundamentalisms committed to white supremacy.

Within this new context of intensified religiosity, Christian ministry provides the gift and discipline of discernment. In the days of the New Testament, the gospel of Jesus Christ confronted not only the challenges of Greek philosophy and Roman politics but also the theological and pastoral questions posed by the mystery religions that pervaded the worldview and ritual practices of popular culture. Mystery religions in the first century promised cleansing to deal with guilt, security to face fear of evil, power over fate, union with gods through orgiastic ecstasy, and immortality (Green 1970). The apostolic message developed in the New Testament responded to similar aspirations of the human heart but was based on the person and work of Jesus Christ and the presence of the Holy Spirit. The time has come in which ministry needs to rediscover the rich streams of spirituality that have always been available to sustain the life of the church.

DIAKONIA IN A POSTCAPITALIST SOCIETY

We were once accustomed to thinking of massive social change as something characteristic of countries in Africa or Latin America, but the United States is also experiencing a social revolution that analyst Peter Drucker (1994) has described as the coming of the postcapitalist society, in which "knowledge workers" are replacing industrial workers. Significant changes are affecting the lives of people because of the disappearance of old communities, such as family, village, and parish. Neither government nor the employing organizations, the classic "two sectors" that hold power in the postcapitalist United States, are able to cope with the effects of this massive social change. Such effects give place to what Drucker calls the "social tasks of the knowledge society."

As a committed Christian who knows well the potential of Christian faith to mobilize active compassion expressed in service, Drucker places the agenda of assuming social tasks in the hands of what he calls "the third sector" in American society. This is constituted by churches and by myriad voluntary organizations that he calls "para-churches," because they have modeled themselves after the nonprofit pattern established by churches. He assigns to this "social sector" a twofold task: to "create human health and well-being" and to "create citizenship." Drucker's scheme presupposes a reserve of volunteerism that is typically American and has unequivocal Protestant roots, though its contemporary manifestations may be secular in outlook and intention.

Thus, a new element has been added with a sense of urgency to the agenda of Christian ministry. Even denominations and churches that in the past were critical of the social agendas embraced by mainline churches are now becoming engaged in new forms of *diakonia*. It is well known that ministers among ethnic minorities have been bound to become involved in different forms of social activism. The challenge is becoming more generalized today. By placing service within the larger conception of ministry, churches will avoid falling into the patterns of the welfare system. The redemptive power of the Gospel transforms people in such a way that it enables them to overcome the dire consequences of poverty. Sociological studies of Christianity in the 1960s and 1970s were usually hostile to churches. The scenario has changed today. As social planners and city governments acknowledge the problems generated by the current economic system, sociologists have come to see churches as the source of hope from which the urban poor gain strength, courage, and a language to cope with poverty.[3]

CLUES FOR THE FUTURE

This reflection on ministry only makes sense within the larger picture of the life of the churches in the United States and the reality of global Christianity. Many points in the narratives of The Lexington Seminar show that concerns that in the past were characteristic of the church in "missionary territories" have become concerns of the church at home. The situation in the United States is not as critical as that in Europe where Christianity is in open decline, but in order to have a future churches clearly must adopt a missional stance. If we accept the fact that the West, namely Europe and North America, is to be considered as a mission field, we also must accept the validity of a search for a ministry approach that will have a missionary thrust and will take seriously the cultural context of that mission field. Let me present here what I call three clues to be pursued in the future.

First, missiologists have been studying with renewed vigor the discipleship process as it took place before the Constantinian experience. They are looking for clues that will help churches prepare Christians to live as a minority in a hostile world. I have found especially helpful the work of Alan Kreider, who has reviewed many recorded stories of conversions in the first three centuries. As he studies the records of early Christian converts, Kreider (1999, xv) writes, "I am struck by the way in which conversion involved change not just of *belief* but also of *belonging* and *behavior*. . . . Often scholars have not given due weight to these dimensions, so that when they tell the stories—some of them very famous—of early Christian converts they overlook the concern for ethics and solidarity, that, to me, is evident in the texts."[4]

Missionary experience and observation confirms what the more systematic work of scholars uncovers, and it is pointing in the direction of a renewed concept of discipleship and education for the faith. Because of our Protestant "modern" bias, we emphasize doctrine and the correct understanding of it as well as the rationalization of the institutional life of the church and even of the public witness of Christians. We are learning now that the redemptive power of the gospel and the power of the Holy Spirit that are active when truth is applied to life can change deep-seated patterns of behavior. Perhaps established churches have lost their connection with that dimension of Christianity. We are also learning that the sense of belonging is a key component of the Christian experience. We are learning it from the joy and meaningful experience of marginal people coming to Christ from the bottom of society, those who have not belonged to any form of community, who have experienced the reality of lostness in a dramatic way, and who have experienced the joy of coming home when they meet Christ.

Second, clues point to the possibility that we are living in the middle of a New Reformation. Sociologist Donald E. Miller, University of California, has written a puzzling description and analysis of three mega-churches that could well be described as postmodern churches because of their ability to understand their context and respond to it with a contextual kind of ministry. Miller's book (1997) is based on careful field work from a team and his own convincing interpretation. The title of the book is eloquent—*Reinventing American Protestantism: Christianity in the New Millennium*—and it offers postmodernity in American culture as a means of understanding the significance of what he calls "the new paradigm churches" that have developed in recent decades. The thesis of his book is that

> A revolution is transforming American Protestantism. While many of the mainline churches are losing membership, overall church attendance is not declining. Instead, a new style of Christianity is being born in the United States, one that responds to fundamental cultural changes that began in the mid-1960s. These New Paradigm Churches as I call them in this book are changing the way Christianity looks and is experienced. (1)

He observes that ministry in these churches has left behind denominational patterns received from the past and is appropriating contemporary cultural forms, such as a new genre of worship music and new structures for the institutional church, and is thus "democratizing access to the sacred by radicalizing the Protestant principle of priesthood of all believers." For Miller we are witnessing the coming of a new era of postdenominational Christianity in the United States.

Third, a group of theological educators and missiologists have taken up the challenge posed by Lesslie Newbigin (1986) and are exploring what it means for Western churches to adopt a missionary stance in their own culture. Some of them are linked in the "Gospel and Culture Networks" and have been working consistently in a critical analysis of the legacy of Christendom in the life of congregations and denominations. Their books take seriously the present forms of ministerial and congregational life and practice, and they outline new models as they record and evaluate emerging forms of ministry, congregational organization, and evangelistic activity. Because of their serious work in the development of a biblical and theological frame for a new missional stance, they deserve the attention of anyone interested in ministerial formation.[5]

IMPLICATIONS FOR PRACTICE

If the ministry toward which we teach is taking on new dimensions as a response to a new era in the history of the church, the theological institutions in which formation for ministry takes place must become laboratories for this new type of ministry. I cannot develop in depth the implications of the reflection I have offered, so I limit myself only to pointing in some directions that are being explored and outlined by the institutions that have participated in The Lexington Seminar.

As the student body in seminaries continues to reflect the demography of the global village, theological education has the opportunity to become a laboratory for a new type of ministry. However, the mere presence of diversity is not enough. An intentional dialogue must be fostered through a participatory pedagogical approach, remembering always that true dialogue requires openness in all participants and that its aim is not necessarily that minorities conform to the thought patterns of the predominant culture but that all participants be mutually enriched. A clear sense of *koinonia* is at the heart of participatory pedagogy.

The ministry of the Word will continue to be at the heart of Christian ministry, and the formation of ministers will still require that they be provided with tools, based on the best available scholarship, that are good instruments for the task of interpreting the text. The need for new communication methods appropriate for people who experience postmodernity does not dispense seminaries from the task of teaching the disciplines that are necessary for understanding the text of Scripture. However, as the narrative of Pacific Lutheran Theological Seminary (2001) reminds us, there is a difference between approaching "texts as texts" from the studious objectivity of a narrow academic perspective and approaching texts as *kerygma* in a theological community. A contribution of postmodern culture is that it has helped remind us of the difference.

Paying due attention to national or international students who come from a more religious and less analytical culture may also be a source of insights into spiritual realities. When free to express themselves in an atmosphere of participatory dialogue for learning, my students from so-called fundamentalist backgrounds have sometimes brought our classes into a deeper and clearer under-standing of New Testament material than critical analytical tools have allowed others to appropriate.

As a growing number of ordained ministers and other experienced church leaders enroll in degree programs, theological education becomes a training ground for "reflection on praxis." The pedagogical process must be con-ducive to the critical learning that comes when the practice and experience of students is placed under the light provided by an adequate grasp of Scripture, history, the social sciences, and other topics. The process requires a careful description of practice from what we could call a hermeneutics of *sympathy* rather than one of *suspicion*. Students must be evaluated not only by their com-mand of the information provided by the classic disciplines but by their abili-ty to reflect on their own practice.

Finally, "agenda-setting courses" should grow in importance, for they allow students to pose questions that arise in concrete situations of ministry and use all areas of the theological curriculum to answer those questions (Eastern Baptist Theological Seminary 2000). These courses require a dialogue of the disciplines among faculty in such a way that the point of connection between theological scholarship and the practice of ministry is constantly visible. By pro-viding courses that address concrete ministerial issues and encourage the appli-cation of knowledge from many disciplines, seminaries can reduce the perception among students that certain disciplines are merely academic hoops through which students must jump in order to get a degree. Further, evalua-tion of students under these conditions should measure their ability to apply academic and scholarly knowledge to pastoral practice.

CONCLUSION

Theologians dealing with ministerial and pastoral issues today are being dri-ven to restudy New Testament teaching about religiosity as well as about the presence and power of the Holy Spirit. For the life of the church, communi-cation technology and techniques as well as an intellectually reasonable faith are not enough. Spiritual power and disciplines such as prayer, Bible medita-tion, and fasting are necessary for mission across new religious frontiers. Theological educators should be open to the ministry of persons who are gift-ed to minister in these areas and may also aspire to develop such gifts in them-selves. On the other hand, the Apostle Paul, writing to the Corinthians, recognized that immorality, abuses, and manipulation could exist even with-in the context of spectacular spiritual gifts.

Working in theological education and training for mission in North America, we have become aware of the importance of spiritual formation for ministers. A change of mind has been taking place at this point. If ministry is conceived simply as the exercise of a set of professional abilities, education for ministry could follow what missiologist Jim Pludemann (2000, 902) describes as an "assembly line paradigm" in which spiritual formation is neglected because it does not fit the paradigm. "The factory paradigm encourages missionaries to set objectives for mere outward behavior. It is primarily interested in quantities." Spiritual formation on the other hand is a process that takes place inside a person; it is not something that can be measured, controlled, or predicted. Theological education must become itself a form of ministry, a way of making available the means of grace that God has provided for the continuous growth of God's people toward the goal of becoming Christ-like persons.

NOTES

1. For two valuable discussions of the subject from very different but coincidental perspectives, see Groome (1991, 299–366) and Engen (1991, 87–130).

2. My analysis of context in this section follows the pattern I develop in "The Global Scenario at the Turn of the Century" (Escobar 2000, 25–46).

3. For a story of how a sociologist in the city of Philadelphia has changed his mind and come to realize the key role of churches, see Stafford (1999, 35–39).

4. Emphasis mine; see also Kreider (1995).

5. Valuable work of the North American network may be seen in Guder (1998) and Hunsberger and Van Gelder (1996).

The Work Ahead

PRACTICAL GUIDELINES FOR MORE EFFECTIVE TEACHING AND LEARNING

· MARY-ANN WINKELMES ·

Formative Learning
in the Classroom

Many seminary faculty can still remember when students' formation happened on the residential seminary campus, guided by interactions among students and faculty who lived and worshiped and learned together. As Professor Jones in the Church Divinity School of the Pacific narrative recalls (2001), "In fact, the traditional . . . seminary approach has been described as 'formation by osmosis,' because so much of it has to do with studying and praying together in community."[1] That community, however real or romanticized it may be, no longer inhabits today's seminaries and no longer supports students' "formation by osmosis" in the spaces between mandatory gatherings such as class meetings or required worship services. Today's seminary communities are fragmented.

As a senior faculty member in the Pacific Lutheran Theological School narrative admits (2001), "We drive up here and teach our classes, then climb back into our cars and flee to our homes." The narrative describes "a community in diaspora, . . . with faculty strung out across the Bay Area and another student residence several miles away . . ." Even if the situation in this narrative is exaggerated for dramatic effect, the hard truth is that formation is not happening adequately for students in today's disjointed seminary communities. The only place and time teachers can ensure that a formative learning community gathers in the seminary is in their very own classrooms during class meetings. The seminary classroom is arguably the most feasible locus for the kind of gradual, intellectual, and spiritual formation that seems to have happened within the supportive, residential seminary communities of generations past.

Yet many faculty are reluctant to engage issues of personal and spiritual formation in courses that focus on other particular subjects. As a result, some seminaries relegate the responsibility of students' formation to an administrative post or an office that acts something like a guidance counselor. This often isolates rather than integrates formation at seminaries, although formation is essentially a process of integrating one's intellectual, emotional, and spiritual development into a wise, coherent whole.[2] Some seminaries cannot agree even to such a generalized definition of formation. With the advent of increasingly open admissions (primarily for financial reasons), seminaries are struggling to redefine what formation means at their individual schools. When students come from a variety of denominational backgrounds and will go on to serve communities of various denominations, successful formation can no longer mean turning out students whose values and views and knowledge are particular to the specific faith of the seminary's unidenominational founders. Most seminaries have yet to reach a definition of formation for their students that all faculty can accept comfortably. This lack of consensus may contribute to some faculty's retreat from actively supporting formation in order to focus more explicitly on course subject matter. As the representation of denominations among the students changes, so do faculty and administrative opinions on what constitutes formation for those students and how much of it is the in-class responsibility of faculty members.

Increasingly open admissions result in increased student diversity not only in terms of their denominations but also in their social, cultural, political, economic, and educational backgrounds. Unidenominational seminaries of generations past educated relatively homogeneous populations of students who shared a particular system of values and beliefs, similar economic and cultural origins, and similar educational preparation before seminary. In today's seminaries, by contrast, faculty are finding the teaching methods that succeeded with the more homogenous student populations of the past (to which some of them belonged) are no longer sufficient today. Creating an environment for successful teaching and learning in seminary classrooms has become more complicated. At the same time, the importance of what happens in those classrooms has increased dramatically. With seminary communities "in diaspora," more of the work of educating the whole student is left for the classroom. If formation doesn't happen there, where else can it happen? Seminary classrooms are perhaps the single most important and most feasible place for formation to occur.

If the work of formation does not happen in classrooms, then the special task and special value of seminaries is in jeopardy. Seminaries will increasingly resemble masters-degree-granting liberal arts institutions—with a very limited curriculum. Individually, faculty will teach courses that focus intensively on subjects like the Bible or preaching skills or church history, and students will graduate with knowledge about those discrete subjects and with a degree or license to practice. At seminaries where faculty and administration cannot agree about the sort of formation issues they want students to engage, a legitimate choice can be to accept the fragmentation of the seminary community and to declare their position as a degree-granting institution. In this context, students would not be required to pass any sort of integrative examination in order to graduate, although they may independently integrate their learning experiences into a wise and coherent worldview that will make them good leaders and mentors for those whom they will serve.

At seminaries where formation is still a desired part of preparing students for their future work, faculty may wish to create an environment in their classrooms that actively encourages formation in a general sense—even while the definition of formation is evolving at each seminary. While formation is a responsibility that is specific to seminaries, research on teaching and learning outside the seminary, in the broader realm of higher education, offers ideas that can help seminary teachers consider how to create classroom environments that support formation according to their own definitions. This essay considers the pedagogical implications of some of the major research on learning in higher education and offers some suggestions for practices that can encourage formation in the classroom.[3]

RESEARCH ON HOW STUDENTS LEARN

Recent research on learning in higher education indicates what most seminary instructors have already experienced: Students are more diverse than they were a generation ago in terms of class, race, religion, educational experience, and styles and strengths of learning. With this variety has come an increased interest in the variety of ways students learn and an enhanced focus on how students perceive, apply, and internalize course content. Research on these areas, while spearheaded and continued by developmental psychologists, is also pursued now by neuroscientists and by professors in virtually all disciplines who study the learning habits of their current students and thus contribute to a nationally supported enterprise of "classroom research."[4]

Theological educators have a specialized sort of teaching wisdom that equips them both to resolve the erosion of formation in theological education and to make a significant, needed contribution in the realm of higher education. Seminary teachers have long concerned themselves not only with teaching course content to their students but also with their students' overall learning experience. They have focused explicitly on the relationships between what happens inside and outside the classroom to shape their students' worldviews and promote the education of a whole person. They have even pondered the role of the seminary in a person's lifelong learning and formation. Until fairly recently, seminary teachers worked as ministers for five years before teaching in seminary and had opportunities to observe the ways people of all ages in a parish community learn. Seminary instructors, more than professors in most colleges, universities, and professional schools, belong to a culture in which the overall educational and developmental experience of students warrants serious consideration.

PHASES OF INTELLECTUAL DEVELOPMENT

The Lexington Seminar discussions have highlighted the fact that seminary teachers, like many of their colleagues in higher education, notice some learning behaviors that concur with categories of learning and development outlined in the 1960s by researchers such as Arthur Chickering and William Perry. Chickering (1969) identified seven "vectors of development" for college students: confidence, emotions, autonomy, identity, interpersonal relationships, purpose, and integrity. Seminary teachers tend to think of these "vectors" together as students' "formation," and they include in that formation an additional category of spiritual individuation.

William Perry (1970) provided another way of understanding students' development when he identified seven phases of intellectual and moral development that he grouped into three main categories: dualism, multiplicity, and relativism. Perry's freshmen experienced a kind of black-and-white dualistic thinking that new seminary students often encounter in terms of a moral dualism of right and wrong. Kiyo, the Japanese student in the Church Divinity School of the Pacific narrative (2001), states his firm belief that it is "not right to criticize [the] Bible." Another example is Judith, a student in the Bethel Theological Seminary narrative (2001) whose personal circumstances reinforce her moral dualism by encouraging her to crave certainty. She tries to garner support from her fellow students in the classroom, commenting, "I am sure that we all agree that it is dangerous to stray too far from the obvious, most widely accepted meanings of the text." The Lexington Seminar narratives also describe students whom Perry would place in his "multiplicity" category. In seminary, these students often have difficulty integrating what they learn in the classroom with a consistent worldview that guides their decisions. Julie, a student who has just failed her integrative examination at United Theological Seminary of the Twin Cities (2001), voices this perspective.

> I really don't have a clue how to do what you are asking of me . . . different parts of me think and feel different things about faith and ministry, and I don't know how to turn them into one person. . . . On the one hand, you want me . . . to have a well-developed theology that informs what I do as a minister. On the other hand, you want me to stay open, "tolerate ambiguity," and allow different contexts to inform my theological perspective. I don't think I can do it. . . . I don't know how to make the connections you are asking me to make theologically between those two principles.

Perry's relativism is a phase in which students have resolved such apparent dilemmas. Relativist students have developed criteria for evaluating and selecting the most convincing or helpful options appropriate to a given context. Clearly, the same sort of guidance that is appropriate for a relativist student is not equally helpful to Kiyo, the moral dualist reluctant to examine the Bible too carefully, and to Julie, mired in the confusion of multiplicity. Yet the three might be classmates in the same course at any seminary. The challenge that this presents for instructors is addressed in the later section of this chapter called "Practices That Encourage Formative Learning in the Classroom."

Recent research has aimed with good reason to problematize the phases of learning and development identified in the 1960s by Chickering and Perry. A number of scholars have drawn attention to the need for studies of more representative groups of learners than Perry's male undergraduates at Harvard College in the 1960s or Chickering's earlier generations of students. Sue and Cross, for example (Sue and Sue 1990; Cross, Strauss, and Fhagen-Smith 1999), have studied the psychosocial development of black and Latino students, primarily before college age, while Treisman (1992) and Steele (1992) have considered the impact of cultural tradition and racial stereotyping on learning by Asian and black students in college mathematics. Gender differences in college learners have been the focus of Belenky et al. (1986) and Baxter Magolda (1992). King and Kitchener (1994) chose an unusually large focus group for their study of students in colleges in the Midwestern United States. Still others are researching the learning practices of more advanced adult students (Merriam and Caffarella 1998).

While these studies have pointed to the limited representativeness of studies published by Perry and Chickering in the 1960s, they still conceive of learning in terms of progressive trajectories of intellectual, social, and psychological development, many of which are close parallels to those established by Perry. For the most part, the pedagogical research and literature on postsecondary learning has yet to adjust for the impossibility of selecting a representative sample of learners, the limitations of conceiving of learning in progressive phases, and the methodological dilemma inherent in categorizing learners. For example, are a student's learning styles and strengths and phase of development intrinsically the student's rather than the result of adaptation to teaching practices which are in turn adaptations to educators' perceptions about learning? Seminaries would be a useful focus group for researchers studying modes of learning and teaching because seminary students represent such a diversity of ages and backgrounds—religious, spiritual, social, cultural, political, economic, and educational—and because seminary instructors are particularly reflective about their students' overall formation.

LEARNING STYLES

In addition to a variety of phases by which we can choose to understand students' development, we can also consider students' different styles and strengths as learners, regardless of which particular phase of development we think pertains to them.[5] Some are strong visual learners, while others learn best by hearing. Some learn best by reading and some by applying new principles in a tangible way. Some understand concepts best when they encounter them in formats that seem chronological, others do better with formats that are typological, while still others organize new information spatially.

One illustration of a predominantly spatial understanding is a geometric diagram-outline produced by a Japanese student preparing for her research paper in a college in the United States (Figure 1). A professor drew up the more traditional outline based on the student's completed paper (Figure 2). While the outlines are dramatically different in form, they correspond to the same paper. This particular student conceived of the paper-in-progress in spatial terms and perhaps could not have produced the traditional outline until after she had completed the paper. Crafting a traditional outline in advance, then, would *not* have helped the student *prepare* her paper, although crafting a geometric diagram *did* help the student organize the structure of her paper in advance. But even a teacher attentive to individual students' learning styles might not have predicted that asking students for a preparatory traditional outline would have put one of the most successful students at a distinct disadvantage! A less restrictive request for a descriptive statement, sketch, or outline demonstrating how the main ideas of the paper would be connected might appeal more equitably to different types of learners.

Among today's varied student populations, traditional methods of teaching and testing, such as lecturing and independent or guided research papers, can certainly be effective but also have the disadvantage of favoring certain types of learners over others. "Everything is structured for a certain type of person, and I'm not that person," laments Jean, a single mother and part-time student in the Austin Presbyterian Theological Seminary narrative (1999). This kind

Figure 1. Mind Map of Lloyd Webber's Production

This map shows how I visualize that Lloyd Webber's *Phantom* production came into existence. Before I could come up with an outline for my argument, I had to pin down all the ideas that I wanted to use in a compact form. Most of my ideas were still fuzzy, and refused to come into focus until I constructed this visual aid to guide the development of my ideas.

The different elements that make up the production are numbered in chronological order, but there is no reason why some of the elements were not created concurrently or in conjunction with another element.

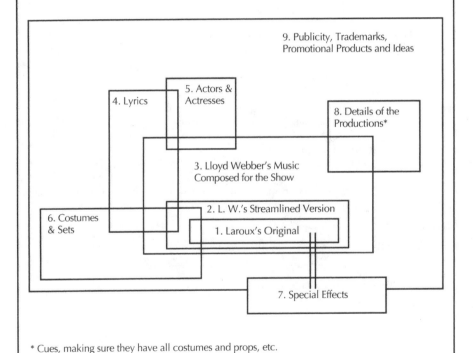

9. Publicity, Trademarks, Promotional Products and Ideas

5. Actors & Actresses

4. Lyrics

8. Details of the Productions*

3. Lloyd Webber's Music Composed for the Show

2. L. W.'s Streamlined Version

6. Costumes & Sets

1. Laroux's Original

7. Special Effects

* Cues, making sure they have all costumes and props, etc.

Source: Miley Nakamura, Mind Map of Lloyd Webber's Production. Reprinted by permission of Miley Nakamura. All rights reserved.

Figure 2. Sample Outline of Mind Map of Lloyd Webber's Production

Topic: Music in Andrew Lloyd Webber's *The Phantom of the Opera*: How it has made the show popular.

Argument: Andrew Lloyd Webber's orchestration relies on conventional Western styles of musical phrasing and instrumentation. It exploits the natural tendencies of music to correspond with the ebb and flow of emotions, and allows the music to reflect the mood and/or tone of a scene, thereby making the musical accessible to a large general audience.

I.   Introduction.
    A.   The popularity of *Phantom* and its music.
    B.   Possible reasons: story, spectacle, characters.
    C.   Success mainly comes from orchestration.

II. Criticisms of Andrew Lloyd Webber's music.
    A.   What reviewers criticize.
    B.   Why they are wrong.

III. Why the music does deserve praise.
    A.   Tactics of Western music that Lloyd Webber uses.
        1.   Exploits the natural tendencies of musical phrasing.
        2.   Orchestrates the numbers with instruments commonly associated with different moods.
        3.   Relies on recurring themes, bringing back melodies associated in audience's memories with certain character roles and types.
        4.   In scenes with romantic implications, couples orchestration with rhythm of the lyrics to amplify sensuous overtones and transmit amatory expectations.

[outline continues]

Source: Sue Lonoff, Sample Outline Based on Mind Map. Reprinted by permission of Sue Lonoff, Derek Bok Center for Teaching and Learning, Harvard University.

of alienation from the learning process leads some students to resist and even resent the teaching methods they encounter at seminary. As the library director from the Eastern Baptist Theological Seminary narrative (2000) explains:

> Our current students . . . already had a voice in the world from which they came. When they arrive here many have the experience of being silenced. They have been interactive, even leaders, in their old world, and when they come to us, in some classes, they are expected to be passive listeners. . . . It isn't working. Many become angry in their silence. They decide to do what they have to do to get out of here. . . .

Students often feel there is no room for the contributions they might make in the classroom. Julie, a student in the United Theological Seminary of the Twin Cities narrative (2001), explains of her classmate, Clarice:

> She gets most angry, she says, over the fact that few people really make an effort to know the truths and realities of her life and the great knowledge that she brings out of that. She doesn't always feel that what she says is taken seriously.

Why should students' own experiences be an essential part of classroom teaching? Recent research in neuroscience suggests an answer.

NEUROSCIENCE AND THE PHYSIOLOGY OF LEARNING

Neuroscience tells us that thinking is a process of activating synapses in the brain, while learning is a process of growing new neural networks between synapses. When a student actively thinks through a new concept, figuring out how to apply it in a particular context, she is physically growing and rerouting the thinking process through the formation of new neural connections between synapses.[6] Past generations of seminary students would receive information in the classroom and then ponder it and apply it outside the classroom in the context of their interactions in the larger seminary community. Today, few seminaries provide the full-time, residential community that can support this kind of formation, and opportunities for students to think through new concepts in the classroom are needed.

Learning, then, is a process of making new connections—both physical (between synapses) and metaphorical (between ideas or between new information and existing knowledge). When a student encounters new information in the classroom, he connects that information with his previous knowledge. More often than we care to admit, that means connecting new knowledge with previously learned misinformation. Once this happens, the new information will be misunderstood. The subsequent process of unlearning misconceptions is even more difficult than learning new information. This is why it is essential to provide students with an opportunity in the classroom to apply a new concept in a way that requires them to think it through actively, encounter any potential conflicts with their preexisting conceptions or misconceptions, resolve those through questions and discussion, and make new connections. Testing these connections in the classroom provides all students an opportunity to connect and apply new information across a variety of real-world contexts simply by taking advantage of the great variety of students' experience and expertise. All students in the group have the opportunity to learn from experience beyond their own and thus move more quickly toward integrating these experiences into their evolving worldview.

The research in neuroscience that points to the necessity of providing opportunities for students to process and internalize information as they encounter it in the classroom is supported by further research in the area of cognitive stress.

Cognitive Stress

Most of us would envy the seminary instructor who has not encountered the point in a semester when even successful students inexplicably seem to forget knowledge and skills they have already mastered. This phenomenon often occurs when students approach a task or topic or discipline that seems unfamiliar to them. Research on this sort of cognitive stress indicates what at first seems counterintuitive: reviewing the previously mastered course content and/or retraining the forgotten skills is not needed because the lapsed knowledge and skills reappear once students feel familiar with the modes of thinking and the terminology of the new context (Colomb 1988).[7] While cognitive stress can never be completely avoided, it can be minimized. The more course content that is delivered in class without an opportunity for students to apply, test, and internalize that content, the more quickly and often cognitive stress will manifest itself. Cognitive stress can be minimized by encouraging students to process and internalize new content in class as it is presented. Students who work to understand and internalize concepts as they are introduced in class will have *learned* the course content and will understand what to *do* with that content in their personal and professional lives.

Implications for Teaching

This kind of learning, application, internalization, and deep understanding of course content is increasingly difficult for students in today's seminaries, most of whom do not live in a residential campus community that constantly stimulates and supports the out-of-the-classroom thought that alters their worldviews and enhances their formation. Too often the expectations of what and how students can learn in their fragmented seminary experience outside the classroom are unrealistic. How likely is it, for example, that Jean, a single parent and part-time student in the Austin Presbyterian Theological Seminary narrative (1999), will have the opportunity to follow Dean Dunn's prescription:

> I think it's great, Jean, when students from different traditions have the opportunity
> to teach each other. Please keep working on those relationships. After all, we want you
> to have a certain ownership in your education. We want you to take your share of
> responsibility in making your educational experience work.

If our goal is to help diverse learners understand the relationships between what they learn in the seminary classroom, how they navigate the larger seminary community, and how they function in the world, we must provide opportunities for them to practice making those sorts of connections as a regular part of their training in seminary—not just through accidental (and increasingly rare) out-of-class interactions at the seminary, but purposefully in the classroom.

Yet many seminary instructors fear that time spent providing such opportunities during class meetings sacrifices time the professor could use to deliver course content to students. A professor in the Bethel narrative (2000) claims:

> Do you realize . . . that once I set a foundation for what we're doing, I only have time in a quarter to spend about ten minutes on each chapter of the Gospels? If I start stealing time from that to deal with all these "process things," the students will leave here under-prepared.

And in the Eastern Baptist Theological Seminary narrative (2000), a Bible professor complains:

> [M]aybe we need to do a better job of getting students more involved with their own education at the beginning, this finding your own voice, or whatever. But some of us are so content-oriented and have so much content to impart, that we need to . . . get a lot of it out there in the beginning.

Coverage of important content, however, is no guarantee of students' retention of that content. Nor does covering this content guarantee students' ability to analyze it and use it in their professional and personal lives. Even the most successful graduates, like the four alumni in the Calvin Theological Seminary narrative who hold positions as ministers in the Christian Reformed Church, struggle after graduation to apply their classroom learning to their work as pastors. These four claim that their "spiritual formation" in seminary was inadequate and that they received too little training in the "skills needed to do the job of ministry." They see their Bible and church history courses as unconnected with "issues faced daily by pastors." And these are the *successful* graduates! These four face a problem that would not have been helped by coverage of additional course content in their Bible and church history classes. The value of the course content they learned has been reduced by the fact that they lacked guidance and practice in what to *do* with that course content.

The experiences of graduates like these, along with our own observations of students' learning and formation inside our ever more fragmented seminary communities, point to the classroom as the locus not just for presenting course content but also for students' application and integration of that content. This necessity is underlined by neuroscience research that tells us learning is a process of making connections between new and old ideas, and by research on cognitive stress which suggests that efficient mastery of content comes with processing and integrating that content as soon as it is encountered. Because our students' styles and phases of learning are so varied, we must use varied modes of both presenting material and encouraging students' understanding of how to make use of that material. Ideally, we aim to educate in a way that appeals fairly to students' diverse styles of learning without excessively favoring any particular style or phase of learning over others.

PRACTICES THAT ENCOURAGE FORMATIVE LEARNING IN THE CLASSROOM

In seminary classrooms populated by a wide variety of learners, what teaching practices encourage students' retention and thoughtful integration of course content? First of all, it is important to recognize that formative teaching/learning environments can exist as well in lecture courses as they do in small discussion seminars, in one-on-one tutorials, or in mentoring partnerships. In each context, the considerable challenge is to know something about students' learning styles, phases, and preparatory experience, and then to employ a variety of teaching/learning techniques that will appeal to students as equitably as possible. This helps to ensure that course content is accessible to all students and also that students multiply their methods for acquiring and internalizing course content.

The framing of course content is a sometimes overlooked method for making information more equally accessible to students of varied learning styles, phases, and levels of preparation, all in the same classroom. At the beginning of any class meeting, a fraction of the students arrive knowing what to expect, understanding the relationship between the content of the readings, the focus of any additional assignment, and the announced topic of the day's lecture or discussion. The majority of students will not make all of these connections independently. This is not necessarily an indication that they have not read or written what was assigned. It only means that they do not think about the organization of the course and the syllabus in the same way the professor does. An explicit introductory comment by the professor about the purpose of each class meeting, its main goals and main issues, its place in the design of the whole course, and its relationship to any readings or other assignments benefits all students in the group—from those whose ample understanding is affirmed and perhaps enhanced to those who see for the first time exactly how the general course themes and particular day's assignments and topics are connected. Some professors accompany this oral explanation with a written diagram or agenda on the blackboard or on a handout, where it is visually accessible to students (some of whom are stronger visual learners) who can refer to it through-

out the class meeting to help them contextualize any part of the lectu
cussion. An explicit comment at the end of the class meeting that summarizes
these connections and introduces the next topics to be examined further clar-
ifies and affirms the students' efforts. In lecture courses as well as in smaller discussion seminars, professors can even involve students in the brief introductory
exercise of contextual framing for the class meeting by inviting them to add the
subtopics they most want to consider to the professor's basic agenda. This can
give students a greater sense of ownership of the class meeting that follows, an
increased sense of the importance of their own role, an added incentive to focus
primarily on those issues the group has agreed are the most important, and an
increased sense of responsibility and control over their own learning.

This sort of contextual framing that can help to focus and define the purpose of each class meeting can be applied to each assignment and each of the
required readings as well. A professor's explicit statement about the purpose
and focus of each piece of work required of students in the course not only helps
students make the connections necessary for internalizing course content, it also
encourages students to be more aware of their learning across the course of the
semester. Making the purpose of an assignment transparently clear to students
can also allow the professor some flexibility in determining *how* students can
acceptably fulfill that purpose. For example, if the professor creates an assignment whose purpose is to help students prepare their papers by making them
describe how the main ideas of the paper will fit together, then the professor
is free to allow students to do that in a variety of ways. For example, the
Japanese student who organizes her thoughts spatially (and not in traditional
outline form) could submit a diagram (Figure 1) or a diagram accompanied
by a brief written explanation (making the diagram accessible to a professor who
doesn't think about ideas spatially) in fulfillment of the assignment. The
assignment thus fulfills its purpose of helping the student prepare her paper
while making that preparatory thought accessible to the professor who can then
provide guidance. When professors make the purpose of assignments transparent to students, then students can measure what they have learned against the
professor's stated purpose for that assignment and then become more aware
of the success of their work.

Frederick Mosteller (1989) asks his students to take this kind of measurement in a different context—at the end of each class meeting. His "minute
paper" assignment requires students to spend a minute before the end of class
answering two questions in writing: (1) what main ideas are you taking from
this class meeting; (2) what question do you still have? Like most teachers who
use this device, Mosteller is often surprised at how much students' main ideas
and questions about the class differ from his own. At the beginning of the very
next class meeting, or even in a between-class communication, he can clarify

Figure 3. Sample Peer Response Sheet

Peer Response Sheet

Writer:

Reader:

RECORD YOUR RESPONSES TO THE FOLLOWING QUESTIONS EITHER IN THE SPACES BELOW OR ON SEPARATE SHEETS OF PAPER.

Read the paper through once, rather quickly, without pausing to write comments. Then put the paper aside and answer the following questions without looking back. (If you can't answer the question, write "I don't know.")

1. What single feature of the paper stands out to you as a reader?

2. What do you think is the writer's main point?

3. Was there anything in the paper that seemed confusing to you? (If so, explain briefly.)

Now reread the paper, making any comments in the margins you feel would be helpful. Try to comment on development and organization of ideas: Do you understand the points the writer is trying to make? Do ideas seem well-connected? **Remember, you are not being asked to evaluate the paper: you are being asked to respond to it with an eye toward helping the writer improve it.**

4. Underline the thesis statement. Is it clearly stated? If not, what seems confusing?

5. Is there any place where the writer needs to support an idea with more concrete details or explanations? Is so, where?

6. How well does the writer make transitions between his/her main ideas? Identify places that need better transitions.

7. List at least two ways in which the essay could be improved.

8. List at least two things you like about the paper.

9. What would you like to know more about? What questions do you still have?

10. Ask of the essay "so what?" after you finish reading. Write a sentence or two paraphrasing the point of the paper, answering the question, "in what way(s) is this interesting, surprising, intriguing, etc.?" If the paper lacks a "so what?" point that out and discuss the possibilities.

Source: Derek Bok Center for Teaching and Learning, Harvard University. Sample Peer Response Sheet. Reprinted by permission of the Derek Bok Center for Teaching and Learning, Harvard University, and the President and Fellows of Harvard College.

any misconceptions and address any questions that, left unaddressed, would quickly lead to students' cognitive stress and their less effective learning. This simple diagnostic tool allows Mosteller to monitor students' understanding in the context of a lecture course, an environment in which a teacher often does not discover student misconceptions or confusions until exams or papers are submitted.

Students who become accustomed to considering their comprehension at the conclusion of class meetings or assignments can begin to take on greater responsibility in evaluating their own work and that of their peers. A professor who makes his or her definition of the characteristics of a successful piece of student work accessible to students can encourage them to evaluate their own work and that of their peers according to commonly understood standards. Students who are aware of the standards of evaluation can understand a teacher's comments and grades as constructive feedback rather than inscrutable, personal judgments. Many professors find that engaging students in a peer evaluation exercise before they submit the final version of an assignment can help students both by honing their critical thinking skills and by providing them with helpful suggestions (from their peers) for revising their work. A careful set of guidelines for peer evaluation exercises (like the one shown in Figure 3) is usually enough to ensure that students are neither too flattering nor too harsh in their evaluations. Peer feedback also provides students with at least one other response to their ideas in addition to that of the professor. These responses will differ at least in style if not in content, thus providing an additional stimulus to the student's critical evaluation of the message.

Opportunities for students to practice their critical, evaluative skills can be provided in large lectures as well as in individual comments on assignments. A lecturer can stimulate students' active thinking by beginning with a dilemma or problem that cannot be adequately addressed without the content that the lecture will provide. First, students recognize that particular information is needed to solve the problem, and they listen for that information. Second, while they listen, they may apply the new information to the dilemma that requires it and even begin to evaluate the results. To further enhance this process of applying and processing the new information, a short amount of time can be allotted during the lecture for students to engage their peers in the process. Eric Mazur (1997), for example, includes three such exercises in each hour-long lecture, allowing two minutes for each one. He invites students in groups of two to apply the concept he has just described in his lecture to a new situation he proposes. Not only does this provide his students with an opportunity to form new neural networks during the lecture meeting, it also enlists the classroom community's diverse perspectives to help the professor reach learners with various strengths at different phases in their intellectual development. No single professor could provide as many possible ways of understanding and explaining new material as Mazur's students provide for each other.

Of course, seminar-style discussion classes provide additional opportunities to enhance students' learning and their critical thinking. An example is case-based discussion teaching—common in many professional schools and also in The Lexington Seminar. A written narrative or case describes a situation to be discussed. Participants identify the topics raised by the case and examine those topics in discussion together, both in the context of the particular situation and also beyond it. The group eventually deduces principles and lessons to be learned, applies those to other scenarios, and refines them. This method maximizes students' access to the many informed perspectives in the class group and to varied styles of understanding. It not only encourages participants to make new connections (a necessary condition for learning, according to neuroscientists) but also allows for the essential step of voicing misconceptions. These can then be understood and corrected, thus minimizing students' opportunities to internalize misinformation along with new concepts. Case-based teaching also provides an opportunity for metacognitive awareness of how learning is happening, because the processes by which content is explored and understood are on display and could be introduced as a topic for the group's consideration. Often case discussions can provide an array of rich and varied means for addressing complicated, real-world questions like those posed to the job candidate in the Pacific Lutheran Theological Seminary narrative (2001):

> "How can you help me make Philippians come alive to the adult Bible study group that meets at my teaching parish? It's a community of Chinese Americans, and I need to contextualize my approach."
> "What do you think Paul meant in Romans 1:26, and how would you explain that in a classroom that included straights, gays, lesbians, and bisexuals?"

A carefully guided classroom discussion can address such relevant questions in ways more imaginative, varied, and broadly accessible to all students in the group than any single professor could offer by herself.

For peer learning to succeed in lectures, case discussions, or written feedback, three criteria must be clearly understood by all participants: the purpose of the exercise (what are the teacher's goals and what should students gain), the exact procedure that will be used (including precise details of timing and roles and responsibilities), and the characteristics and proposed uses of any product participants must create (like a written comment, list, diagram, or spoken argument). These three essential preconditions for peer learning—a commonly understood purpose, procedure, and product—can be applied just as well to all pedagogical practice. Before a professor provides a lecture or requires any work of students, the purpose, procedure, and product must be thoroughly defined and commonly understood for the project to succeed.

This sort of clarification requires a greater transparency with students about teaching and learning strategies than many seminary professors are accustomed to providing. While seminary faculty can be exceptionally thoughtful and precise when discussing their teaching and learning goals with colleagues, surprisingly few are as forthcoming about their teaching strategies with their own students. Greater transparency invites students' greater awareness of their learning practices and encourages students to take a more responsible role in their own education. Transparency about pedagogical aims and practices also enables teachers to treat their students as junior colleagues in the pursuit of satisfying teaching and learning experiences in the classroom. For example, once teachers have established with their students a transparency about teaching and learning goals, students can provide useful and informed feedback about the effectiveness of teaching methods and particular assignments. Professors can then adjust accordingly. Frederick Mosteller's "minute papers" are a valuable example. This sort of informal assessment allows teachers to benefit from the prompt and frequent feedback that is so beneficial for students.[8] In this context, students are cast as the experts on which aspects of a professor's teaching are most effective for their particular learning, and teachers take on the role of learners as they gather data about which aspects of their teaching work best for their diverse students.[9]

CONCLUSION

By making pedagogical goals and methods transparent to students and by valuing students as junior colleagues and experts on their own learning experiences, seminary instructors can create a classroom environment that encourages the kind of integration essential to formation. This symbiosis of teaching and learning offers even more than a place for formative learning. It also allows a teacher to model the kind of formative educator and mentor his seminary students will need to be—one who enables learners to educate themselves.

Seminary teachers and administrators who have participated in The Lexington Seminar discussions engaged each other in just such a symbiotic, formative environment for learning. As peers, they provided for one another a variety of perspectives and different styles of explaining and understanding. They guided one another in forming new conceptual connections. They experienced as learners many of the teaching practices that research on learning in higher education suggests are most effective for today's diverse populations of students. They also recognized that students can be helpful colleagues to professors in their efforts to provide a satisfying seminary education. One common resolution among participants was to prioritize at their seminaries discussions of learning and teaching among teachers and between teachers and students.

Just as The Lexington Seminar participants have experienced formative learning, so seminary students must learn in their own diverse styles how to understand and adjust to information that comes not only from their professors but from a variety of sources in many different forms. With our guidance, students in increasingly fragmented seminary communities can provide this for each other and themselves in the classroom. With their guidance, we can learn increasingly effective ways of providing them with classroom environments that encourage their formation.

NOTES

1. All narratives cited in this book can be found in the Archives section of the Seminar's Web site: http://www.lexingtonseminar.org/.

2. For more on formation, see the essay in this volume by Victor Klimoski.

3. In the case of virtual, online classroom communities, or actual classrooms that incorporate some online students, the principles considered in this chapter are equally helpful, while the teaching techniques may involve a variety of tools that allow for communication with and inclusion of off-site students. The challenges of including off-site students in the learning community are examined in a separate essay by Richard W. Nysse.

4. On this scholarship of teaching program, see Hutchings and Babb (2002) and Hutchings (2002).

5. On learning styles, see Kolb (1984), Gregorc (1998), Gardner (1983), and Schmeck (1988).

6. Several accounts of the brain physiology of learning that are accessible to non-neuroscientists are Bloom, Lazerson, and Nelson (2001), Sousa (2001), Wolfe (2001), and Zull (2002).

7. Colomb's research on college students writing for the first time in an unfamiliar discipline demonstrated that efforts to review basic skills are almost always wasted because students recover apparently forgotten writing skills as soon as they understand the new context in which they must use them. Furthermore, focusing on the ideas students wished to communicate rather than on the mechanics of their papers helped students gain familiarity with the new context quickly.

8. Richard Light's Assessment Seminars (Light 1990) indicated that students learn best in college when they receive frequent and prompt feedback on their ideas (in the form of oral feedback from peers in small study groups or other peer assessment exercises, or prompt feedback from a teacher), when they have frequent small assignments, and when they have opportunities to revise their work.

9. This kind of student-faculty communication about teaching and learning accomplishes many of the goals for good educational practice outlined by Chickering and Gamson (1998). They maintain that good practice in undergraduate education (1) encourages contact between students and faculty, (2) develops reciprocity and cooperation among students,

(3) encourages active learning, (4) gives prompt feedback, (5) emphasizes time on task, (6) communicates high expectations, and (7) respects diverse talents and ways of learning. For more on the constructive, formative kind of assessment described here, see Angelo and Cross (1993), Banta and Paloma (1999), and Gordon Smith's essay in this volume.

·GARTH M. ROSELL·

Engaging Issues in Course Development

Over a half century has passed since John Wisdom, the noted English philosopher, first told his well-known "parable of the gardener."[1] The story centers
on two people and a plot of land—land that appears to be a long-neglected
garden. While the garden still shows evidence of some "surprisingly vigorous"
plants, it has, however, become overgrown with weeds and filled with vermin.

The first man says to the other: "Look at the way these are arranged. There
is purpose and a feeling for beauty here. I believe that someone comes, someone invisible to mortal eyes. I believe that the more carefully we look the more
we shall find confirmation of this." As they examine the garden, they sometimes come upon evidence suggesting that a gardener comes and sometimes
they come on new things that suggest the contrary and perhaps "even that a
malicious person has been at work." Each learns all that the other learns
about the garden. "Consequently, when after all this, one says, 'I still believe
a gardener comes' while the other says 'I don't' their different words now
reflect no difference as to what they have found in the garden, no difference
as to what they would find in the garden if they looked further and no difference about how fast untended gardens fall into disorder."[2]

Wisdom's parable, as the reader is undoubtedly aware, was originally
intended as a way of engaging issues surrounding God's existence and character. When applied to matters of teaching and learning, however, it has
become for me, over my thirty-five years of teaching, a kind of paradigm for

course development—reminding me regularly of the importance of testing my assumptions, of taking time to think, of setting my goals, of designing my courses, and of evaluating the results.

Testing Our Assumptions

Wisdom's story, of course, is basically about assumptions—about how it is possible for two radically different conclusions to be drawn from exactly the same body of evidence. A very similar problem exists for those of us who teach (Grunert 1997). Before we ever set foot in the classroom, our assumptions about how we teach, about how students learn, and even about what content should be presented have already begun giving shape and direction to our classes.

Most of us, I suspect, simply teach the way we were taught. Those who were fortunate enough to have studied under master teachers might have an advantage over those who were not so fortunate. In either case, however, few seminary professors have ever given much attention to how they teach. Doctoral programs, quite properly, tend to focus primary attention and resources on helping students master a particular field of study. In doing so, however, they sometimes fail to prepare their graduates adequately for the one activity in which they will be spending the major portion of their professional lives—namely, teaching. The assumption seems to be this: If a person knows his or her field, that person will be able to teach it effectively. As any student can tell us, however, such an assumption cannot always be sustained and is either naïve or simply obstinate. Yet many of us continue to enter the classroom without ever having read a book, taken a course, or even attended a workshop on the subject of pedagogy. Surely the assumptions that lead to this curious irony need to be tested (Chickering, Gamson, and Barsi 1989).

Even less attention, it would seem, has been given to the ways in which students learn (Davis 1993c; Gardiner 1996). This unfortunate state of affairs, as Robert Diamond (1998, 154) has reminded us, appears to be changing as higher education gradually moves "from being teaching-centered to being learning-centered." My first awareness that such a shift was under way came during the early 1970s when I attended a summer workshop sponsored by the Case Study Institute. There in the heart of Cambridge, in something akin to an epiphany, it first dawned on me that lectures and seminars were not the only arrows in my educational quiver. While lectures and seminars have remained central in my teaching since that time, I have found great delight in using additional methodologies in my teaching—from the use of case studies to the development of on-site courses.

Testing our assumptions about teaching and learning, however, remains insufficient by itself. There is also a need to evaluate our presuppositions about the content of the courses we teach. John Wisdom's "garden," I would suggest, can serve as a useful metaphor for many of the fields in which we labor. It seems all too apparent, for example, that church history contains both that which is beautiful and that which is desolate, both flowers and weeds, both saints and scoundrels. One could, I suppose, choose to see only the good, the right, and the fit, or, like Bertrand Russell (1957), see only the seamier side. It might even be possible for an enterprising soul to divide the "goods" and the "bads" of church history, adopting the first category as part of "our tradition" and attributing the second category to "their tradition."

In the end, however, I am convinced that scholars must embrace the whole of the field in which they are teaching. Unfortunately, such an approach presents almost insurmountable problems for course development. Because we must all be selective in what we can cover, we must be especially vigilant in testing the assumptions that guide the selections we make. The sheer amount of available information continues to grow exponentially, and we must guard against the temptation to overlook less familiar arenas of evidence. The composition of the student population in most of our seminaries is increasingly diverse, so we must pay special attention to ensuring that their voices are heard and their traditions are honored.[3]

TAKING TIME TO THINK

Over the course of my teaching career, I have become increasingly convinced that the careful testing of assumptions—about how we teach, about how students learn, and about the content of our courses—is an absolutely essential preamble to the development of effective courses. Such testing takes time. There are no shortcuts. Before we can construct a course, we must spend time thinking about what we are doing and why we are doing it.

Such an idea is, of course, all too obvious. Educational institutions, one might suppose, are places devoted to thinking—quiet enclaves of learning in which scholars pursue the life of the mind. For growing numbers of faculty and students, however, the life of quiet reflection is tantalizingly out of reach. Busy schedules, unexpected interruptions, and overloaded calendars have left many of us with little time for careful thought.

As participants in The Lexington Seminar have gathered each summer in Maine, these very same concerns have been expressed in conversations repeatedly. The life of the mind is increasingly difficult to pursue in the midst of busy schedules and growing institutional obligations. Students struggle to coordinate the demands of study, work, ministry, and family. Faculty members struggle to find space for research and writing in the midst of countless committee meetings, speaking engagements, family responsibilities, and outside jobs. Administrators struggle to keep up with the growing pile of paperwork, endless reports, and continual meetings. In the midst of it all, little time seems to remain for serious reflection.[4]

Such problems should come as no surprise. More than twenty years ago John Fletcher warned us of "the coming crisis in theological seminaries." As late as the 1950s, he argued, most seminaries had a single educational goal—namely, to train pastors for the church. By 1980, when Fletcher reported his findings in the Alban Institute's *Action Information*, virtually every theological institution had expanded its programs to offer continuing education for clergy, theological education for laity, and ethical and theological reflection for churches, community leaders, and the professions. "Seminaries are slowly but surely walking into a minefield," he continued, if one takes seriously the significant changes that are occurring in student demographics, church membership, faculty aging patterns, growing economic pressures, and the trend toward professionalization. "In an era of increasingly fragmented seminary life and part-time attendance," Fletcher (1980, 6–10) suggested, "opportunities for serious self-knowledge and mutual reflection on the student's ethical, educational, and emotional background will be markedly fewer."

Given these realities, it would be helpful if more of us—as those entrusted to prepare leadership for the church—were to set aside an hour each week for serious thought and focused reflection. The ground rules would be simple: Find a comfortable place where we can work without distractions; select a time when our minds are especially fresh; bring paper and pen to record our thoughts; and then systematically explore who, what, where, when, and how we are teaching. As the Scriptures remind us (1 Cor. 10–15), "each one should be careful how he builds."

SETTING OUR GOALS

Having tested our assumptions and having thought about our task as teachers, the next step in course development is the setting of our educational goals.[5] It is essential, as Diamond (1998, 125–67) has phrased it, that we develop "a clear statement of instructional goals" for our courses.[6]

For many of us, however, setting goals is no easy task. Throughout the history of theological education, in fact, fierce battles have been fought over the establishment of educational goals. At America's oldest colleges, as George Marsden (Marsden and Longfield 1992, 15) has reminded us, "higher education simply meant expertise in the classics."[7] Heavy emphasis was given to subjects such as "Latin, Greek, and mathematics" (Ringenberg 1984, 37), and a focus during the classroom sessions tended to be upon "reciting classical authors" (Marsden and Longfield 1992, 13).

At Yale College, for example, students were receiving this kind of classical education well into the nineteenth century (Noll 1979, 7–8). Augustus Hopkins Strong (1836–1921), who graduated from Yale in 1857, described his educational experiences in fascinating detail. "In those days there was almost no instruction," he wrote in his autobiography (Douglas 1981, 62–63).

> Professor Hadley and President Woolsey . . . are the only teachers whom I can remember to have given actual information to their pupils. The system . . . consisted simply of learning lessons from a textbook and reciting them to the tutor or professor. No discussion was permitted at any time. I do not recall that a single question was asked by any student of an instructor during the whole four years of my college course. It was a dead-alive system, which of itself did much to make scholarly work a drudgery and almost nothing to make it attractive. Great as Professor Hadley's merits were as a drillmaster and an example of thorough investigation, he never so much as intimated to us that Homer was a poet. . . . [Professor] Dwight taught us Plato, but he never told us that Plato had a system of philosophy, that there was a difference between the philosophies of Plato and Aristotle, or that either of these had a following down the ages. Never was it suggested to us that a subject might have light thrown upon it by side reading; never were we referred to books for illustration; never was the history of a science spoken of. . . . When I think what might have been done in the way of making study interesting and how completely the student was left to his own devices, I feel that I was treated hardly, and I thank a good Providence that prevented me from utterly despising the regular studies of my course.[8]

For educational reformers like Charles G. Finney, however, the kind of curriculum offered at Yale was like "David in Saul's armor"—forcing students to stagger under the weight of an educational system that Finney described as essentially irrelevant, scattered, impractical, and out of touch with common folk (Finney 1989, 88).[9] Oberlin College, under Finney's leadership, sought to provide an alternative—what they called a more "thorough education"—one that not only combined physical, mental, and moral training but that also opened its doors to both women and African Americans.[10] "Suppose you were going to make a man a surgeon in the navy," Finney argued. "Instead of sending him to the medical school to learn surgery, would you send him to the nautical school to learn navigation? In this way, you might qualify him to navigate a ship, but he is no surgeon. Ministers should be educated to know what the Bible is, and what the human mind is, and know how to bring one to bear on the other. They should be brought into contact with mind, and made familiar with all the aspects of society. They should have the Bible in one hand, and the map of the human mind in the other, and know how to use the truth for the salvation of men" (McLoughlin 1960, 188).

Such practical wisdom, as Finney understood it (1989, 89–90), required far more than the memorization and recitation of classical authors. Consequently, Finney adopted what we might today call an interactive seminar method of teaching (Foster 1888, 104). Rather than the traditional emphasis on classroom recitation, each student was assigned a specific topic or issue on which they were expected to read and reflect and about which they were to prepare an oral presentation for class. During the class sessions, Finney would put the names of the students in a hat, shake them together, and pick one out at random. The student who was thereby selected would be asked to make his/her oral presentation to the class. This would be followed by a time of lively and intense interaction—as the instructor and other members of the class asked questions, raised objections, and presented alternative interpretations. On occasions, according to student reports, the discussions could continue over several days.[11] After class, students would frequently "swarm" around Finney "like bees," as Hiram Mead (1877, 11) described it, anxious to pursue some issue or other a bit more fully.

"It is our custom in this institution," wrote Finney, "to settle every question, especially in theology, by discussion. I have now for twelve years been going annually over my course of instruction in this manner, and owe not a little to my classes, for I have availed myself to the uttermost of the learning and sagacity and talent of every member of my classes in pushing my investigations. I call on them to discuss the questions which I present for discussion, and take my seat among them and help and guide them according to my ability; and not infrequently, I am happy to say, do I get some useful instruction from them. Thus I sustain the double relation of pupil and teacher" (Hardman 1987, 357–358).

The contrasts between the "Oberlin" model and the "Yale" model, at least during the mid-nineteenth century, are instructive. While both have their strengths and weaknesses, they remind us that the decisions we make about our educational goals can have an enormous impact on what happens in the classroom. If our goal is to teach the content of a field, then the methods we use to accomplish it will likely take a particular shape. If our goal is to help students think for themselves, then the structure of our syllabus will likely flow out of that set of values. If our goal is to make our students more globally aware, then our reading and paper assignments will likely include those kinds of priorities. If our goal is to sensitize our students to the realities of poverty, then our classroom may have to move outside our buildings.

Most of us do not reduce any of our courses to a single goal—or even to a single set of goals. Most of us, I suspect, want our students to be physically, mentally, socially, and spiritually healthy graduates, and we hope that our teaching can contribute in some way to making that possible. Yet, we know in our hearts that no single course can accomplish all those goals. Nor can an individual faculty member, working in isolation, bring about the desired result. The glory of an educational institution, after all, is that it provides an entire curriculum and an entire faculty and an entire library and an entire community to accomplish all that needs to be achieved.

Such a realization places a special premium on lively conversation and good communication. This, at its core, is the reason for The Lexington Seminar—to remind the academy and the church that it is possible to build a community of learning in which life can be enriched and multiple goals can be achieved. Like a great symphony orchestra, different sounds and tempos and passions can, in fact, be blended to the glory of God and the good of society.

DEVELOPING OUR COURSES

Because we naturally gravitate toward subjects that interest us, because we prefer to focus on fields in which we are professionally trained, and because we like to teach materials that stir our intellectual passions, our best courses tend to emerge from the very core of our being. Therefore, our best courses, I am convinced, take many years to develop. In a sense, one might argue, they take a lifetime.

My fascination with teaching began around the kitchen table in a Minnesota home. For it was there, as our family gathered each evening for good food, lively conversation, probing questions, Bible reading, and prayer, that loving parents taught us to think, helped us to express ourselves, gave us our core values, and introduced us to a world of immense variety and wonder. Having grown up in that environment, it is no surprise that all three children became professional teachers.

Since leaving my Minnesota home, I have been privileged to study under many fine teachers—from gifted Sunday school instructors like Frank and Edith Johnson to a college mentor like Arthur Holmes to graduate thesis advisors like Lefferts Loetscher and Timothy Smith. Their high expectations and gentle promptings helped to sharpen my growing interest in the study of philosophy, then of theology, and ultimately of Christian history. I had long been fascinated by ideas and systems—but my teachers helped me to discover that my deepest passions centered on an exploration of how those ideas and systems operate within living human communities. Through the guidance of good teachers, history became my intellectual home—nourishing my spirit and engaging my mind.

Quite naturally, then, I want my students to love history as much as I do. I am aware, of course, that in our current postmodern culture the study of history is often neglected and sometimes dismissed. Consequently, I have tried to find ways in which to engage my students with those traditions that have shaped their lives and the communities in which they live and work. I actually believe that students need to understand the personalities, issues, themes, and literature of Christian history if they are to be effective in their life and work.

Much of this task can be accomplished through the more traditional settings and methodologies of classroom lectures and intensive seminars, particularly when they engage students with primary documents and reliable historical evidence. Indeed, in my judgment, nothing can ever replace the learning environment created by a gifted teacher, an eager student, and good library.

About fifteen years ago, however, it began to dawn on me that the "classrooms" in which we conduct our courses can also "teach." My American Puritanism class, for example, takes place entirely outside the traditional classroom. Dubbed "Rambling with Rosell" by my students, a variety of lectures, discussions, and dramatic presentations take place at the actual sites where historic events occurred and where the participants in those events lived. Debating the theology of Anne Hutchinson in the shadow of Cyrus E. Dallin's famous statue of her near the Boston Common, listening to the re-creation of a George Whitefield sermon at Pulpit Rock, or discussing an Anne Bradstreet poem at the very site where it was composed tend to engage students in fresh and exciting ways. Ancient gravestones, unusual styles of music, and changing patterns of architecture often produce the sorts of questions rarely heard in the traditional classroom. Most notable, perhaps, is the power that on-site learning seems to have in helping students integrate their studies. Historical, theological, pastoral, sociological, and political questions are woven together into a single fabric. Indeed, as students have told me, it is difficult to think and talk on one level only when confronted by a complex and multidimensional world.[12]

THE SEVEN-STEP PROCESS OF COURSE DEVELOPMENT

In developing my own courses, I have found a seven-step process to be especially helpful, and as an example of the process, I present the steps as I followed them through the design of my course on American Puritanism.

1. Make Use of Existing Models

I began by looking for existing models. Fortunately, in this case, I had a senior colleague in history, Nigel Kerr, who had taught a similar class for over a decade. Knowing of my interest in the subject, Nigel invited me to team teach the class with him. It turned out to be a marvelous experience for both of us as we shared responsibilities, discussed teaching strategies, and argued over divergent interpretations. Of most importance for me, however, was the opportunity to observe the complex dynamics of on-site teaching. Although I have subsequently changed many aspects of course content and methodology, having a tested model with which to begin was an enormous help.

2. Test Your Assumptions

The second step in the process was the testing of assumptions. I had assumed, for example, that traveling courses would be less effective in teaching content than the more traditional forms. What I discovered, to my surprise, was that students seemed significantly more interested in detailed information about the people, events, and issues connected with the sites than was normally true in my campus-based classes. I had also assumed that students would tend to read less in these contextually oriented classes than they did on campus. What I found, again to the contrary, was that they tended to read more. I had further assumed that the students whose performance was average in on-campus courses would continue to perform essentially at that same level in the field. I discovered instead that some of these "average" students became intellectual stars in the field. I found that different styles of learning tend to respond differently to various contexts for learning.

My biggest surprise, however, was the discovery of how much time it takes to prepare to teach an on-site course. I had assumed, to be quite candid, that such classes would be the least demanding on my time and energy. After all, I supposed, I wouldn't have to be talking all the time. What I discovered, to the contrary, was that on-site courses were the most difficult I had ever taught—both in terms of preparation and organization. For lectures and seminars, in which the teacher essentially controls what is presented or discussed, preparation can be more focused. Standing in a cemetery, however, one is confronted by a huge array of possible topics—from the theology of gravestone art and the nature of colonial medical practice to the problems of dating historical events and identifying those who were buried beneath our feet. The instructor's knowledge, I found, must be significantly broader, deeper, and more fully integrated than is usually the case in more traditional settings. Quite simply stated: When preparation is thorough, on-site courses appear deceptively simple; when preparation is weak, they flirt with disaster.

3. Identify Your Educational Goals

For the American Puritanism course, five primary goals emerged.

Knowledge of Field. My first goal was to engage the students with the personalities, issues, and themes of a movement that helped to shape the culture of New England. In order to accomplish this goal, I asked each member of the class to do detailed research (using both primary and secondary materials) on two individuals and two themes connected with colonial New England (such as John Winthrop, Anne Bradstreet, Puritan architecture, and the Salem Witch Trials). The students were then expected to present their findings at the appropriate historical site in a lively, well-organized, ten-minute oral presentation and provide their classmates with appropriate written materials that supported their presentations. In effect, they were expected to become mini-experts on those topics throughout the course. Because their peers came to rely on them for information on those individuals and themes, they tended to work exceedingly hard on their assignments. Many of these presentations, in fact, have been outstanding.

Familiarity with the Literature. My second educational goal was to introduce the students to some of the enormous literature in the field. Not only was each student expected to read Heimert and Delbanco's excellent anthology of Puritan literature and Leland Ryken's *Worldly Saints,* a fine interpretative study of the movement, but through the student presentations and my mini-lectures they were exposed to perhaps sixty or seventy additional resources. As a result, the students finish the course with a working knowledge of much of the important literature in the field.

Move beyond Mythology. A third educational goal was to help students move beyond legend and myth. While every movement has had it critics, few have suffered more than have the Puritans at the hands of their detractors. Consequently, one of my goals for the course was to help students come to know the Puritans as they really were, not as many modern critics want them to be. This goal could be achieved (I was convinced and remain convinced) by encouraging students to read what the Puritans wrote rather than simply what has been written about them.

Create Community. My fourth educational goal was to create a learning and sharing community. Many elements of our educational system tend to encourage competition and strengthen intellectual individualism. While there are obvious benefits to these emphases, they should not be the only kinds of experiences to which our students are exposed. In American Puritanism, students learn from each other, from the sources, from the sites, and from the instructor. Such learning fosters a spirit of interdependence, a building of friendships, and an appreciation for differing perspectives.

The final session of the course is always held at my home. The purpose of this session is threefold: to consolidate the learnings of the course, to encourage students to continue their explorations of these subjects, and to help bond the community. I am no longer surprised when students in the class tell me that the course was transformative for them.

Stimulate Further Study. Because any course is finite, my last goal is to encourage further study. In order to accomplish this goal, I have constructed a detailed notebook for each student containing bibliographical suggestions (organized by categories), detailed descriptions of all the sites on our itinerary, and a variety of background documents (not readily available in standard anthologies). I also encourage students to incorporate into the notebooks the written materials that other students have provided with each of their presentations, and I have constructed the notebooks to provide room for written comments and any notes that the students might wish to record.

The results have been heartening. Many students in the class actually revisit the sites either by themselves or as tour leaders for family, friends, or groups. This process greatly enriches the educational experience for the students and reinforces those learnings that have already taken place. A number of these students have become so fascinated with the Puritans, in fact, that they have chosen to focus on some aspect of the movement in their doctoral studies.

4. Select the Appropriate Methodology

American Puritanism can be taught as a traditional seminar, a lecture course, a case-study course, or an on-site course. The selection of one or more of these educational methodologies, however, should grow directly out of the educational goals one has selected. Each methodology, as most of us have discovered, has its own inherent strengths and weaknesses.

If a primary goal is to provide a general overview, a lecture format might be the best choice. If one wishes to immerse advanced students in primary documents, the seminar might be the way to go. When discussion of various interpretations are the target, case studies might be selected. If the educational goals are those I have identified in Step 3, then an on-site course might be the best choice. The instructor might even want to use a variety of methodologies to accomplish the educational goals. Each approach has its benefits and drawbacks. Consequently, it is important to select your methodology with great care.

5. Set Appropriate Requirements

Many of us, I suspect, follow a familiar pattern in setting requirements for our courses: namely, one midterm exam, one final exam, one twenty-five-page paper, and two thousand pages of reading. Were you to check my syllabi, in fact, you would discover that these are exactly the requirements for most of my lecture courses. Why require anything else, we might ask, when this pattern has worked well enough for us and others in the past?

Change for the sake of change, of course, is seldom wise. It is equally foolish, however, to set the requirements for our courses without first asking ourselves if these are the most effective means of helping our students achieve their educational objectives. Requirements, like the selection of methodologies, should flow out of clear educational goals.

In American Puritanism, for example, I decided to eliminate formal exams. This was a risky move for someone like myself who deeply values classical and traditional educational structures. What I discovered, to my great relief, was that students' presentations became a kind of informal test of the quality of their work. Moreover, the absence of exams seemed to contribute to a greater sense of community and mutuality of learning among the students.

6. Clarify Your Expectations

In designing our courses, we need to be absolutely clear as to our expectations for students in the class. The syllabus, I am convinced, should be seen as both a legal contract and a moral covenant with our students. We should require nothing that is not recorded there in writing. We should honor all that does appear. And we should strive to be as precise as we can regarding dates, times, topics, assignments, and standards for evaluation.

7. Evaluate the Results of the Course

Although I will be saying more about evaluation in a moment, a brief comment about this final step in the course development process would perhaps be helpful with reference to the American Puritanism course. Our seminary, like many others, requires formal course evaluations at the end of every course in the curriculum. Standard forms, appropriate to each type of classroom setting, have been approved by the faculty. Students remain anonymous. The machine-scored results, authorized by and completed under the guidance of the academic dean, are available to the instructor only after submission of final grades for the course.

While these formal evaluations can be helpful, a less formal course such as American Puritanism should also be evaluated in less formal ways. Over the years, in fact, I have sought out as many members of the class as time would allow to solicit their comments and suggestions for the course. These conversations have been enormously helpful in shaping the course and in providing useful feedback on how individual students are experiencing the course. Because these classes tend to be relatively small, usually involving twenty to twenty-five students, such a process is possible to pursue.

EVALUATE THE RESULTS

John Calvin's *Institutes* went through a variety of editions between 1536 and 1559.[13] Although composed in twenty-four days, G. F. Handel's *Messiah* also went through many revisions between its first performance in 1741 and the composer's death in 1759 (Larsen 1972). If these great works require much time and revision, it should come as no great surprise that our courses also need time to come to full maturity.

If we are sufficiently wise to accept the gift of evaluation, however, our teaching can be strengthened and our courses can develop into little symphonies that will inform the mind, enrich the spirit, and promote the common good. Unfortunately, for many of us the experience of evaluation is anything but welcome. Like the fearsome angel with the flaming sword that blocks our way back to Eden, we have come to see evaluation as largely punitive and enormously discouraging.

What is needed, perhaps, is a kind of paradigm shift in the way we understand course evaluations.[14] Some years ago, it was my privilege to publish a brief *Classroom Observation Form* (Rosell 1978). Not only did I find it helpful in my own courses but to my great surprise it began to be used by many colleagues as well.

The concept is disarmingly simple. Begin by asking a colleague to attend one of your classes—to observe what happens in the class, to keep notes on those observations, and to discuss with you what he or she observed. The goal is not so much to judge as to describe what took place in the classroom.

The insights that can come from this process are amazing. On one occasion, for example, I was asked to observe a colleague who had expressed a concern that he was never able to get a good discussion going in his classes. "It always seems to end after a sentence or two," he told me, and he asked if I could offer any suggestions that might help. The class had barely started when a student raised her hand to ask a question. The teacher, who happened to be wearing a three-piece suit, responded immediately to the student, but while doing so he also buttoned his suit coat and stepped behind the lectern. Following his brief verbal response, no further discussion ensued. I noted the incident in my notes but thought little about it, and the class went on. Ten minutes later another student raised his hand, and the same suit-buttoning, retreating-behind-the-lectern process was repeated. Indeed, this happened several more times before the class was over, and the results in each instance were the same.

In our discussion following class, I mentioned what I had observed. My friend was clearly surprised to learn of his behavior, and we chatted a bit about why he might have been prompted to respond in that way. As a result of those discussions, however, we decided to try an experiment. I would observe the class once again, but when a question came up this time he would (without being too obvious) unbutton his coat and step out from behind the lectern and toward the student who was asking the question. As he did so, the class literally came alive with discussion. Our eyes met, and his expression was one I will not soon forget.

Most of us have mannerisms that either enhance or detract from what we are trying to accomplish. Often we are not even aware of them and only rarely will our students tell us about them. What a gift it is, therefore, to have a colleague who can make us aware of what we are doing and can discuss with us how we might improve.

Such observations can also help us develop skills in setting the pace of a class session. In my experience, faculty members frequently spend so much time on preliminary or even logistical comments that they are forced to rush through the most important parts of their lecture. A time line, noting significant points of transition, can be of great help in correcting this problem.

A good observer can also be a great help in charting the kinds of interactions that are going on in class. It is possible, for example, to draw a box on a plain sheet of paper for each student in the class—keeping track of how many times each interacts with the teacher or with other members of the class. By the end of the class, my chart looks something like a sociogram with interaction lines (including times of the interactions) drawn from box to box. In the middle of each box I put the total number of times each student participated verbally in the class.

Such a chart can help a teacher in many ways. There are times, for example, when I have observed a class in which students on only one side of the room were active participants. In some cases, such a pattern is a result of where a teacher focuses when he or she looks up from the notes. On other occasions I have discovered that only the male students participated in the class discussions. Such patterns, and many others, are vitally important for a teacher to know if he or she is to make the class as effective as possible.

Other things that a good observer can watch for are the time and manner in which the class is started and concluded, the energy level of the students, the use of technology, the sensitivity with which the instructor interacts with the students, and how many students arrive late or leave early from the class.

Over the past thirty years, it has been my privilege to observe scores of my colleagues as they teach their classes. I have also benefited from the observations of faculty and student colleagues who have done me the honor of observing my classes. Not only have they rescued me from a multitude of practices that would have damaged my teaching, but many of them have also become very special friends in the process. What I have discovered, to my surprise, is how fascinating the issues of teaching and learning can be for those of us who labor in what are often called the classical disciplines.

Education is not my field, and it would be foolish for me to pretend to possess the kind of expertise that I do not have. My life has been spent as a historian whose primary time and energy has been directed toward research, writing, and teaching in that field. In pursuing those tasks, however, a wonderful circle of academic friends has developed, friends who seem glad not only to help each other professionally but who also share a common passion for teaching.

IMPLICATIONS FOR PRACTICE

Much more could be said about the process of course development. These brief reflections, therefore, are simply intended to begin the conversation and to stimulate further thought on how we develop our courses.

It is a daunting task, whatever our discipline, to gaze out on a field filled with more than can possibly be packed into any course, indeed, far more than any of us could master in a lifetime. The task of testing our assumptions about how we teach, about how students learn, and even about what we should include in our courses can sometimes seem overwhelming. The job of setting appropriate goals for our classes and our institutions can wear us out. Even the need to invest more of our busy schedules in the work of quiet reflection can prove to be a weariness to the soul.

Yet we need not despair. For all around us, if we have ears to hear them, are friends and colleagues who are ready to share the load. All around us, too, if we have eyes to see it, is the providential care of a gracious God. In a fragmented world, often divided by anger and strife, it is good to know that we are not alone.

And so we return, at the end, to John Wisdom's fascinating garden, grateful for the questions about teaching and learning that it has raised and grateful for friends who stand ready to help us discover the answers. For the parable is not only about a garden. It is also about a conversation.

NOTES

1. First published in Wisdom (1944/45, 191–192) and reprinted in Flew (1951) and Wisdom (1953).

2. Quotations are taken from Hick (1957, 145–146).

3. Church history, for example, has been taught for many years from a largely Western perspective. The field, happily, is gradually becoming more global in its perspective as assumptions about the proper locus of historical study begin to change.

4. This section is adapted from Rosell (2002, 3).

5. This does not mean, of course, that the task of testing assumptions and thinking about what we are doing is finished. On the contrary, it is a process that continues throughout life.

6. A variety of helpful guidebooks have been published providing practical tips on course development. Among the most useful is Grunert (1997).

7. America's nine oldest colleges are Harvard (1636), William and Mary (1693), Yale (1701),

Princeton (1746), Columbia (1754), Pennsylvania (1755), Brown (1765), Rutgers (1766), and Dartmouth (1769). For the development of education in America see Miller (1990), Ringenberg (1984), and Veysey (1965).

8.   For an excellent study of Strong, see Wacker (1985).

9.   For a fuller discussion of the Oberlin College model and Finney's role in its development, see Rosell (1993, 55–74).

10. See Fletcher (1943, 173), *The Woman's Journal* (1890, 385), and Finney (1989, 88).

11. For example, see Clark (1876, 49–53) and Blackwell, Oberlin College Archives, General Files, Box no. 12, 2.

12. One of the most fascinating discoveries of on-site teaching was my growing realization that students perform differently in different environments. Some of the students who tended to struggle in a traditional classroom setting became veritable "stars" when on the road. See Smith and Kolb (1986) and Gardner (1993).

13. See Calvin (1989) and McNeill (1960) for the first and final editions.

14. A shift much like that described by Kuhn (1962).

·RICHARD W. NYSSE·

Online Education

AN ASSET IN A PERIOD OF EDUCATIONAL CHANGE

"Sin, death, and the devil will not be banished by the introduction of computers in the process of education. The *eschaton* did not arrive with the World Wide Web. With that said, I'm finished making concessions to naysayers. Web-based technology has already facilitated fundamental change; this is not a fad, and the change is not simply a marginal enhancement or a costly diversion."

The words above opened a brief opinion piece I wrote six years ago (Nysse 1998, 419). Today I would not change a word, except that I might add several exclamation marks. As was the case six years ago, students continually teach me new possibilities for online learning, and I, unfortunately, discover new shortcomings in my online teaching. Increasingly I recognize the latter to be personal failures, not limitations that an online environment imposes on course design and implementation. The use of online media for the core of teaching and learning continues to unfold. The number of online courses continues to grow, because students continue to enroll in those offered. The dotcom meltdown did not end the more quiet growth in online education.

Faculty and student objections continue to be voiced, but during the past six years I have sensed that a corner has been turned. Increasingly, I hear colleagues express curiosity about online education, not opposition. Most may be no closer to teaching online, but they no longer dismiss the methodology as a fad. Satisfied students are telling their faculty advisors that they have learned much in their online classes, and such classes are now recognized as a valid option at certain seminaries, including my own. The methodology, however, is not yet part of the mainstream; in many respects it remains an add-on, and there are still days when the pace of progress seems glacial. We have used computers to automate record-keeping functions, and we have adapted to innovations in communication, but we have not transformed the way we work. We still tend to do what we have always done, only faster and in greater volume.

In this essay,[1] I begin by describing the changing educational context in which online education is being introduced. I then compare online education with traditional classroom education—the standard against which online education is typically judged—and try to acknowledge the strengths and weaknesses of each as a means of ensuring student learning. Finally, I describe some of the means of student support that are needed to make online learning most effective.

THE CURRENT CONTEXT OF EDUCATIONAL CHANGE

While vigorous discussion about the nature and quality of online teaching continues,[2] larger shifts are occurring within higher education. From ominous teaching methodology to learning theories to assessment practice, the focus in higher education is shifting from teaching to learning,[3] and the introduction of online capabilities as an educational medium is occurring within this larger shift from teaching to learning.

One concrete manifestation of the change is the assessment practices of accreditation agencies.[4] They are asking educational institutions what they are intending to do. What is their articulation of their own mission? How do they know whether or not their intentions are actually being accomplished? Responding by citing evidence of a low teacher-to-student ratio with all classes taught by teachers with Ph.D.s is no longer taken as definitive proof that the mission is being accomplished. Such teacher-centered, input-based assessment is no longer the norm. Such indicators of quality are not being jettisoned; they simply are not being granted the same presumptive privilege. The focus is on outcomes. What are students actually learning? When, where, and how are they learning?[5] Further, the possibility of high-quality learning is assumed to occur in a wider range of educational environments than was acknowledged in the past.[6] The cocurricular dimensions of a student's learning experience are being given increased visibility (American Association of Higher Education et al. 1998). The cocurricular dimension is not reducible to mere support or enhancement of the classroom experience. It is part of the core that constitutes a holistic learning experience; the entire seminary is termed a learning community. Online education and traditional classroom education are each but a part of a larger learning environment.

For my institution, Luther Seminary, and for my denomination, the Evangelical Lutheran Church in America (ELCA), significant non-classroom-based components have always been present. In one form or another, Luther Seminary has for many years required students to work in congregations while enrolled in degree programs. In addition, the ELCA requires a one-year internship for ordination. Traditionally, internship has been placed after the second year of seminary study, with students returning for a third year of study after internship. Yet even with this tradition, when students return for third-year classes, faculty struggle to integrate or even acknowledge the learning that has occurred during internship. How do we structure differently a class on the Psalms or on the Gospel of John because of the internship experience? We have difficulty stating what the differences should be between students who have and have not participated in the internship experience. Covering content is still a powerful impulse. It is a deeply embedded default switch that inhibits our imaginations. Experiential learning still struggles to find legitimate space at the center.[7]

None of this stirring depends on the existence of the Internet; technology is not driving these changes and transitions. If all online education disappeared tomorrow, the shifts and debates—encapsulated in expressions like "learning-centered, not instruction-centered" or "student-centered, not teacher-centered"—would continue unabated. Nevertheless, frustrations and anxiety over the transitions quickly target online education as a major perpetrator of unwanted change. It is not. It simply makes the changes more evident. The key issue with regard to online education is its role in the transitions, not whether it is itself generating the transitions.

COMPARING ONLINE AND CLASSROOM EDUCATION

Despite the turmoil over traditional classroom contexts, online educators are still challenged by the longstanding question: Is online education as good as classroom education? Despite my desire to avoid a binary construal, the question must be addressed for at least two reasons. First, despite current reevaluation, classroom education has a record of considerable accomplishment that must be acknowledged, even honored. Matching its accomplishments is a significant achievement. Second, the deference to classroom education is so high that it is the assumed benchmark in conversations about online education, even when online education is not portrayed as a concession.

If classroom education is to be the benchmark by which online learning is to be measured—and not all educators concede this point (Kassop 2003)—just what is that benchmark? How do we know what we claim to know about the learning that occurs in the classroom? How much of what is attributed to classroom teaching is actually the result of student reading and writing outside the classroom? For example, if students are expected to put in three hours of preparation time for each hour of classroom time (that is, three-quarters of the total hours spent learning are at a distance from the classroom), how can we justify attributing all the learning that occurs to the classroom environment? More methodologies are at work in what we call traditional teaching and learning than simply person-to-person exchanges in a classroom; more "distance" is involved in classroom education than we generally acknowledge, making the "distance learning" in online education much less novel than it seems at first glance.

The assumption that classroom instruction sets the standard by which online instruction is to be measured raises issues that run deeper than the previous paragraph suggests. Certainly, it does not acknowledge the growing number of guidelines that now define quality in online education. One such set of guidelines was produced by the Institute for Higher Education Policy (2000).[8] The IHEP promulgated twenty-four benchmarks (from an initial list of over forty) as "measures of quality in internet-based distance learning." Three of the twenty-four (Nos. 4–6), termed "course development benchmarks," are listed below.

4. Guidelines regarding minimum standards are used for course development, design, and delivery, while learning outcomes—not the availability of existing technology—determine the technology being used to deliver course content.
5. Instructional materials are reviewed periodically to ensure they meet program standards.
6. Courses are designed to require students to engage themselves in analysis, synthesis, and evaluation as part of their course and program requirements.

I do not suggest that every online course meets these standards, but I do question how many classroom-based courses hold themselves to comparable standards, much less meet them. After twenty-five years at Luther Seminary, I know of no explicit, publicly available, statement of "minimum standards" for course "development, design, and delivery" for classroom courses. (While I suspect that some seminaries are significantly different from the portrait I draw here, I doubt that Luther Seminary is entirely an aberration.) The faculty at

Luther Seminary has worked on statements of learning outcomes (or objectives), but such statements function more as suggestions than standards. Some teachers have embedded these outcomes in their syllabi, and the outcomes are employed to some extent in evaluative activity when tenure and promotion decisions are made. But the faculty as a whole has not held itself accountable to the very objectives it has developed.

Further, the faculty has never systematically examined what constitutes the best match between methodology and learning outcomes. Does lecture provide the best methodology for a given learning objective? Are small groups better than lectures for a given outcome? If, then, we have not addressed correlations between instructional methodology and learning outcomes in the classroom, on what basis do we assume that the classroom is a superior environment to online education?

Other than perhaps a self-study for ATS reaccreditation every ten years, when is classroom instructional material reviewed to ensure that it meets program standards? Would not most faculty regard such a review as an invasion of their educational domain? Do they not shrink from the thought of reviewing their colleagues' instructional material? I have been unable, after repeated invitations, to get my biblical division colleagues to review my online course pages in a systematic, evaluative fashion. It seems so unnatural to critique each other at the level of instructional materials, as if it were a breach of faculty etiquette. But if we cannot routinely work together at that level, how can we extol the communal virtues of the classroom when compared with the supposed isolation of online education?[9]

Finally, how often are courses and programs examined and held accountable for requiring "students to engage themselves in analysis, synthesis, and evaluation" as is called for in IHEP Benchmark No. 6 above? In my experience educational institutions determine which courses are to be required—what subject matter domains are to be engaged by students—but not what analytical, synthesizing, and evaluative abilities students should attain as a result of those courses, especially not in a way that could lead to calling into question a course that fails to be so designed (not to mention actually achieving those outcomes). Many individual faculty members do design for these outcomes and do assist students to meet them, but program directors would be viewed with great suspicion if they were to evaluate each course with those expectations in mind. It would be regarded as a sign of distrust.

The persistent resistance to assessment raises questions about our commitment to community, for such resistance can readily be construed as the assertion of individual prerogative over communal accountability. This may be a perennial debate in the history of academic freedom, but the balance seems tipped too far in the direction of the prerogatives of those with power, in this case individual faculty. Students are generally not accorded a symmetrical privilege. The character of our educational community is shaped by how we handle the particulars of accountability.

THE MYTH OF THE CHARISMATIC TEACHER

Communal character is also shaped by how we understand the roles of student and teacher. The classroom is often regarded as an ideal community of learning, with ideas freely exchanged and tested. And yet we teachers do so much of the talking! I know things, and I love to inform others about what I know. I think it would be helpful for them to know what I know. And pretty soon, despite my best intentions, I am doing all of the talking and, as a result, the "exchanging and testing" of student ideas drops by the wayside. Online teaching helps to quell my dominating voice.

This is not a small matter, and it is not a caricature. In May 2003, I sat with five colleagues discussing teaching and learning over a pleasantly served lunch. We had just left a session in which we discussed team teaching. As the conversation shifted to what fosters student learning, all five insisted that a charismatic teacher was the *sine qua non* of student learning. I dissented with oblique comments about pedagogical design variables and active student learning principles, but their insistence only grew stronger. And yet, what does such insistence imply about lifelong learning apart from a classroom and a teacher's presence? What does it say about student effort and motivation? What does it say about all the knowledge faculty (and students) have attained by reading throughout their years of learning? At a minimum we faculty need to recognize how much is learned by reading and writing and then more fully apply that process to assisting the learning of our students. If we sustain our own learning by reading and writing, why do we insist that students learn best by listening? We care deeply about our students' learning, and most of us do not wish to be so much at the center of the learning experience, but the methodology is so ingrained! Teaching online classes has helped me glimpse another way of being.

DIFFERENT METHODS FOR ACHIEVING LEARNING GOALS

For a significant number of students, classrooms present formidable pedagogical obstacles, and some of these can be overcome by online education. The two key questions are: What type of learning do we need and want? And how do we get there given the circumstance under which we work? The issue in the end is not which mode is better. Both classroom and online education are methodologies for achieving certain ends. Many instances of poorly managed

classroom environments exist, against which a goodly number of online classes would shine in comparison. And the opposite is also true. In each case the
key issue is the pedagogical practice. Thus, comparing "delivery systems" is
probably wrongheaded from the beginning, for best pedagogical practice may
require a different conception of education. It is not about delivery; it is about
learning.

By now it is undoubtedly obvious that I would not wish to limit my
online classes to what works best in my classroom (assuming, based on the lack
of reliable benchmarks, that I even know what the latter is). Some teachers
would agree, but at the same time they wish to retain as much of the classroom
as possible as they enter the distance education milieu. They would be happi-
er if online connections could transmit more of the classroom experience. With
faster digital connections (called "high bandwidth"), we could offer streaming media which would allow instructors to present themselves as talking
heads on a computer screen. The advantage of this technology is that it could
be done in real time and thus allow students and teacher to speak with each
other as the class progressed. But I fear we would quickly attempt to push too
many of our existing classroom pedagogies through the faster connections.
Relatively slow digital connections impede the replication of the classroom,
which can be a distinct advantage in the online environment. Being "restricted" by low bandwidth forces one to rethink pedagogy, stripping down the technological wish list to the pedagogically necessary. If low bandwidth prevents
us from replicating what we do routinely in the classroom, we are forced to
think anew about what is pedagogically needed to help students maximize their
learning.

THREADED DISCUSSIONS AND REACH VS. RICHNESS

As a teacher moves from classroom to online courses, "obvious" answers to
pedagogical questions no longer seem so obvious. For example, when lecturing is inhibited by low bandwidth, we can stop to ask how important the
teacher's voice is for maximizing student learning. Is the teacher's voice actually crucial? If so, at what junctures? It may not be in the quantity or places we
have assumed. Perhaps the teacher's voice might equally serve student learning by merely posing and focusing the questions to be pursued, thus guiding
the learning process more than being the source of it. Low bandwidth limits
the possibility of effective lecturing, but it also makes possible a high degree
of student interaction around engaging, open-ended questions.

I know of classroom-based teachers who have tried to shift toward greater
student interaction but have found class discussions too superficial. Some
have tried to overcome this obstacle by replacing at least some of the verbal

discussion with the exchange of written work between students, but exchanging the papers soon becomes a logistical nightmare. A threaded discussion (something that does not require high connection speeds) readily solves the logistical problem. A threaded discussion (also called an "electronic bulletin board") allows students to post their comments in a central online location where an index of all the written exchanges is automatically produced, thus allowing participants to see what has gone before and to add their comments at the appropriate juncture in the conversation rather than only after the most recent comment, as is the case with email. By removing the logistical obstacles, this learning activity can be utilized frequently in a course. In short, technological limitations can lead to productive rethinking of pedagogical practice.[10]

But another question waits in the wings. What about the visual, auditory, and tactile richness of a face-to-face classroom? That question tends to drag us back to the impulse to replicate the classroom. The impulse should be resisted. Instead, we need to ask relentlessly, What maximizes student learning? We need to ask this question for every environment in which teaching and learning can be undertaken. When we do so, we may find that educational richness is not limited to the narrow reach of the physical classroom. If low bandwidth and physical and temporal distance from a classroom are givens, we need to ask how we can maximally assist student learning under such circumstances. How can we create richness within the reach provided by online technology? That is the question that comes to the forefront.

This shift in focus is not easily attained. Historically, we have thought of the classroom as offering rich interaction while at the same time conceding its restricted reach. According to this paradigm, only those who can get to the classroom have access to educational richness. Scholarships and grants have been used to ameliorate the problem of restricted reach and limited access. The Internet reopens the debate about a tradeoff between richness and reach because the Internet dramatically increases reach. But does it do so at the expense of richness?[11] In the past, most of my colleagues would have immediately answered with a resounding "Yes," as would most students who had limited experience with online learning. For many teachers and students, the increased reach afforded by the Internet was imagined only as the kind marketed on late-night radio and television—highly isolated, individual learners mastering a batch of data disconnected from meaningful contexts.

The increased reach of online learning, however, does not have to be at the expense of educational richness. And threaded discussions are a prime example of a means to attain both richness and reach. The amount of exchange and interaction between students in a threaded discussion can easily exceed what is possible with the geographical and temporal restrictions of a classroom. Exchange does not need to end when the period is over. No bell rings at the end of each of the weekly three units of fifty minutes—the standard Carnegie seat-time units for calculating what constitutes the necessary instructional period. Face-to-face, small-group discussions can be deeply engaging, but a transcript of a fifty-minute discussion would reveal how little temporal allotment is available for each student to offer deeply considered comments. In contrast, a threaded discussion allows time for everyone to contribute; everyone can "hear" by reading what everyone else has stated. There is no speaking over each other, and nothing is lost if there is a lapse in attention. If small groups are formed, the teacher can "hear" the contribution of every student. Unlike classroom discussions, there is no need to spend time traveling to one place, and even more significant, the entire exchange is fully retrievable and thus available for later review. Students can contribute to each others' learning as they formulate for each other what they have learned in their individual preparation for contributing to the threaded discussion.

Further, faculty "censorship" of the discussion by means of their body language or nonverbal cues is limited, students cannot as easily vie for faculty approval, and it is easier to provide "correction" (via private email) should it be deemed necessary, without doing so in front of peers and risking shaming. Students who are having difficulty performing are quickly noticeable, and assistance can be given sooner. Finally, in threaded discussions students have a definable audience for their ideas. They are writing to peers, which removes the artificiality of traditional papers, which are written for a theoretical audience that the professor tries to define for the students. Writing to peers who will be colleagues in ministry is not nearly so artificial. In addition, the writing that is being done is an attempt to communicate with, to learn from, and to sway an actual audience. This can develop a collaborative, collegial practice that is sorely needed in the contemporary church. Thus, richness and reach no longer need be a tradeoff.

The extended reach offered by education is not limited to spanning geographic and temporal obstacles to student-to-student interaction. It includes reaching across learning styles and personality types. That shy students, for example, can more readily enter an online threaded discussion has become nearly legendary, but equally important is the reflective time that is available between comments for students who sometimes respond too quickly in classroom discussions. Students who term themselves as talkative have commented appreciatively in self-evaluations that they had never thought so much before expressing their views. Most importantly, though, the increased richness of a threaded discussion does not reside inherently in the technology. The questions discussed need to be thought-provoking and life-engaging. Once again, technology facilitates a sound pedagogy; it does not produce the engagement or the learning.

Online teaching and learning is only one more avenue by which we pursue educational transformation. The status quo, as good as it may be, is not good enough to cease the pursuit of improvement; it is not yet the best that we can do.

STUDENT SUPPORT

The traditional classroom learning environment for a program of theological education, even for a single course, exists in a matrix of interlocking support. Teacher and students are surrounded by other participants, who are needed to complete the learning environment. Janitors, librarians, secretaries, registrar, grounds crew, counselors, supportive friends and family members, congregations, and service organizations, among many others, are part of the fabric that constitutes the learning environment. These participants have considerable impact on students and are integral to their success whether or not faculty acknowledge or work closely with them.

If this is the matrix that constitutes the traditional educational environment, what is the matrix that constitutes the online learning environment? Maintenance personnel keep classrooms in good repair. Who keeps the online environment (servers, hard drives, software, etc.) in good repair? Supporting students involves much more than physical space and computer capacities. The social environment is a fundamental component of student support. A concern that most people have who are resistant to online education is that online students are severed from necessary social support. Students, it is claimed, are too isolated in online education. The dynamism and support of the social matrix is assumed to be lost.

For online teachers this is a crucial issue, especially for those who overtly acknowledge the extra-course matrix in which the learning environment exists. They recognize that they cannot single-handedly provide all the support that is needed for online students to flourish. All too often, however, the *de facto* expectation is that teachers can do exactly that, especially when seminaries start tentatively with one or two pilot classes. Either the faculty member personally (and heroically) provides the extra support or students are left largely on their own. In the first scenario, the situation is unsustainable. The faculty member is likely to experience burnout and, if not that, will confirm colleague suspicion that online teaching constitutes much more work than classroom teaching. In the second scenario, the heroic effort is shifted to the student; the self-driven students will succeed as they do in nearly any environment and the less self-directed will drop out. The latter will report that online education is cold and impersonal. Too frequently the result in both scenarios is that teachers dismiss online education as nothing more than a collection of "electronic correspondence courses."

A defensive response to the charge that online education leaves students inadequately supported is to question the extent to which faculty teaching in classrooms actually align their efforts with those of the larger matrix. Too often we work in isolation from the larger learning environment, and there is something disingenuous in faculty objections to online education because of the alleged lack of student support when they themselves tend to ignore the larger matrix in relationship to the classroom. In my early years as a teacher, although I regarded the cocurricular dimension of seminary life as a necessary backdrop for education, I did not perceive it as a core component of student learning. It could enhance (or inhibit) good teaching and learning, but it was not a constitutive part of it. Student experience of the learning environment of a school is not as compartmentalized as it often is for faculty. The curriculum and cocurriculum are united in a student's evaluation of the worth of their seminary education.

Minimally, student support in online education needs to replicate the intensity of the support offered in a traditional context. "Intensity" is the key word; "replication" by itself is not the goal. Students deserve to feel equally supported in both environments. The mechanisms of support—the delivery systems—may change; in fact, they will change. For example, placement services which might have been as minimal as putting notices in a three-ring binder in the dean of students' office now need to be placed on the institution's Web site. This will require attention to Web design and navigational principles. Tutoring and assistance with writing skills are other supports that need to be in place. The manner of their availability will be quite different when students do not meet directly with a tutor or writing center personnel. Providing these support services digitally involves a shift in administrative thinking proportionate to the shift in faculty thinking discussed in the previous section.

Chapel services might be a good illustration. The campus pastor (or whoever oversees on-campus worship) needs to imagine ways to connect with the worship life of distance students. Whatever form that "connection" takes need not become a replacement for the local worship community in which the student participates, but it must communicate care for the worship life of students. It might require the campus worship community to connect with local worship communities. It needs to be more than video streaming on-campus chapel services, helpful as that at first may seem. The problem with video streaming on-campus activities such as worship services is that nothing really changes. On-campus worship leaders continue to do what they have always done, except that they have added a camera. To the distant student it says, "Too bad you couldn't be here." The distance learner is merely allowed to peek in on where the action *really* is taking place. It shouts, "Concession!" Broadcasting the on-campus environment is doing nothing more than trying to make the walls of the campus elastic, stretching them to reach across geographical distances. The Internet is a new "location," a new place of meeting, not simply a new form of broadcasting or delivering across distances. I have added a "place" for praying in my online classes, but that is hardly the limit of what could be done. Others will have to join the exploration for new forms of inhabiting the online environment. More important than a proliferation of training events is gathering support staff, faculty, and students together to explore new ways of interacting in an online environment. Our imaginations have not been exhausted!

As we develop comparable levels of support by new means, we will need to think through the core values that are offered to students in cocurricular interactions. Better, we will need to have students tell us what the core values are. Means and ends need to be distinguished. Do the means of these interactions service the social needs of faculty and staff more than they do the needs of students? For example, having cookies or popcorn available at the registrar's counter may create a delightful, supportive ambiance, but if a student has had to take off three hours from work to drive to and from campus to fill out and sign a form, the value may be irrelevant. The ambiance created by the snacks is better than being gruff, but, in truth, the staff may derive more value from the face-to-face interaction than the student, especially when the latter calculates the overall cost of the interaction (such as time, fuel, energy, and childcare). Better than offering cookies is to offer students the convenience of taking care of more administrative tasks online (such as registering for courses or establishing passwords). Fortunately, such student support is finally being offered on a regular basis, and not just for online students and commuter students but for residential students as well.

Faculty and staff are not the only ones who need to rethink the ways in which student support can be provided. A significant number of seminary students need to alter (not lower) their expectations for support in online education. Seminaries, like all other schools, are highly scripted social environments, and these scripted environments have shaped student expectations. Even though seminary students are generally autonomous adult learners who are able to draw upon their own rich, postcollege learning experience and who, in every other aspect of their lives, no longer act as they did in their early twenties, many of them still tend to carry forward expectations for support that were shaped or scripted by prior school experiences. They fall too easily into passive behavior and too readily defer to authority figures, whether teachers or staff, whom they expect to tell them what they are allowed to do. That is the way it was in college; why not expect the same in seminary?

Further, because of the "caring" mission of the seminary, students are too ready to let themselves be "taken care of," with all the latent dimensions of paternalism implied by such care. Despite our best intentions, educational institutions have been scripted toward conformity and compliance, and the product too often is passive learners. After all, such learners are the ones who are rewarded by the social system embedded in the schooling. As a result, even active adult learners are inclined to surrender too much initiative to the institution. Faculty and staff consciously want active learners but unconsciously fail to surrender the prerogatives of the script they have inherited and now replicate. On the other hand, if all scripts are removed entirely, the less self-directed students will feel cut adrift. Finding the right balance between providing necessary support and not discouraging independence is a difficult task that often leads to tensions that were not created by the introduction of online teaching and learning.

RETHINKING STUDENT NEEDS

As educators and students move into an environment that is unfamiliar, seminaries must determine which services are vital, even crucial, and which are nice but not necessary. Students, teachers, administration, and staff need to rethink and reframe standards and expectations and return to a central question: What is the core value in each of the interactions that constitute education—in teaching, learning, and support? Online education forces us to rethink our entire system, rethinking that is, in fact, long overdue. As our student body shifts increasingly to commuting, second-career, part-time adult learners, the need to take up this rethinking and reconfiguration grows more urgent.

My first glimpse of the reframing that should take place occurred in two conferences I attended within two months in 1998. The first was the Distance Teaching and Learning Conference held each August in Madison, Wisconsin. The reframing began with the very first workshop I attended, an introduction to standards for quality in distance education (American Council on Education 1996). While I had gone to this conference to pick ideas to improve the online course in the Pentateuch that I had begun to teach, it was soon evident that my initial interest in the conference was far too atomistic. Improving a freestanding, individual course was not sufficient. Rather the questions were about how the library, counseling services, the registrar's office, and the business office would be present to the learners in any given course. An online course should not be offered in isolation from the support systems of the institution. But that is exactly what we were doing in my pilot class at Luther Seminary. The school was not online even though a course was. It is a testament to those early online learners that they achieved as much learning as they did with so few support resources.

Despite the accomplishments of these early students, however, it became immediately clear that we did not have a sustainable system for online education. We could not continue to add courses without addressing the support issues. No single teacher could adequately provide the needed support. The entire seminary had to develop an online presence. In fact, more than a presence was required; the school needed to work in a Web environment. In a sense, the institution needed to create a second seminary, a fully online one.

Placing such emphasis on online education allows an institution to plant its feet firmly in the Internet environment and reduces the likelihood that it will regard online activity as a concession and thus shortchange the online requirements. When the fully online seminary is constructed, the two institutions can flow together. New efficiencies emerge and students in both environments are better served. Robust hybrid possibilities can be developed. During the transition, however, the amount of work involved may certainly feel like a burden to faculty and staff.

That first conference I attended pointed out the need to take a more complete approach to online education. The second conference made it clear that meeting the need would not be easily accomplished. At the October 1998 conference of Educom (now called Educause after a merger with Cause), two University of Minnesota officials (Kvavik and Handberg 2000) described the university's shift to a "one-stop" system for access to student services. Student information at the University of Minnesota was spread over more than twenty different database systems and was very dependent on the movement of paper, but that was only a technical problem. The deeper problem was conceptual.

Too frequently staff regarded their job as guarding and housing data. An immovable counter, real or imagined, was maintained between the staff and the learner. There might be cookies on the counter, but they did not dissolve the obstacles that the counter represented. The staff had to rethink its role, changing from guarding information and bringing it to the counter when requested to presenting information in a form that could be accessed by the student when needed, regardless of where the students were. Organizing information in a navigable, digital form was the key task, not carrying it back and forth between its repository and the counter. Of course, appropriate password protections had to be set up, but again those were technical issues. The chief resistive force was at the conceptual level because of the recasting of traditional roles. In the first month of existence, the system had a few thousand hits (not particularly impressive for a large university), but within a short period of time the hits reached into the millions. Clearly there was a student desire for information that far exceeded what could be accessed across a counter.

The scale of large universities exposes the compartmentalization of information more quickly than is the case at the average seminary. Students shuffle from one office to the next tracking down the information and forms they need. The movement is almost invisible when the offices are all within one building or when one staff person implements several different steps. At Luther Seminary, staff members often bridge the divides while talking over coffee. Our informality masks our inefficiencies and covers over the frustrations students encounter.

This may seem minor in a small system, and digitizing the process may seem to cost more than could be saved in staff and student time, provided the students are nearby and willing to undergo the inconveniences. But the issues are quickly exacerbated for online and commuting students who do not regularly travel to campus. My contention is that, if a seminary makes its support systems available online for distance learners, it will find that it has greatly added to its service for all other students.

IMPLICATIONS FOR TEACHING AND LEARNING

Several actions are indispensable if this era of educational change is going to bear fruit.

- To avoid an unproductive debate over whether the traditional classroom is superior to online environments, we need to focus on what learners need to know, which requires a thoughtful analysis of the context and situations in which learners find themselves. What are the questions they bring to their education? What questions do they need to consider? How best can essential questions be explored?

- The effective use of instructional technology depends solely on its pedagogical impact. More is not better even if one has the speed and bandwidth to dazzle the learner.

- Seminary faculties need to take seriously the science of instructional design and the lessons it offers for bridging a concern for disciplinary knowledge and the strategic, purposeful ways of helping learners actively engage that knowledge.

- Teaching reflectively in a variety of settings (weekend courses, course intensives, courses that combine traditional and Web-based components) and paying attention to what one learns from those settings (not simply whether one prefers one setting over the other) provides a coherent basis for considering the opportunities and challenges of the online environment.

▪ We need to reflect on the matrix into which our individual courses fit, and we need to develop a collective consciousness as a faculty about what we are learning as we teach, no matter the environment. We squander the insights individual instructors are gaining when we lack a regular practice of talking about our teaching.

CONCLUSION

Online theological education provides a means to address the transitions that are occurring in our institutions and systems. No seminary is immune, and no seminary can wait until everything is in place before engaging those transitions. Faculty cannot wait until support systems and training are perfectly in place. Administrative and support personnel cannot wait until there is money for more staff. Students cannot wait until support systems are perfected. We need to abandon the notion of mastery for a moment and begin thinking together—administration, faculty, and students—about the dynamics of learning and explore how the Internet affords us new ways to learn together for the sake of ministry in communities of faith and service in God's world.

With all that said, I hope my enthusiasm for online education is obvious. I am fervent about the possibilities but realistic as well. The obstacles have been and will continue to be overcome only by hard work. So why continue to bother? The briefest and most deep-seated reason is the students I have served through online education. They are gifted, and they will be a gift to the church. They have blessed my life, and I want to continue to work with and for them.

NOTES

1. For other valuable articles, see Bellinger (2003), Amos (1999), and Williams (2002b).

2. One place to note the continuous debate is in the pages of *The Chronicle of Higher Education*. The articles span the spectrum from wild enthusiasm (fewer of these now appear) to disdainful ill-boding. One notable debate was generated by David Noble (1998), who considered online teaching as fully and only destructive. Responses to his "sky is falling" article quickly appeared (Noble et al. 1998).

3. For a quick introduction to this shift, see the helpful—and frequently cited—article by Barr and Tagg (1995). For more extensive treatments, see Tagg (2003) and Weimer (2002).

4. See the essays regarding accreditation in *Theological Education* published by the Association of Theological Schools (McCarthy 2003). In addition, eight regional agencies recently produced a joint statement on online standards (Regional 2000).

5. "Scholarship of teaching" is a commonly used phrase for research on learning as it is occurring. The class itself becomes a research project for the teacher. The Carnegie Foundation for the Advancement of Teaching [http://www.carnegiefoundation.org/] has had a major role in advancing this work. Convenient starting points are their "eLibrary" (Carnegie 2003) and Hutchings, Bjork, and Babb (2002). A seminal book in this movement is Boyer (1997 [1990]). See also *The Journal of Scholarship of Teaching and Learning* [http://www.iusb. edu/~josotl.].

6. Service learning is one such impetus. See Stanton, Giles, and Cruz (1999) or Jacoby (1996). For someone new to service learning, one place to begin is the National Service Learning Clearinghouse [http://www.servicelearning.org]. A significant evaluation of service learning has been conducted by the W. K. Kellogg Foundation (2000).

7. Change has been a major factor in many institutions. Higher education has no grounds for claiming exemption. It is not, in fact, entirely surprising that the work headed by Peter Senge moved from corporate environments in *The Fifth Discipline* (Senge 1990) to educational institutions in *Schools That Learn* (Senge 2000).

8. The study, released March 21, 2000, was commissioned by the National Education Association (NEA) and Blackboard, a course management software vendor. The recourses available for the evaluation of online education are developing rapidly. A fine example is Graham et al. (2000) and (2001). Questions have been raised about the reliability of studies that have shown no significant difference between classroom-based and various distance education modalities (Institute of Higher Education Policy 1999). Interestingly, the latter study was also conducted by the Institute for Higher Education Policy. It was commissioned by the American Federation of Teachers and, again, the NEA.

9. My own practice is to *build* my courses on a publicly available Web and *conduct* my courses in Blackboard. Thus all the course material—its design, assignments, discussion questions, etc.—are available for browsing by prospective students, colleagues, graduates, donors, and congregations. If someone finds the material useful for lifelong learning or continuing education, they are free to use it. Blackboard is used to provide password protection for what students write to each other. Their exchanges are kept private.

10. Thinking about threaded discussions led me to *Discussion as a Way of Teaching* (Brookfield and Preskill 1999). Brookfield and Preskill address classroom-based courses, but there is much that can be applied to online discussions. This is an example of the productive interchange that can occur if we focus on pedagogy before technology. Classroom teachers might benefit from reading *Facilitating Online Learning* (Collison et al. 2000) or *E-Moderating* (Salmon 2000).

11. The interplay of "richness" and "reach" in business are discussed by Evans and Wurster (1999).

Rehabilitating Prejudice

FRAMING ISSUES OF DIVERSITY IN THEOLOGICAL EDUCATION

In 1969, as I entered my freshman year at a coed and racially mixed Christian high school in an integrated Milwaukee neighborhood, I decided to join the school's Madrigal Singers, a group of eight to ten students that sang most often at nursing homes on occasional weekends. We were a motley crew for sure, representing a broad spectrum of ethnic, cultural, and class backgrounds and a range of musical skills from the unusually talented and previously trained to those (like myself) who had never learned to read musical notation and could barely stay on key. Fortunately, the sole criterion for admittance to the Madrigal Singers was simply the love of music. As we learned to sing various musical pieces from diverse ethnic and cultural traditions, our audience of senior citizens around the city never wavered in their support or displays of affection and appreciation for our musical gifts. In fact, our performances could sometimes take on an almost mystical aura, effectively connecting us not only to one another but to an elderly generation with whom few of my youthful generation ever connected or tried to connect.

Two months later, I also joined the youth choir at my parish church. The choir director was a young Polish American woman who helped us share in the joy of singing gospel; jazz; rock (yes, we performed *Jesus Christ Superstar*); the *Bossa Nova Mass*; traditional folk tunes; early Christian hymns in German, French, and Spanish; charming American spirituals; and moving Latin motets. And when we sang, we sang mightily—all of us young people: black, white, yellow, and brown—we, who were children of one of the most successfully integrated churches in the city of Milwaukee, would make a boisterous noise unto the Lord.

These two musical groups proved there were powerful ways to bring adolescents together to experience and witness the presence of God (and his grace) in our lives, and the creative wisdom displayed by the two choir directors was far ahead of its time. I cannot help but think that perhaps at least one reason that I spent fifteen years working in urban youth and young adult ministry in Milwaukee, New York, and Boston arose from the substantial influence of these two musical groups and the two extraordinary women who directed them, with one of whom I have sustained a lifelong friendship.

It did not matter that both my choir directors were young, European American women or that we students were black, white, Asian, and Hispanic, male and female, lower-, middle-, and upper-middle income, or that I lived at "Eleventh and Burleigh," a predominately black and working-class neighborhood that was located adjacent to a part of the city that was easily recognizable in that era as the urban ghetto of Milwaukee. The important thing was that "I came as I was" to my church and high school communities to connect with others in a common desire to worship and praise God through our love for music and community. By the outpouring of our disparate musical voices, we connected with one another through both our individual strengths and in our particular brokenness. Through the chorus of our human experience, we entered into deeper dialogue with others in our parish and civic community, and because our church was called to be a Christ-centered community of diversity in faith (Watts 2001), we adhered to the dictate expressed by Paul in his letter to the Galatians (3:28), "In Christ there is neither Jew nor Greek, there is neither slave nor free, there is neither male nor female; for you are all one in Christ Jesus." As people who were trying to lead a Christian life, we found common ground with one another as God's children by ensuring that every voice was present at the altar of worship.

By retelling this old story of mine, I do not wish to imply that conditions in Milwaukee in 1969 were especially conducive to multicultural diversity. After all, it *was* 1969. The level of intolerance and prejudice was certainly more obvious and more destructive then than it is today. No, my point is to demonstrate how a group of diverse people were able, at a particular point in time, to find a sense of unity in the midst of diversity. And if I portray life in my portion of middle America then as having a certain level of diversity, think of the diversity in which we live today. Back then we categorized difference around race, ethnicity, nationality, and class. Today, for better or for worse, we continue to use such categories, but we also perceive diversity as it relates to gender, sexual orientation, marital status, age, religion (including denominations within religions), and (in the case of seminaries and higher education in general) student status—full-time, part-time, residential, commuter, online.

I believe, nevertheless, that by reaching back to my experience as a young person in Milwaukee, I can begin the process of reframing issues of diversity in theological education. But relying on personal experience alone is not a sufficient basis on which to develop a better understanding of these issues, and so I will also reach out to the hermeneutical theory of Hans-Georg Gadamer. This unlikely—though, as I hope to demonstrate, entirely appropriate—connection between interpretive theory and mundane experience suggests the kind of connections we must make in order both to draw upon our own lives and at the same time to perceive our experiences from angles of interpretation that frame and illuminate the significance of what we may know only indirectly. My aim is to help us better engage diversity in modern seminary life and redefine our understanding of prejudice and misunderstanding.

THE REHABILITATION OF PREJUDICE

The word "hermeneutics" comes from the Greek verb *hermeneuein*, translated as "to interpret," and according to Richard Palmer (1966, 13–32), the origin of the word is best portrayed in the mythical story of the Greek god, Hermes, the translator of language and writing—"the tools which human understanding employs to grasp meaning and to convey it to others." From early in its history, hermeneutics was intended to decipher meaning in the literary classics of antiquity, legal jurisprudence, the Bible, and other sacred texts. It was not until the nineteenth century, however, that the work of Friedrich Schleiermacher pointed to ways in which hermeneutics might be applied more broadly—to interpret and clarify diverse messages and convey multilayered and textured meaning to others so that understanding between the conveyor of the message and its intended recipient would ultimately result. As Nakkula and Ravitch (1998, xix) assert, "hermeneutics, when connected to human interactions, opens up important possibilities for deeper understanding and respect in relationships."

Schleiermacher, generally regarded as the founder of modern Protestant theology (Mueller-Vollmer 1988, 72), defined hermeneutics as "'the art of understanding,' an art or practice that related discourse and understanding (*verstechen*) to each other" (Gallagher 1992, 3). He also coined the phrase, "the hermeneutic circle," through which he indicated the interrelationship between whole and part in interpreting any material of a textual nature. Shaun Gallagher (1992, 59) explicates Schleiermacher's essential rendering of the "circularity of understanding" by stating that, "the meaning of the part is only understood within the context of the whole; but the whole is never given unless through an understanding of the parts. Understanding therefore requires a circular movement from parts to whole and from whole to parts." A hermeneutics of ontology (Ricoeur 1989, 197–221) translates the relationship of whole and part of circular understanding into a paradigm of meaningful human action which is rendered in the metaphor of "the person as text" (Gergen 1980, 29).

GADAMER'S "PREJUDICE" OF PREJUDICE

One way of summarizing this relationship between part and whole is to suggest that each of us is unable to be understood independently of our contextualized experience in the world at any particular point in time: We are historically situated creatures who spring from different temporal, social, geographical, ideological, and philosophical locations, and we hold firmly to the diverse perspectives and assumptions that we each bring to our relationships with others. This is where the work of the German philosopher Hans-Georg Gadamer and his radical reframing of the concepts of prejudice, bias, and misunderstanding come into play. According to the Gadamerian perspective, one essentially *is* one's interpretation of the world, and it is through the socializing influence of language that this condition primarily occurs.

Gadamer developed much of his early hermeneutic thinking from the philosophical influence of his mentor and teacher, Martin Heidegger,[1] for whom existence or being *is* understanding. Heidegger asserts that "the essential meaning of being human . . . is making meaning of the world and of one's being in the world" (Heidegger 1996, 57). Heidegger's ontology is fulfilled in the meaning-making individual who constantly interprets her place in the world and what it means to be situated in the world in particular ways (Nakkula and Ravitch 1998). Heidegger's most profound contribution to hermeneutics is that of moving it from a primary concern for interpreting the hidden messages in written texts to understanding what it means to be human in the world in all aspects of one's existence.

Gadamer, according to Browning (1995, 2), "accepted Heidegger's view that all attempts by humans to understand something must necessarily and inescapably begin with, and be contrasted to, the pre-understandings, pre-judgments, and veritable 'prejudices' that we bring to the understanding process. Rather than pre-judgments getting in the way of understanding, as Enlightenment and empiricist epistemologies claimed, Heidegger and Gadamer held that they are essential to it. We only understand something in relation to the pre-understandings and prejudices that we bring to what we are attempting to understand."

As Gadamer ([1960] 1999, 270) asserts, "'Prejudice' means a judgment that is rendered before all the elements that determine a situation have been finally examined." "Thus," he says, "'prejudice' certainly does not necessarily mean a false judgment, but part of the idea is that it can have either a positive or a negative value." Gadamer's "rehabilitating" of these phenomena allows us to view them as unavoidable processes that should be embraced and reflected upon, rather than denied and avoided. This revised notion of these concepts is essential to understanding the hermeneutical process. This view describes prejudices, biases, and misunderstanding as events, objects, and experiences that we have come to know up to the moment and that are subject to constant revision and change. From Gadamer's perspective, one is always *projected* into new situations with accompanying misunderstanding, but misunderstanding that is open to reinterpretation, given our access to new information and our increased self-understanding. Gadamer asserts that we encounter every situation and object through our "forestructure of understanding" of what has previously been learned and internalized in preparation for the ongoing assimilation of new experiences. He refers to this forestructure as "prejudgment, prejudice, bias, and misunderstanding," which occurs within the context of human action and interaction as an unavoidable part of what it means to be human.

THE PLAY OF LANGUAGE

Gadamer argues that this internalization of meaning and experience occurs primarily through the socializing influence of language. He suggests that language is used primarily as a vehicle through which the world becomes less alien: it is the process by which we ourselves become "de-alienated" from unfamiliar people, places, ideas, experiences, and things in the world previously unknown to us—so as to effectively make the *alien familiar*. Gadamer (1976, 9) further argues that "prejudices . . . constitute the initial directedness of our whole ability to experience" and that "language is the fundamental mode of operation of our being-in-the-world and the all-embracing form of the constitution of the world" (3). We define ourselves in the world, and our relationship in connectedness to others, through the medium of language.

Gadamer places language within the broader context of "play" and suggests that language is ultimately organized like a "game" through which a player ultimately becomes lost. But this loss, which is the result of the development of linguistically more complex functioning, is viewed as only a temporary condition until the player becomes played by the game itself because the rules have become thoroughly internalized. Through the play of language we are able to liberate ourselves (from our earlier internalized preconceptions) and become transformed, thus re-creating our understanding of the world (and ourselves) as we move toward possibility for more authentic engagement. Gadamer asserts that we should begin with open exploration of our prejudiced assumptions about a phenomenon or experience and move from this prejudiced (or interpreted) position to explore what is unknown and less familiar to us through further reflective questioning. This process of ongoing questioning and critical self-reflection should lead to the generation (and integration) of even deeper questions, which should lead to the uncovering of more meaningful data and to further questioning of our prejudiced positions and worldview. Thus, our understanding of the world should be in a process of constant revision as we integrate new information for deeper and more complex understanding (Nakkula and Ravitch 1998).

The process of engaging this "circle of understanding" defines what it means to be human. A paramount question for us becomes, How might we encourage faculty and students to examine their natural human prejudices and thereby find opportunities to engage more fully with the diversity of the world around them?

My experience as a teenager in Milwaukee moved me toward the kind of understanding that Gadamer offers. Despite the effects of racial and class prejudices, I knew that what was paramount, though I obviously could not articulate this as an adolescent, was the fundamental truth of a shared humanity: we all sing in the same chorus. While this did not mitigate the harsh realities of racism in the society at large, it placed this prejudice within a definition that did not give the final word to the limited and partial perspective of a racist society. Through the perspective of such a personal and theoretical lens I present the particular issue of diversity in theological education.

TRANSFORMATIVE LEARNING:
THE PEDAGOGY OF CRITICAL ENGAGEMENT

In their final project report to The Lexington Seminar, the faculty at McCormick Theological Seminary (2000) wrote, "[We] need to connect in a more personal way with students, recognizing the significance of personal relationships for learning and formation as well as building community." And, in recognition of the school's racial, ethnic, theological, and cultural diversity—while simultaneously embracing a strong desire to continue in its affirmation of its own institutional identity as a seminary of the Presbyterian Church (USA)—the faculty also remarked, "We speak often of being inclusive, yet we could do much more to understand our students and their contexts." Faculties from other seminaries that have participated in The Lexington Seminar have voiced similar sentiments regarding the best practices for their teaching and learning.

The black feminist writer and educator bell hooks (1994, 13) asserts that "to educate as the practice of freedom" is "easiest to those of us who teach who also believe that there is an aspect of our vocation that is sacred; who believe that our work is not merely to share information but to share in the intellectual and spiritual growth of our students." Parker Palmer (1993, xi–xii) reminds us that "to teach is to create a space in which the community of truth is practiced." Certainly, the spaces in which faculty exercise their craft as teachers and scholars of the church lend themselves to the pursuit of truth as it is revealed to them. Faculty in seminaries and theological schools are very much aware of the vocational aspect of their work. Desiring that their work with students be somehow transformative in nature is often a core expectation of their teaching.

Therefore, based on insights gained through my experience in professional education, my reading of the literature, and my participation at The Lexington Seminar, I suggest that in order for seminaries to adapt successfully to the changing world in which they exist, they should strive to do the following things:

- Celebrate diversity and find similarity in difference.
- Employ the hermeneutics of engagement.
- Encourage critically reflective teaching.
- Make diversity a regular part of conversation among faculty, students, and administrators.

CELEBRATE DIVERSITY AND FIND SIMILARITY IN DIFFERENCE

No doubt, any one of us can find ways in which our personal and professional lives could be made easier if diversity were not, well, so diverse. Given the proper mixture of stress and circumstance, any one of us can muse nostalgically and think how reassuring it would be to turn the clock back to a supposedly simpler time when students came to seminary with similar expectations and training. But there is no going back, and rather than focus on the difficulties caused by diversity, we should think instead of the richness of experience that our changing environment ushers in and celebrate God's grace in granting us this bountiful gift. We should explore ways to find similarity within difference.

For a very individualized example, consider that I am a middle-aged African American male with no children and strong ecclesiastical roots in Roman Catholicism and have lived for twenty-five years in fast-paced Manhattan and Boston. Therefore, I may never know exactly what it means to be Mark, the fictional character in the narrative of the United Theological

Seminary of the Twin Cities (2001),[2] who is described as a "white, middle class, United Church of Christ student. He is married with teenage children and serves as a student pastor in a rural setting. He is approximately 40 years old, moderately liberal theologically, and has experienced 'positive stretching' but minimal struggle in his time at seminary." But were Mark and I ever to cross each other's paths, I believe a necessary starting point for our interaction would be those characteristics of our life experience that, though different in form are indeed quite similar at their very core: We are both native-born American men who are of middle age and who share a belief in the relevancy of the Christian faith and a strong love of the church. I would also imagine that Mark and I could commune around our respective understandings of what it means to be men who have now crossed over into middle-age, with all the concomitant realities, concerns, issues, and responsibilities that define who we are at this unique juncture in our lives, though these things may express themselves differently for each of us. It is in the similarities of our individual experiences through which we reach common ground as persons made in the image and likeness of God.

In a more institutional context, teachers should look for ways to connect with the diversity of experience in their classrooms. For example, this might involve

- A restructuring of the classroom experience in light of student diversity,
- The discovery of ways to democratize the classroom experience to make space for student voices previously not heard, or
- Dramatically changing the actual format for teaching content in light of recent research in brain neuroscience and students' diverse learning styles.

Because so many of the students in seminary today are adult learners who bring with them a wide array of talents and experience, it is vitally important to create sufficient time, space, and opportunity within the classroom to draw upon this fund of rich experiential knowledge. This might take the form of students (either singly or as teams) leading a portion of seminar classes in which they present a theological topic and offer their own fund of experiences as a starting point for applying their understanding. Or, for example, a teacher might build into a course on preaching opportunities for students to reflect on the way in which their personal and cultural experiences affect the way in which they are inclined to approach preaching. For instance, a teacher might set aside the first several sessions of a seminar to allow students to introduce themselves, describe their background, and identify what they hope to gain from the course. Such a strategy would give the students (as well as the teacher, who should also participate) opportunities to name their differences (and prejudices) but also to see the similarities in their experiences and gifts.

Employ the Hermeneutics of Engagement

Gadamer's rehabilitation of prejudice embodies a less-threatening perspective on a word that is often imbued with existential discomfort and personal unease. By construing prejudice as a regular and necessary part of everyday human functioning as opposed to a stigma of personal failing or a point of moral attack, we develop ways to become more fully engaged in the world. It is important that individuals be allowed to give voice to their concerns about diversity as they understand them to be, for only through a process of self-questioning do we arrive at a deeper understanding of the issues about which we critically reflect.

Each of us is the product of our cumulative history. There is no such thing as a value-free or neutral individual; we are the composite of both our unique biological makeup and the social contexts and backgrounds that help create who we are as individuals. And it is from the starting point of our own particularity in the world that we come to understand our prejudices. Faculty can be quite instrumental in class by exhibiting a willingness to share some of their own particular experience in the world and thus help students formulate a context for reflecting on their own prejudices and misunderstandings and develop relationships with one another and with faculty. By admitting to students, at the outset, his or her particular strengths and weaknesses, a teacher sets the context for mutually transformative exploration. Encouraging students to interact socially outside of class (with one another and with the course instructor) is yet another excellent way to encourage the development of our own hermeneutical skills.

Gadamer's view on prejudice also necessitates that we recognize that understanding is never final or complete. Our everyday engagement and activity in the world is subject to ongoing interpretation and revision that come to represent who we are and what we will become. When we open ourselves up to embrace the possibilities for learning, we broaden our worldview and help to shape the kingdom of God on earth. But embracing possibility does not negate the fact that we are also embedded and steeped in our individual traditions—the assumptions that help to shape who we are up to a particular point in time. Given this, it is important that faculty help students understand that interpretation is our continuing project. Faculty should be encouraged to help students engage this interpretive task. For example, planning classroom exercises in which students might name aspects of their own thinking, perspectives, or recently modified behaviors can help facilitate this type of learning. Students may also be encouraged to think about differences in these very same attributes as observed in other individuals, such as their parents, spouses, partners, coworkers, fellow students, or children.

In my work in the Boston Public Schools, I often conduct workshops to help teachers engage more effectively with challenging children and adolescents from diverse cultural backgrounds. The reality is that most of the teachers in the Boston school system come from different racial, ethnic, and social class backgrounds than the majority of the student population, which often leads to tension and conflict. In my workshops, therefore, I usually ask teachers to reflect momentarily on the specific challenges they face in working with urban students. These are students whom the teachers generally perceive as a "problem" to be addressed rather than as developing individuals with young minds to be intellectually engaged through transformative learning. This attitude held on the part of many teachers who are otherwise quite capable individuals in their respective disciplines unfortunately sets the stage for a limited capacity to engage with students from diverse backgrounds.

In my workshops, I ask teachers to name the assumptions they hold about their students. I help them interrogate the reasons for which they hold these assumptions and encourage them to challenge themselves through critical self-reflection. They spend an extraordinary amount of time talking with one another, not about these students *per se*, but about themselves as individuals, as spouses, partners, mothers, fathers, sisters, brothers, friends, and educators. They spend time looking at where they come from, exploring why they decided to become teachers and why they believe in the things they do. I help teachers explore the ways their beliefs and attitudes help to facilitate or hinder their capacity to work effectively with their students each day. We discuss what they would like to accomplish with students, and I invite them to name ways of getting to "there from here." We brainstorm about different ways to teach their subjects, issue grades, and manage student classroom behavior while still meeting curricular deadlines, administering standardized tests, and, ultimately, facilitating student academic success. I help teachers give voice to their own particular strengths and help them see the diverse assets and talents of their students.

We spend little time talking about the negative behaviors of students or reflecting on trouble spots. Rather, I try to help teachers use the rich experience of the students' lives in their classroom teaching and see their experiences as substantive material for engaged classroom teaching and learning. The goal in my professional work is to help teachers transcend boundaries of all types and explore new ways of being with their students and, ultimately, with themselves. This task is often a slow process because most teachers are generally grounded (as are we all) in their own particular ways of teaching, doing, and being—their own particular prejudices. It is often hard to break out of old habits and learn how to incorporate fresher ways of being in the world.

I believe similar strategies that I use in my workshops with Boston educators can be used in workshops for seminary faculty. Such faculty workshops might include having small groups of three or four faculty meet together to accomplish the following:

1. Generate a list of faculty questions and concerns about issues of diversity in theological education.
2. Engage faculty in a discussion that focuses on the kind of challenges that diversity presents in the classroom.
3. Encourage faculty to acknowledge and name some of their assumptions about issues of diversity and comment on how these assumptions may have developed.
4. Help faculty identify the kind of skills and knowledge needed in their classrooms to meet the challenge of diversity.
5. Direct faculty to the appropriate educational and community resources that provide the necessary skills and knowledge needed to effectively work with diversity.

After faculty have had an opportunity to reflect and learn from one another in these small groups, they may serve as consultants to each other, suggesting ways to respond to the challenges raised during their discussion. Later, in a larger plenary session, faculty could report back to the larger group on some of the learning and insights gained in the small groups.

BECOME A CRITICALLY REFLECTIVE TEACHER

According to Stephen Brookfield (1995, 1), "We teach to change the world." Doing critically reflective teaching, though, is not simply a matter of thinking deeply about issues in education or the specific subject areas of our own academic disciplines. Critical reflection, according to Brookfield (8), involves "[understanding] how considerations of power undergird, frame, and distort educational processes and interaction" and "[questioning] assumptions and practices that seem to make our teaching lives easier but actually work against our own best long-term interest." Classrooms are not politically neutral spaces but contested locations that exist to support the forces that seek to maintain ideological hegemony and power. Working to interrogate and understand these conditions within educational practice should be an ethical imperative for each of us and a central part of our educational practice.

Make Diversity a Regular Part of Conversation

Across the country many schools have embarked upon efforts to deal with issues of diversity. For some schools this has included the sponsorship of small-scale initiatives, such as faculty colloquia during which invited guests offer various perspectives on cultural competencies and other aspects of diversity and engage faculty in conversation on these important issues. Other institutions have undertaken large-scale and longer-range projects that focus on concerns about diversity that have included assessing the consequences of racial, ethnic, class, and gender issues within the classroom and across the institution itself. One institution that has exercised extraordinary leadership in promoting diversity at its school, in part as a response to new and increased expectations among concerned students of color and others, is the Harvard Graduate School of Education (HGSE),[3] which should be especially acknowledged for its commitment to "examine how the institutional culture affects, and the learning environment supports" its increasingly diverse student body (Mapp and Johnson 1997, 3).

Former HGSE Dean Jerome Murphy established a five-year Faculty Recruitment Committee, from 1992–1997, which was charged as part of the school's faculty recruitment initiative with the responsibility of bringing faculty of color to the school to be visiting professors. This effort was underwritten by a $2 million endowment given to the School of Education by former Harvard University president Neil Rudenstine. The Faculty Recruitment Committee was subsequently extended from 1997–2003. In addition, in 1996, HGSE began a series of "faculty diversity seminars" in which faculty met each month to discuss their teaching in light of issues of diversity. This effort was also spearheaded and supported by the Dean's Office at HGSE.

Other schools have become involved in large-scale efforts to address diversity issues by sponsoring occasional daylong "diversity retreats" for faculty and students alike, or by involving all areas of the institution in publicly held "diversity dialogues" and roundtable discussions in which institutional issues on diversity are discussed and explored in greater depth. Focus groups have been used in some schools to solicit students' views on diversity as they experience it. Several schools have sponsored faculty papers on topics related to diversity.

Also, at HGSE, the dean's office established a Teaching Curriculum Quality Fund that provides diversity grants for faculty to identify readings with more diverse points of view for use as part of the course syllabus or to develop case studies that center on issues of diversity for use in the classroom. These occasions have enabled faculty to discover more effective ways to bring diversity issues directly into the curriculum and to enrich the overall educational experiences of students.

In 1996, a special assistant in the HGSE deans' office, Karen Mapp, researched the experiences of diversity at seven other academic institutions and was later assisted in reporting her results by Susan Johnson. According to Mapp and Johnson (1997, 3):

> The reports from these schools confirmed that our experience at HGSE is by no means unique. A more diverse student body brings new perspectives that inevitably reveal shortcomings in current curricula and teaching practices. Faculty members at various institutions have learned that, although they have made changes in their courses and are committed to effectively serving diverse groups of students, their efforts often are not initially successful and students find them inadequate. This process of inquiry and review is often unsettling, even painful, and faculty members who believe that they are making real progress often discover that they still have much to learn and much to do.

Mapp later convened seven focus groups of students at HGSE to assess their experience of diversity at the school. Six of the focus groups comprised students who represented diverse racial and ethnic groups; the seventh group represented international students. These focus groups included a total of five master's students and thirty students enrolled in the several doctoral programs at HGSE. A Working Paper on Diversity, which summarized the results of the students' responses in the focus groups and comments by faculty, was subsequently made available to the HGSE community in 1997. This document proved pivotal in facilitating HGSE to move forward with plans for the school's diversity initiatives. Diversity projects emanating from this initial investigative inquiry included the establishment (in 1997) of the Diversity Innovation Fund, which has supported, with small grants, student-initiated ideas that are designed to broaden the diversity conversation at HGSE.

Other projects and programs that resulted from this initiative included the following:

- The Teaching Fellow Training on Diversity in which the director and the teaching assistants of the Student Writing Center explored ways to incorporate issues of diversity in student assessment and ways to provide helpful feedback on student writing.
- A Standing Committee on Diversity (SCOD) was also established not long after publication of the working paper to respond to two questions: Where should HGSE be in five years? How do we get from here to there?
- The Harvard Education Forum, a series of public guest lectures on topics of relevance to education, sponsored numerous sessions in which issues of diversity were the main focus. The sessions included panels on ethnicity, gender, race, and language-based learning, to name just a few.

- The Inter-Area Research Study Group used a grant from the Pew Charitable Trusts to learn about the experiences of various research-based groups engaged in exploring diversity as it relates to various aspects of education.

CONCLUSION

Because of the increased diversity of experience and learning skills among today's seminary students, theological institutions are challenged in myriad ways to meet the needs of this growing constituency while also, somehow, finding ways to remain true to their own sense of mission and tradition. Fortunately, despite our own perceptions of our students' biases, misunderstandings, and prejudices (different in form but similar in kind to our own), students continue to come to seminary to engage in theological reflection and achieve a better understanding of their Christian faith and heritage. By joining them in the chorus of human experience, we give ourselves the opportunity to embrace a new student-constituent reality, a reality that is truly reflective of the goodness of God from whom we have all been similarly blessed by the awesome love and grace expressed in the gift of our own diverse and prejudiced humanity.

NOTES

1. One is still left in much pain and amazement in trying to understand how one of the foremost intellectual pillars of our time allowed himself to diminish his contributions and credibility to twentieth century philosophical thought through his sympathetic affiliation with fascist Germany's Nazi Party. Heidegger was a self-ascribed member of the Nazi party during World War II. It is a paradox of our times how someone like Heidegger could exhibit such absolute genius in one aspect of his life and yet become a participant in moral corruption of such monumental proportions as his undisputed involvement in this part of history demonstrates.

2. All narratives cited in this book can be found in the Archives section of the Seminar's Web site: http://www.lexingtonseminar.org/.

3. I wish to thank Rosemary Downer of the dean's office at Harvard Graduate School of Education (HGSE) and Dr. Nancy Nienhuis of HGSE's Office of Student Affairs for making available to me documents on the school's diversity initiatives.

·GORDON T. SMITH·

Faculties That Listen, Schools That Learn

ASSESSMENT IN THEOLOGICAL EDUCATION

Most faculties of theological schools struggle to know what to do with assessment.[1] Faculties want to be learning communities; they want to learn how to be more effective at the work that matters so deeply to them. And they assume that good assessment is essential. But this assumption is matched by a persistent perception that assessment is an imposition arbitrarily required by accrediting agencies or administrators and not inherent to their work as scholars and teachers. Assessment for some is a minor annoyance; as one faculty member put it, "One more damned thing we have to do before the summer break!" For others, assessment is an outright violation of true theological education—something that undermines teaching and learning because it is viewed as trying to measure and commodify learning.

In what follows, I demonstrate that such a reaction to assessment is unfortunate. In its very nature, assessment can and must be inherent in what it means to be teachers and learners. Assessment is integral to the character of our work. If we take the work of theological education seriously, we take assessment seriously because we take learning seriously. Theological education matters because the church matters and because leadership—theological and ministerial—matters. It matters enough that we want to have some degree of confidence that what we are doing makes a difference, that it actually does fulfill the ends for which it is designed, that it actually does provide effective ministerial leadership for the church.

As theological educators, we *want* to make a difference. From this naturally flows a desire to know if what we are doing *is* making a difference. Does learning toward effective ministry actually happen in our schools? Does our work, as theological teachers and as theological schools, actually accomplish what we say and pray is the goal of our endeavors?

In other words, thinking about assessment and doing good assessment matters. It merits our time and energy. Good theological schools attend to matters of assessment not because accrediting associations require it, but because they believe in their work and want to be confident that the work of teaching and learning serves its intended objectives. Having said that, it follows that accrediting agencies recognize that effective assessment is something that theological faculties do. The Association of Theological Schools (ATS), with its delineation of what makes for a good theological school, specifies: "The institution offering the M.Div. shall be able to demonstrate the extent to which students have met the various goals of the degree program" (ATS, *Degree Program Standards* A.5.1.). Further, standard A.5.2. specifies that the school sustains a continual process of evaluation which determines the extent to which the degree program meets the needs of the students and the goals of the program.

What the ATS standards highlight is that we cannot take for granted that assessment is given its rightful place of importance in institutional priorities. The standards are a means by which theological schools call each other to demonstrate that good assessment procedures are happening. But in the end, we will not engage the practice of assessment and embrace it as something integral to our work as the faculty of a theological school unless we can come to an appreciation of why it is pivotal. Without an effective program of assessment, we will never move beyond good intentions; we will not have a solid basis on which to make decisions about matters of curriculum or points of complaint or criticism regarding our academic programs.

The work of theological education merits good assessment for at least two reasons. First, good practices of assessment provide schools with a form of intentional accountability, a means by which we demonstrate that we are doing what we say we are doing. Accountability is a fundamental spiritual discipline, and assessment is a means by which we practice what we preach. We have an obvious accountability to the ecclesial bodies that we serve and with which we partner in the formation of women and men for ministerial leadership. But we are also accountable to the wider community of higher education, for we are degree-granting institutions. Further, we are accountable to our students who invest time, money, and energy (and their hopes and dreams) into a curriculum that they trust is oriented toward effective ministry. (I say this even though I stress below that as adults students need to take responsibility for their own learning.) Finally, we are accountable to donors, who rightly expect us to be good stewards of their investments.

We do assessment because in the end we lecture not so that teaching occurs but so that *learning* happens. We need, then, to find ways to gauge and confirm that what we intend to accomplish actually occurs. The bottom line is that we are accountable to the mission of the school, and assessment is a means by which our accountability finds expression.

The second reason that assessment merits our time and energy is that good assessment fosters learning. One of the objectives of a good education is that each student should become committed to continuous learning. This outcome should become evident in each student's capacity to evaluate his or her own experience and learn from it. We cannot reasonably expect this outcome in our students if, as theological schools, we are not fostering the same outcome in ourselves—to learn from our experience as we attend to what is actually happening in our academic programs. Good intentions are no more than good intentions; good learning is necessarily the fruit of intentional practices that not only foster good learning but also assure that it is happening. Thus, we lead by example and become, in the language of Peter Senge (1990; 2000), not only schools where learning happens but "schools that learn." We learn from our own experience through a process of intentional reflection on what has happened and what it means, and we adjust our programs as our experience indicates.

Beyond these two core reasons for assessment, I would also add the following. Many faculty have a deep and hidden fear that they are failures and that they are ineffective in enabling women and men to prepare for religious leadership in the church. One reason for this fear is that criticism is plentiful; there is much too little affirmation that highlights the value of the work that a theological faculty does. Further, the fear is often unstated, deflected, and based on incomplete information that provides no guidance for faculty to become more effective. Assessment, therefore, is, a vital aid to help faculty members and theological schools see the positive work they are doing. It is an integral practice—native, not alien, to the identity and purposes of any good theological school. The challenge then is to cultivate an approach to assessment that is congruent with our work as theological educators, linked clearly for each school to its particular vision of Christian ministry, and oriented around and through the routines and rhythms of our academic lives. Assessment is a practice that encourages us to think theologically about our work; the focus is not so much oriented toward a product as it is to a means of approaching our work in a manner that fosters both accountability and learning.

THE CHALLENGE OF ASSESSMENT

Doing assessment well requires persistence, diligence, and care. This is so because of a variety of challenges that face theological schools, including (1) overemphasis on the measurable, (2) complexity of theological schools' objectives, (3) variables over which theological schools have little control, (4) the uniqueness of each theological school, and (5) the time required to do assessment well.

OVEREMPHASIS ON THE MEASURABLE

In his recent publication, *The Answer to How Is Yes*, Peter Block (2002) has effectively demonstrated that one of the great temptations of contemporary organizations, including academic institutions, is to idolize pragmatism.[2] Western society values the concrete, the tangible, and the measurable. We are heirs of both the industrial age and modernism. Yet what matters most in theological education may not be that which "works" or that which is (immediately, at least) quantifiable. The danger is that we might pursue practices that are measurable while we unwittingly overlook or neglect the practices that foster what matters most and which, in the long run, are most beneficial.

Block (2002, 4) does not question that we need to attend to what "works." But he suggests that our pragmatism moves us there prematurely; we are inclined to focus either too quickly or too exclusively on that which is measurable. We easily make "what works" the defining issue to be addressed.

Elliot Eisner (1985, 184–85), in the same vein, insists that the outcomes of good teaching are multiple and not always measurable. There is something ineffable and hard to define, let alone measure, when good teaching happens. And Parker Palmer (1997) in his *Courage to Teach* stresses that good teaching can never be reduced to technique—to methods or approaches to classroom instruction that are either measurable or immediately obvious. Rather, speaking only of the classroom, it is imperative to stress that the character of good teaching itself cannot be assessed in quantifiable terms. The Lexington Seminar report prepared by Associated Mennonite Biblical Seminary (2000)[3] puts it this way: "One of the primary learnings from this project has been that the more important factors in successful education of seminary students are also among the more difficult to quantify or measure."

Is assessment then impossible? No. But these observations remind us that we will not do good assessment unless we learn to attend to what truly matters, what truly enables someone to become an educated and self-educating person. A sports analogy may enlighten this point. The genius of playing baseball is the skill of a team to "advance the runner." While the objective is, of course, to score runs, great teams have learned to focus not so much on scoring runs, but on that from which scoring runs is derived, namely advancing the runner. This *a priori* commitment is necessary and elemental to winning. The genius of the game, in other words, is not to focus on "winning" but to cultivate the practices that make winning a likely outcome. In much the same way, it is essential that assessment in theological education focus on those factors that will likely foster long-term growth in wisdom, the capacity for continuous learning, and the inner dispositions that sustain ministerial effectiveness.

COMPLEXITY OF THE OBJECTIVES

When we discuss assessment of learning in theological schools, we have a unique challenge: How to respond to the multiple objectives of our ministerial academic programs, notably the M.Div. degree? We are well past the thinking that a good education is merely a matter of attaining good grades. We do not assume that if a student has high marks in our classes that "learning" is taking place nor that someone with low marks is not learning. As is stressed below, the grading of student work is only one dimension of effective assessment, and, further, it is only effective when it is integrated with other sources of information. Yet, it is amazing how frequently grades are the only criteria for measuring learning that students and faculty have in hand. The Lexington Seminar report from Regent College (1999) highlights that students tend to place disproportionate emphasis on the significance and diagnostic capability of a grading system.

The goals of theological study are much more complex. Theological schools often speak of goals that relate to being, knowing, and doing. In other words, the conversation about assessment tends to center around different kinds (or categories) of formation. The Roman Catholic Program of Priestly Formation (PPF), for example, speaks of spiritual formation, a "well-ordered" pattern of personal and communal prayer; intellectual formation, with reference to academic studies; and pastoral formation, which "introduces students to the practical, pastoral life of the Church" (National Conference of Catholic Bishops 2001, 43–46).

What complicates the matter of assessment is that different goals need different kinds of assessment. And, of course, the form of assessment needs to be congruent with that which is being assessed. We recognize, for example, that we cannot assess a student's emotional maturity in the same manner we assess that student's understanding of the theological tradition of the church. However, having said this, it is also important to add that we must not press or make too rigid distinct categories or goals. It is apt, for example, that the more recent editions of the PPF speak of the need for clarity—doctrinal and otherwise—regarding the priesthood itself. In this way various streams or aspects of formation are located within a particular conception of the ministry. Individual dimensions are understood as parts of a whole. One could rightly wonder if a person really understands Chalcedon if this has not, in some substantial way, led to the ordering of the affections. In other words, each of the three categories of formation (spiritual, intellectual, and pastoral) needs to be assessed in tandem with the others; each is informed by the others.

The observation is often made that the contemporary theological school attempts to be three things simultaneously: an academy, a trade school, and a monastery. And because each of these foci have a different ethos and character, theological schools are faced with a tremendous challenge, and yet, in significant measure, schools have no choice but to be all three.

VARIABLES OVER WHICH THEOLOGICAL SCHOOLS HAVE LITTLE CONTROL

The variables that make for long-term effective ministerial leadership are many, and theological schools need to accept that they are but one of these variables, not as a denial of hope and vision, but as an affirmation of limits, for they are partners with undergraduate programs, family systems, and church bodies, and in come cases with houses of spiritual formation and community, but most importantly with the students themselves, who, in the very nature of things, only learn if they are engaged and take personal responsibility for their learning. While a program of theological study may be deeply formative, theological schools still need to accept that they do not have control over the outcomes. We cannot orchestrate the ends we seek through our educational programs, or, as Elizabeth Liebert (2000, 60–61) aptly puts it, we cannot "engineer" change. All we can do, as will be stressed below, is observe what is happening through our academic programs and do what we can to encourage the outcomes we are seeking. And we do this with a modesty in our claims of what theological education has done and is able to do. Theological schools need to affirm their limits as well as the limits inherent in the educational process itself.

UNIQUENESS OF EACH THEOLOGICAL SCHOOL

Each theological school has a distinctive charism, a distinctive way of engaging the challenge of theological education. The narrative prepared by Pacific Lutheran Theological Seminary (2001) exemplifies how this distinctiveness is more than just a matter of theological or denominational heritage; a Lutheran seminary in California has a different sense of its mission than does a Lutheran seminary in the Midwest. Consequently, no educator should espouse a single model or approach to assessment. Each theological school remains unique; each will have its own emphases and own range of convictions about theological education that will find expression in how its various goals are weighted, even how they are assessed. Each school is a unique confluence of monastery, academy, and trade school, and each has a different range of associations and partnerships with undergraduate colleges and ecclesial bodies, all of which will inevitably shape the way in which assessment happens such that the approach to assessment is congruent with the mission and ethos of the school.

Time to Do Assessment Well

Finally, one of the biggest challenges to doing assessment well is finding the time—the leisure and space in the schedule to design the questions, solicit the feedback, and reflect on the data collected. Assessment demands the careful work of those who collect the necessary information, but it also requires that schools establish assessment as a priority in their regular routines and that faculty view it not only as integral to their work but as worth the investment of precious hours throughout the academic year. Assessment should not be an exercise that dominates our lives as faculty, and it should not feel like an imposition. But we need to make appropriate time for this vital practice. If we value our common commitment to the mission of the school and wish to verify that together we are making an impact toward that mission, and if we value good conversation about how our students are learning, then we need to find the time—actually set aside the time—to do assessment well.

Good Assessment Is Worth Pursuing

Assessment is worth the time and energy that we devote to it. But we must learn to do assessment in a way that is minimally disruptive, most congruent with our vision and values as a theological school, and most likely to foster our capacity to be a school that learns and cultivates good teaching and learning. Achieving this outcome requires certain commitments and certain best practices. The commitments, at the very least, are the following: (1) thinking theologically about theological education, (2) maintaining clear objectives for theological education, (3) establishing broad faculty ownership of assessment, (4) fostering good conversation with ecclesial bodies and field supervisors, (5) assessing both competencies and dispositions, and (6) enkindling the joy of good teaching and learning.

Thinking Theologically about Theological Education

The task of theological education is a *theological* task. The call to do assessment is but an invitation to think theologically about our work as scholars, teachers, and educators—to think about what it means to do higher education in a way that is informed and sustained by our theological affirmations, convictions, and passions. This commitment to think theologically needs to be matched by a resolve to learn and excel at what it is that we are doing. Thus, we are learners, ever seeking to process new information and adapt to what we see and what the information we glean through assessment is telling us. Theological reflection without a willingness to learn and adapt is missing something that is inherent in the very meaning of theological education.

Thinking theologically about learning necessarily means that we think about education and study with a distinctive and purposeful orientation toward the practices of ministry. Essentially, all courses, not just those that are designated "applied" or "practical," should be oriented toward the work for which students are preparing. We can then discard the flawed distinction between academic and applied courses and recognize that nothing may be so practical as a course in theology and nothing quite so intellectually stimulating as a course on preaching. This tension between the "academic" and the "practical" is highlighted in the narrative of Austin Presbyterian Theological Seminary (1999) in the apt response of the dean to the complaint that John Wesley was not a systematic theologian but a preacher: "Yeah, but some people think the reason he preached so well is that he knew an awful lot about the Bible, and theology!"

Maintaining Clear Objectives

The practice of assessment requires a greater level of clarity about the objectives of our theological schools. It only makes sense that assessment be linked not to vague or abstract expectations or ideals but to specific objectives—the values and commitments of a school at a particular point in its history. Admittedly, this is not necessarily easy, as is demonstrated by those Lexington Seminar narratives that show faculty debating and disagreeing about the fundamental purposes of their theological school.

However, for assessment to be done well, these values and commitments need to be framed in terms of what is rightly called "student outcomes" (Palomba and Banta, 1999), which suggests that schools must understand both the intended outcomes that professors have established for their courses and the actual outcomes achieved by the students. The Lexington Seminar report by Claremont School of Theology (2000) arose from the question, "What happens for our students in the Master of Divinity program?" It then moved to the realization that "we needed somehow to hear from students more fully than we had done to date." The report for Eastern Baptist Theological Seminary (2000) begins by declaring a resolve to move from "teaching-centered to learning-centered pedagogies."

Further, the focus of assessment should be programmatic rather than student specific. Students have multiple responses to the same courses and academic programs, and a variety of factors are involved in a student's own learning over which the theological school has little if any control. Yet, the school does have the capacity and responsibility to assess its programmatic offerings and to consider these offerings in the light of the objectives of program.

Finally, academic programs should be viewed and reviewed as more than just curricular offerings. Cocurricular or extracurricular variables may well be as crucial to the programmatic objectives, if not more crucial, as courses might be. The common worship, the informal discussions over coffee, the student discussion groups for which there is no academic credit, are all significant means by which fundamental values and dispositions are formed.

ESTABLISHING BROAD FACULTY OWNERSHIP

Both experience and the testimony of the best writing on assessment emphasize the need for broad faculty ownership and commitment to assessment. The role of ecclesial bodies and administrators is vital to the assessment and evaluation process. Further, students need to be encouraged to take seriously their own self-evaluation. (Indeed, part of what we need to do is to cultivate in students the ability and willingness to think clearly and effectively about their own capacities and sensibilities.) Yet the faculty have the primary role and responsibility in assessment. The Roman Catholic Program of Priestly Formation document stresses this point. Palomba and Banta (1999, 71) also highlight the crucial role of faculty in assessment and insist that assessment needs to be housed with the faculty, declaring, "Turn it over to them!"

The faculty design and deliver the curriculum. Therefore, they must, in the end, assume responsibility for their work, a responsibility that they carry together. If they do not accept the need for and the approach taken to assessment, then it will be ineffective. If faculty perceive assessment as imposed by an accrediting agency, they will not embrace the need for assessment nor will they do it well. If they view assessment as driven by administrators or "education experts," it will be less than effective, because they will not own it. They will perceive it as something imposed upon them and thus not their responsibility. Conversely, faculty care about their work. They want to make a difference, and theological schools can appeal to these fundamental values and commitments. Thus, schools need to design, with the faculty, an approach to assessment that is congruent with the faculty's vision for theological education yet still consistent with the mission of the theological schools to which they belong.

While the faculty need to own the program and plan of assessment, they will only be able to do assessment well if key administrative personnel—notably the president and dean—are equally committed to the process and to bearing the weight of the load for the administrative details. There may be an assistant or associate dean who does the bulk of the work. But assessment cannot be done for the faculty; we cannot merely delegate this away to an administrative staff person so that we do not need to be bothered with it. The faculty must own the process, and those in academic leadership need to bear the weight to make sure that it happens, that this remains a priority on the agendas of faculty meetings. The president and dean will assure that the work of the faculty in assessment is actually used to inform key administrative and curricular decisions. Faculty need to be able to see that assessment makes a difference.

FOSTERING GOOD CONVERSATION WITH ECCLESIAL BODIES AND FIELD SUPERVISORS

Theological schools will not be able to do good assessment of their academic programs unless they recognize the critical need to give a privileged voice to the practitioners—those who actually do the ministry for which the degree program is designed. This applies equally to the formation of women and men for religious leadership as it does for social work and medicine.

While denominational officials and church bodies can certainly have either unreasonable or misinformed expectations of the full character of academic programs and culture, they are an indispensable source of insight and encouragement. Taking assessment seriously necessarily means that we recognize the critical place of field supervisors in both the learning of students and the evaluation of their learning. The critical piece in assessment, then, is the conversation between the practitioners and the academic faculty, which ultimately leads to the meaningful capacity of practitioners to inform the shaping of an academic program. Such conversation can be structured in a variety of ways, but how it happens is probably less crucial than that it happens, although I would stress that whatever form is developed needs to allow for faculty (and not just administrative personnel) to be in discussion with those in the field.

ASSESSING COMPETENCIES AND DISPOSITIONS

Good assessment is only possible if, as noted above, we appreciate that we are seeking multiple competencies for our students. But it is also vital that we affirm that effective religious leadership is the fruit of a set of competencies that are, in turn, complemented and sustained by certain *dispositions* without which the competencies are not only meaningless but potentially harmful. Thus, our approach to assessment needs to emphasize that we are evaluating growth and development on both fronts.

If we are seeking to form wise women and men for pastoral ministry, then our "measurements" need to be consistent with this objective, requiring that we learn to work with both the "hard" data of grades as well the intuitive judgments that may in the long run be as significant as anything we have to offer to the process of assessment. Grades matter. But as noted above, they may not actually measure whether the most significant sort of learning is happening. Further, the manner in which grading is done may well undermine the most important learning that is sought.

In *The Answer to How Is Yes*, Peter Block presents an idea that strikes me as pertinent to theological education. He suggests that Western society, in its passion to judge the world by what works, has elevated the archetype of the "engineer" to such an extent that it encourages a one-dimensional perspective that fails to account for some of the most critical aspects of life and work. Things need to work, but they also need to sustain the core values and dispositions that make life worth living. In response, he proposes the archetype of the "architect" as one that faithfully integrates the vision of the engineer, who can make a structure safe and secure, with the vision of the "artist," who has the capacity to cultivate soul, thus accounting for the aesthetic, affective, and spiritual dimensions of life (165–169).

Enkindling the Joy of Teaching and Learning

Whatever image or archetype we use, one critical sign that we have moved in the right direction will be when our assessment is designed around competencies and dispositions (both of spirit and character) rather than courses (which are a means to an end). In this regard, the New Testament highlights that we cannot learn—we cannot hear and respond to the Word—if we are angry; we either hear and respond with meekness or we do not learn at all (see Jas. 1:19–21). In 1 Thessalonians, Paul suggests that he knew his readers had experienced a genuine conversion in the Spirit because they received the Word with joy despite the presence of hardship and persecution.

Furthermore, the classic sources or texts on discernment in the history of Christian spirituality—whether in the "Rules of Discernment" in St. Ignatius Loyola, Jonathan Edwards's *Religious Affections*, or the sermons on the inner witness of the Spirit in the works of John Wesley—consistently stress that what is happening to us affectively is not incidental to our capacity to both teach and learn. The gift of learning—a gift made possible through the gracious work of the Spirit—will only be experienced through diligence and hard work, but it should be filled with joy. Surely, then, one of the indicators or signs that good learning is happening is that both teachers and students experience the joy of exploration and discovery.[4] While the "rules of discernment" remind us that the presence of joy in itself means nothing and may, in fact, be a "false" consolation, the lack of joy is a sure indicator that something is amiss. Thus, surely, one of our resolutions must be that we will delight in our work of teaching and learning, such that both faculty and students "experience a deep joy."

BEST PRACTICES

While each school needs to find an approach to assessment that is congruent with its distinctive charism—its mission, ethos, and values—we can nevertheless discern certain "best practices" that guide those schools that do assessment well and that are applicable for all when it comes to how assessment is done. Among the most important of these best practices are (1) the active participation of students in assessment, (2) the presence of intentionality without excessive intrusiveness, (3) the asking of good questions, (4) the use of multiple sources of information, (5) the effective use of grading and student evaluation, and (6) the effective design of programs and curricula.

ACTIVE PARTICIPATION OF STUDENTS IN ASSESSMENT

Student involvement in assessment should have two distinct dimensions. First, as noted above, schools are wise to encourage and assist students in taking responsibility for their own learning. Attending to one's own learning is itself a sign that one is an educated and self-educating person, capable of continuous learning well beyond one's days of formal theological study.

But second, student participation is also critical to programmatic assessment. "Assessment must be seen as an activity done with and for students, rather than to them," Palomba and Banta (1999, 71) rightly insist. Theological schools most committed to doing good assessment have actively sought to find multiple ways to solicit student feedback not only on specific courses but also on the program as a whole. They need to be in conversation about their own learning—not merely through forms or questionnaires but in actual conversation at regular intervals during their program of study and at key intervals after the completion of their degrees (through longitudinal studies, for example, done two, five, and even ten years after receiving their diplomas).

But students can only play an active role in assessing their own learning and helping the school assess its teaching if schools make explicit the intended outcomes of their academic programs. For example, a school should describe to each incoming class in an M.Div. program what the school is seeking to accomplish and how students can expect to assess not only their own learning and development but the school's process of assessment. If students are going to contribute to the assessment process, they need a clear list of criteria for critical reflection.

INTENTIONALITY WITHOUT EXCESSIVE INTRUSIVENESS

Assessment can only be effective if the goals of the assessment process are clear, the approach to assessment is explicit and intentional, and the means of soliciting information are simple. Schools that are managing to do assessment well *describe* what is happening, *interpret* the information they gather, and follow accepted criteria by which they *evaluate* how lessons learned should shape the academic program.

While good assessment is necessarily "intrusive" in that it forces us to stop and consider what is happening, it should be an intrusion that is both integral to the work that we do as well as to the process of learning itself. Rather than an artificial or contrived mechanism for soliciting feedback, a process of assessment can be integrated into the experience of learning so that both students and faculty find it to be an essential part of what they are doing. This requires that the methods adopted for the assessment be accessible to both students and faculty—not so technical that only educational theorists are able to use and interpret them. Further, the approaches to assessment that we adopt cannot be labor intensive. Faculty in theological schools consistently report that they feel overworked and overextended; therefore, schools cannot assume that they can add a whole new layer of work—hours and hours of assessment—and expect faculty to graciously accept their part in the task at hand.

ASKING GOOD QUESTIONS

Good information about student learning is obtained by asking the right questions; good questions are the only way to get good information. Bad or misconstrued questions are not just useless; they can be counterproductive. Therefore, the instruments we use for collecting data and doing assessment need to be carefully developed. We should not collect information that cannot or will not be used. Our approach to assessment needs to be simple and accessible enough that it is clear how the information we are seeking through our questions will actually inform and, as necessary, change the way we do theological education.

Two kinds of questions need to be asked, from two different perspectives. We can and must ask questions that enable us to attend to both competency development on the one hand and the formation of dispositions on the other—always with the assumption that our academic programs are geared to both. Second, we can and must ask questions about both the final outcome—the objectives we seek—and what we have determined to be the essential elements of the program that are likely to foster that outcome. This in no way discounts the significance of the intuitive judgments and observations we make about our classes and the progress of our students. But good questions enable us to be sure that our intuitive judgments have a legitimate foundation.

I would also observe that good questions include what is going well for a student, what experiences he or she is having that are positive, encouraging, and particularly effective in advancing his or her development. The questions are not designed to encourage a round of complaining; they are meant to determine whether effective learning is happening.

Further, it is important to indicate up front how we as a faculty will respond to any negative information that arises from our enquiries. Not all criticism merits the same kind of response; some negative reactions may actually indicate that good learning is happening! And so, as questions are posed for the work of assessment, it is helpful to identify what kinds of positive and negative responses might arise and to consider in advance what each of these might mean for the work of course and program development.

Finally, when it comes to establishing the questions we will ask, we might also want to consider the following: We cannot assess or respond to everything; therefore, might we be wise to consider one aspect of our courses and programs each year and focus only on that aspect? We might even have three, four, or five critical questions that we will ask in a cycle, over the course of three to five years, all with the thought that we cannot address the whole of our programs each year, but we can agree on a critical question about which we will seek dependable information.

This suggests that it may well be that the standardized form—the same form every year for every class—is not the most effective way to solicit student commentary on courses and programs. Student evaluation forms might help an academic administrator determine that a problem exists with a particular course. But the downside is that faculty frequently see these forms as a means by which students will judge their competence to teach. And so, as often as not, they do not value the forms or view them as a means of their own learning. Conversely, if faculty could agree first on what they all as a faculty want to know about their courses and programs each year—and if an individual faculty member could, perhaps in consultation with the dean, design a form that is course specific—then the student responses could be made integral to both the course and to critical reflection about the school's academic programs.

MULTIPLE SOURCES OF INFORMATION

Our decisions about programmatic changes—curricular and cocurricular—need to be based on corroborating information from multiple sources. What we seek is to make good judgments based on good feedback from diverse perspectives of our work. Most schools recognize that good assessment weaves together a variety of sources of information—from hard data to anecdotal reports, from specific information gleaned from a student questionnaire to comments made in an alum focus group. It would seem that the schools that do this most effectively are those that build their assessment around core competencies.

Further, good assessment requires that we not only integrate the various data culled from multiple sources but also synthesize what we are learning so that we do not solve one problem and inadvertently create more problems. Our hard data must be corroborated by what we are learning anecdotally. Thus we must be patient and recognize that the perspective arising from one source of information needs to be verified by what is being heard from another source.

Finally, schools must take particular care that they do not inadvertently give greater weight to a few loud negative voices when many positive, if less insistent voices, may actually represent the majority view.

GRADING AND STUDENT EVALUATION

One of the critical factors in a program of assessment is how a school chooses to integrate its grading and evaluation system. The review and evaluation of student assignments is an essential element in educational assessment, but if it is the sole criterion for evaluating learning, it has little meaning. Alfie Kohn (2002) makes a compelling case for setting aside some of the common shibboleths about grading—particularly the assumption that grades mean little if anything because there is so much grade inflation and, conversely, that grades are a measure of how effectively a person will do in parish ministry. Grading can be an effective monitor of how well students are processing their opportunities for learning. But we must not overstate the significance of grading as a measure of what students know and how effective we are in our instruction.

Grading is most effective when it is actually done by the one teaching the class. The use of teaching assistants for grading can only, in the end, indicate if students have completed the assigned work. It cannot provide faculty with a means of hearing their students, processing their work, and considering the quality and character of their learning. Grading at its best is an exercise that requires intuitive judgments and a nuanced appreciation of student learning. Only as a faculty member does his or her own grading can he or she attend to a class of students and determine how this class is engaging the material and responding to the lectures, readings, and class discussions. Grading at its best provides an opportunity for mid-course adjustments; faculty read their student assignments and accommodate their lectures accordingly. In other words, the grades that are given midway through a semester are an indication not only of the students' learning but also of the teaching that is (or is not) happening. Thus these grades help a faculty member assess his or her own teaching and adjust how he or she is approaching the material—all with the assumption that this year's class is unique, that it is approaching this material differently, and that what the teacher is most concerned with right now is to know what learning is happening in this class.

Grading is also most effective when students have a clear appreciation of why they received the grades they received. Grading only has value as a means of assessment if it is clear to the student that the grading has been completed according to a clearly defined rubric—equally available to both the student and the teacher.

Grading is most effective when faculty appreciate the need for grading but use it only as a *secondary* means of motivation toward excellence in learning. Students will strive to learn if they care about their subject matter and experience joy in doing well.

Finally, grading is most effective when it is clear to all involved that the final assessment of a student's learning will incorporate more elements of evaluation and review, including the student's own reflection on the learning thus far. And this means that grading is always done with the goal of enabling students to be self-reflective, to monitor their own learning and study. Thus it cultivates the capacity of the student to be self-educating.

Bottom line: Grading is effective if it is not merely a measure of learning but is a means to cultivate learning for student and teacher alike.

PROGRAM AND CURRICULAR DESIGN

Schools that do effective assessment not only ask good questions and learn from the responses to those questions, but they also have found a way to incorporate their learning into the design and implementation of their academic programs. These schools have found an effective way of "closing the loop"—of appropriating insights, responding to feedback, and adjusting programs accordingly. The abiding question in assessment is not only "What data is collected?" but also "How is it used and incorporated into institutional planning?"

Good assessment leads to a responsive faculty with a responsive program and curriculum. But "responsiveness" does not mean a knee-jerk reaction or a simplistic fixing of a problem. We can and must avoid the reductionism that assumes, for example, that a deficiency can be fixed or a "gap" in the curriculum can be resolved by adding a course. We should not assume that if we have "gaps" in spirituality, we need another course on prayer; or if we have "gaps" in biblical understanding that the solution is another course on Scripture. It may be as much a matter of *how* we teach our courses as which courses we teach. Simone Weil's impassioned plea for the study of the ancient languages (1951, 66–76) is a reminder that the study of Hebrew may be as valuable for learning how to pray as any other course in the curriculum, depending on how it is taught. In the same manner, biblical literacy may be fostered as effectively by a good course on preaching as by another course in Scripture.

CONCLUSION

Assessment is not an option; we need to do it and do it well. We have no choice if we are going to be accountable for our work. As Dan Aleshire (2002) has put it, "Our choice as theological schools is to learn to do this kind of educational work grumpily because it has been externally mandated, or to learn how to do it faithfully because we care about our work, our graduates and the communities which they serve." We need to embrace this challenge as something that is both integral to our work and as something in which we actually find joy. Why? Because our work matters. But also because assessment is ultimately about learning, and there is a deep joy that comes in learning. If we do assessment well, we will find that it brings joy to our work and enables us to foster excellence in theological education.

NOTES

1. Palomba and Banta (1999, 4) define assessment as "the systematic collection, review, and use of information about educational programs undertaken for the purpose of improving student learning and development." Following Palomba and Banta, then, I am using "assessment" in this essay to speak of both the systematic collection of data and the means by which this data informs the teaching-learning process.
2. See also an earlier publication by Schon (1987).
3. All narratives cited in this book can be found in the Archives section of the Seminar's Web site: http://www.lexingtonseminar.org/.
4. Raymond Williams (2002a, 3) rightly makes the following observation: " . . . students who catch a glimmer of what it means to be a truly educated and self-educating person, and the potential that opens up for them, experience a deep joy."

References and Recommended Reading

ASSESSMENT

Angelo, Thomas A., and K. Patricia Cross. 1993. *Classroom Assessment Techniques: A Handbook for College Teachers,* 2nd ed. San Francisco: Jossey-Bass.

Banta, Trudy, and Catherine Paloma. 1999. *Assessment Essentials: Planning, Implementing, Improving.* San Francisco: Jossey-Bass.

Berquist, W. H., and J. L. Armstrong. 1986. Planning Effectively for Educational Quality: An Outcomes-Based Approach for Colleges Committed to Excellence. San Francisco: Jossey-Bass.

Bock, D. G., and E. H. Bock. 1981. *Evaluating Classroom Speaking.* Urbana: ERIC Center, Univ. of Illinois.

Centra, John A. 1993. *Reflective Faculty Evaluation.* San Francisco: Jossey-Bass.

Cross, Patricia. 1999. "What Do We Know about Students' Learning, and How Do We Know It?" *Innovative Higher Education* 23 (4): 255–70.

Diamond, Robert M. 1998. Designing and Assessing Courses and Curricula: A Practical Guide. 2nd ed. San Francisco: Jossey-Bass.

Eisner, Elliot W. 1985. The Educational Imagination: On the Design and Evaluation of School Programs. 2nd ed. New York: MacMillan.

Gardiner, Lion F., Caitlin Anderson, and Barbara L. Cambridge, eds. 1997. *Learning Through Assessment: A Resource Guide for Higher Education.* Washington, DC: American Association for Higher Education.

Greenwood, A., ed. 1994. *The National Assessment of College Student Learning: Identification of the Skills to be Taught, Learned, and Assessed.* NCES #94–286. Washington, DC: National Center for Education Statistics, U.S. Department of Education.

Jones, E. A. 1994. *Writing Goals Inventory.* University Park: National Center on Postsecondary Teaching, Learning, and Assessment, Pennsylvania State Univ.

Kaufman, R., and F. W. English. 1979. *Needs Assessment: Concept and Application.* Englewood Cliffs, NJ: Educational Technology Publications.

Kohn, Alfie. 2002. "The Dangerous Myth of Grade Inflation." *The Chronicle of Higher Education,* 8 November, B8.

Magruder, J., M. McManis, and C. Young. 1996. *The Right Idea at the Right Time: Development of a Transformational Assessment Culture.* Kirksville, MO: Office of the President, Truman State Univ.

Miller, Allen H., Bradford W. Imrie, and Kevin Cox. 1998. *Student Assessment in Higher Education: A Handbook for Assessing Performance.* London: Kogan Page.

Palomba, Catherine A., and Trudy W. Banta. 1999. *Assessment Essentials: Planning, Implementing, and Improving Assessment in Higher Education.* San Francisco: Jossey-Bass.

Pike, G. A. 1996. "The Watson-Glazer Critical Thinking Approach." *Assessment Update* (July/August).

Walvoord, B. E. and V. J. Anderson. 1998. *Effective Grading: A Tool for Learning and Assessment.* San Francisco: Jossey-Bass.

CHRISTIAN FAITH AND PRACTICE

Ahlstrom, Sydney E. 1993. *A Religious History of the American People.* New Haven, CT: Yale Univ. Press.

Bass, Dorothy C., ed. 1997. *Practicing Our Faith: A Way of Life for a Searching People.* San Francisco: Jossey-Bass.

Bass, Dorothy C. 2000. *Receiving the Day: Christian Practices for Opening the Gift of Time.* San Francisco: Jossey-Bass.

Berger, Peter L., ed. 1999. *The Desecularization of the World.* Grand Rapids: Eerdmans.

Bridston, Keith R., Fred K. Foulkes, Ann D. Myers, and Louis Weeks, eds. 1974. *Casebook on Church and Society.* Nashville: Abingdon.

Calvin, John. 1989. *Institutes of the Christian Religion: 1536 Edition.* Grand Rapids: Eerdmans and the Meeter Center for Calvin Studies.

Chittister, Joan, OSB. 1990. *Wisdom Distilled from the Daily: Living the Rule of St. Benedict Today.* San Francisco: Harper & Row.

Clark, George. 1876. *Reminiscences of Rev. Charles G. Finney.* Oberlin, OH: E. J. Goodrich.

Clarke, Andrew D. 2000. *Serve the Community of the Church; Christians as Leaders and Ministers: First-Century Christians in the Greco-Roman World.* Grand Rapids: Eerdmans.

Douglas, Crerar, ed. 1981. *The Autobiography of Augustus Hopkins Strong.* Valley Forge, PA: Judson.

Dowsett, Rosemary. "Dry Bones in the West." In *Global Missiology for the 21ˢᵗ Century,* edited by William D. Taylor. Grand Rapids: Baker.

Dykstra, Craig R. 1999. *Growing In the Life of Faith: Education and Christian Practices.* Louisville, KY: Geneva.

Engen, Charles Van. 1991. *God's Missionary People.* Grand Rapids: Baker.

Escobar, Samuel. 2000. "The Global Scenario at the Turn of the Century." In *Global Missiology for the 21ˢᵗ Century*, edited by William D. Taylor. Grand Rapids: Baker Academic, 25–46.

Finke, Roger, and Rodney Stark. 1992. *The Churching of America, 1776–1990: Winners and Losers in Our Religious Economy*. New Brunswick, NJ: Rutgers Univ. Press.

Finney, Charles Grandison. 1989. *The Memoirs of Charles G. Finney: The Complete Restored Text*, edited by Garth M. Rosell and Richard A. G. Dupuis. Grand Rapids: Academie.

González, Justo L. 1995. *When Christ Lives in Us: A Pilgrimage of Faith*. Nashville: Abingdon.

Green, Michael. 1970. *Evangelism in the Early Church*. Grand Rapids: Eerdmans.

Groome, Thomas H. 1991. *Sharing Faith*. San Francisco: Harper.

Guder, Darrel, ed. 1998. *Missional Church*. Grand Rapids: Eerdmans.

✓Harbaugh, Gary L. 1984. *The Pastor As Person*. Minneapolis: Fortress.

Hardman, Keith J. 1987. *Charles Grandison Finney*. Syracuse: Syracuse Univ. Press.

Hauerwas, Stanley, and William H. Willimon. 1989. *Resident Aliens*. Nashville: Abingdon.

Heidegger, Martin. [1972] 1996. *Being and Time*, translated by Joan Stambaugh. New York: State Univ. of New York Press.

Hick, John. 1957. *Faith and Knowledge*. Ithaca, NY: Cornell Univ. Press.

Hunsberger, George R., and Craig Van Gelder. 1996. *The Church between Gospel and Culture: The Emerging Mission in North America*. Grand Rapids: Eerdmans.

Hunter, George M., III. 2001. "The Case for Culturally Relevant Congregations." In *Global Good News*, edited by Howard Snyder. Nashville: Abingdon.

Kreider, Alan. 1995. *Worship and Evangelism in Pre-Christendom*. Cambridge: Grove.

Kreider, Alan. 1999. *The Change of Conversion and the Origin of Christendom*. Harrisburg, PA: Trinity.

Liebert, Elizabeth. 2000. *Changing Life Patterns: Adult Development in Spiritual Direction*. St. Louis: Chalice.

Machen, J. Gresham. 1923. *Christianity and Liberalism*. New York: Macmillan.

Malherbe, Abraham J. 2000. *The Letters to the Thessalonians*, AB 32B. New York: Doubleday.

Manning, Brennan. 2002. *Ruthless Trust: The Ragamuffins' Path to God*. San Francisco: Harper.

Marsden, George M. 1994. *The Soul of the American University*. New York: Oxford Univ. Press.

Marsden, George M., and Bradley J. Longfield, eds. 1992. *The Secularization of the Academy*. New York: Oxford Univ. Press.

McLoughlin, William G., ed. 1960. *Lectures on Revivals of Religion by Charles G. Finney*. Cambridge, MA: The Belknap Press of Harvard Univ. Press.

McNeill, John T., ed. 1960. *Institutes of the Christian Religion*, 2 vols., by John Calvin. Philadelphia: The Westminster Press.

Mead, Hiram. 1877. "Charles Grandison Finney." *The Congregational Quarterly*. [Boston] (January), 11.

Mehl, Roger. 1970. *Sociology of Protestantism*. Philadelphia: Westminster.

Miller, Donald E. 1997. *Reinventing American Protestantism: Christianity in the New Millennium*. Berkeley: Univ. of California Press.

Mueller-Vollmer, Kurt. 1988. *The Hermeneutics Reader: Texts of the German Tradition from the Enlightenment to the Present*. New York: Continuum.

Newbigin, Lesslie. 1986. *Foolishness to the Greeks*. Grand Rapids: Eerdmans.

Niebuhr, H. Richard, and Daniel Day Williams. 1956. *The Ministry in Historical Perspective*. San Francisco: Harper & Row.

Noll, Mark A. 1979. "Christian Thinking and the Rise of the American University." *Christian Scholars Review* 9 (1): 3–16.

Norris, Kathleen. 1998. *The Quotidian Mysteries: Laundry, Liturgy and "Women's Work."* New York: Paulist.

Orsi, Robert A. 1994. "'Have You Ever Prayed to Saint Jude?': Reflections on Fieldwork in Catholic Chicago." In *Reimagining Denominationalism*, edited by Robert Bruce Mullin and Russell E. Ritchey. New York: Oxford Univ. Press.

Palmer, Richard E. 1966. *Hermeneutics: Interpretation Theory in Schleiermacher, Dilthey, Heidegger, and Gadamer*. Evanston: IL: Northwestern Univ. Press.

Peterson, Eugene H. 1992. *Under the Unpredictable Plant: An Exploration in Vocational Holiness*. Grand Rapids: Eerdmans.

Pludemann, Jim. 2000. "Spiritual Formation." In *Evangelical Dictionary of World Missions*, edited by A. Scott Moreau. Grand Rapids: Baker.

Rice, Howard L. 1998. *The Pastor As Spiritual Guide*. Nashville: Upper Room.

Ricoeur, Paul. 1967. *The Symbolism of Evil*, translated by Emerson Buchanan. Boston: Beacon.

Ricoeur, Paul. 1989. "The Model of the Text: Meaningful Action Considered as Text." In *Hermeneutics and the Human Sciences*, edited by J. B. Thompson. New York: Cambridge Univ. Press.

Rosell, Garth M. 1993. "A Speckled Bird: Charles G. Finney's Contribution to Higher Education." *Fides et Historia* (summer), 55–74.

Russell, Bertrand. 1957. *Why I Am Not a Christian*. New York: Simon and Schuster.

Smith, D., L. E. Wolf, and T. Levitan. 1994. *Studying Diversity in Higher Education*. San Francisco: Jossey-Bass.

Stark, Rodney, and Roger Finke. 2000. *Acts of Faith: Explaining the Human Side of Religion*. Berkeley: Univ. of California Press.

Strudwick, Vincent. 2001. "A Great Christian Century to Come: But Will Our Ministry in the Church of England Be Up to It?" Lecture given at the Student and Staff Reunion of the St. Albans and Oxford Ministry Course, 14 July 2001 (Oxford: Diocesan Church House), 11–12.

Sumney, Jerry L. 1999. *"Servants of Satan," "False Brothers," and Other Opponents of Paul*, JSNTS 188. Sheffield: Sheffield Academic Press. 229–52.

Temple, William. 1976. Reprint. *Christianity and Social Order*. London: SPCK. Original edition, Harmondsworth: Penguin, 1942.

Volf, Miroslav, and Dorothy C. Bass, eds. 2002. *Practicing Theology: Beliefs and Practices in Christian Life*. Grand Rapids: Eerdmans.

Wacker, Grant. 1985. *Augustus H. Strong and the Dilemma of Historical Consciousness*. Macon, GA: Mercer Univ. Press.

Wisdom, John. 1944/45. "Gods." *The Proceedings of the Aristotelian Society*. 191–92.

Wisdom, John. 1953. *Philosophy and Psycho-Analysis*. Oxford: Oxford Univ. Press.

Curriculum

Briggs, L. J. 1970. *Handbook of Procedures for the Design of Instruction*. Pittsburgh: American Institutes for Research.

Diamond, Robert M. 1989. *Designing and Improving Courses and Curricula in Higher Education*. San Francisco: Jossey-Bass.

Grunert, Judith. 1997. *The Course Syllabus: A Learning-Centered Approach*. Bolton, MA: Anker.

Hutchings, Pat, ed. 1998. *The Course Portfolio: How Faculty Can Examine Their Teaching to Advance Practice and Improve Student Learning*. Washington, DC: American Association for Higher Education.

Kemp, J. E. 1985. *The Instructional Design Process*. New York: HarperCollins.

Kemp, J. E. 1995. *Designing Effective Instruction*. Upper Saddle River, NJ: Prentice-Hall.

Lowman, Joseph. 1995. "Planning Course Content and Teaching Techniques to Maximize Interest." In *Mastering the Techniques of Teaching*. 2nd ed. San Francisco: Jossey-Bass.

Lowman, Joseph. 1996. "Assignments that Promote and Integrate Learning." In *Teaching on Solid Ground: Using Scholarship to Improve Practice*, edited by Robert J. Menges, Maryellen Weimer et al. San Francisco: Jossey-Bass.

Lunde, J. P., ed. 1995. *Reshaping Curricula: Revitalization Programs at Three Land Grant Universities*. Bolton, MA: Anker.

Mager, R. F. 1975. *Preparing Instructional Objectives*. Belmont, CA: Fearon.

McKeachie, Wilbert. 1999. "Countdown for Course Preparation." In *Teaching Tips: Strategies, Research, and Theory for College and University Teachers*. 10th ed. Boston and New York: Houghton Mifflin.

Molenda, M., J. Pershing, and C. Reigeluth. 1996. *Designing Instructional Systems: Training and Development Handbook*. 4th ed. Alexandria, VA: American Society for Training and Development.

Parkay, Forrest W., ed. 1999. *Curriculum Planning: A Contemporary Approach*. London: Allyn and Bacon.

Popham, W. J., and E. L. Baker. 1970. *Establishing Instructional Goals*. Upper Saddle River, NJ: Prentice Hall.

Project Advance. 1995. *Planning Your Course Resource Manual*. Syracuse: Syracuse Univ. Center for Instructional Development.

Ramsden, Paul. 1992. "The Goals and Structure of a Course." In *Learning to Teach in Higher Education*. London and New York: Routledge.

Schoenfeld, A. Clay, and Robert Magnan. 1994a. "Choosing Materials." In *Mentor in a Manual: Climbing the Academic Ladder to Tenure*. 2nd ed. Madison, WI: Atwood.

Schoenfeld, A. Clay, and Robert Magnan. 1994b. "Creating a New Course." In *Mentor in a Manual: Climbing the Academic Ladder to Tenure*. 2nd ed. Madison, WI: Atwood.

Schoenfeld, A. Clay, and Robert Magnan. 1994c. "Your Course Outline." In *Mentor in a Manual: Climbing the Academic Ladder to Tenure*. 2nd ed. Madison, WI: Atwood.

Sigsbee, D. L., B. Speck, et al., eds. 1997. *Approaches to Teaching Non-Native English Speakers across the Curriculum*. San Francisco: Jossey-Bass.

Smith, P. L., and T. J. Ragan. 1993. *Instructional Design*. Upper Saddle River, NJ: Prentice Hall.

Tanner, David, and Laurel N. Tanner. 1994. *Curriculum Development: Theory into Practice*. Upper Saddle River, NJ: Prentice Hall.

EDUCATION, GENERAL

American Association for Higher Education (AAHE), American College Personnel Association and National Association of Student Personnel Administrators. 1998. "Powerful Partnerships: A Shared Responsibility for Learning." <http://www.aahe.org/teaching/tsk_frce.htm>. (Accessed August 4, 2003).

American Council on Education (ACE). 1996. "Guiding Principles for Distance Learning in a Learning Society." <http://www.acenet.edu/calec/dist_learning/dl_principlesIntro.cfm>. (Accessed August 4, 2003).

Barr, Robert B., and John Tagg. 1995. "From Teaching to Learning: A New Paradigm for Undergraduate Education." *Change* 27: 1–25. <http://critical.tamucc.edu/~blalock/readings/tch2learn.htm>. (Accessed August 4, 2003).

Blackwell, Antoinette Brown. Oberlin College Archives, General Files, Box no. 12, 2.

Bloom, B. S., et al. 1956. *Taxonomy of Educational Objectives*. New York: McKay.

Brown, A. L., D. Ash, M. Rutherford, K. Nakagawa, A. Gordon, and J. C. Campione. 1993. *Distributed Cognitions: Psychological and Educational Considerations*. Cambridge: Cambridge Univ. Press.

Christensen, C. Roland, David A. Garvin, and Ann Sweet, eds. 1991. *Education for Judgment: The Artistry of Discussion Leadership*. Boston: Harvard Business School Press.

Fletcher, Robert Samuel. 1943. *A History of Oberlin College*, 2 vols. Oberlin, OH: Oberlin College.

Fuller, Timothy. 1989. Introduction to *The Voice of Liberal Learning: Michael Oakeshott on Education*, edited by Timothy Fuller. New Haven: Yale Univ. Press.

Gagne, Robert M. 1987. *Instructional Technology*. Hillsdale, NJ: Lawrence Erlbaum.

Hansen, Eduard, and James A. Stephens. "The Ethics of Learner-Centered Education: Dynamics That Impede the Process." *Change* 2000 (Oct): 41–47.

hooks, bell. 1994. *Teaching to Transgress: Education as the Practice of Freedom*. New York: Routledge.

Institute for Higher Education Policy (IHEP). 1999. "What's the Difference? A Review of Contemporary Research on the Effectiveness of Distance Learning in Higher Education." <http://www.ihep.com/Pubs/PDF/Difference.pdf>. (Accessed August 4, 2003).

Institute for Higher Education Policy (IHEP). 2000. "Quality On the Line: Benchmarks for Success in Internet-Based Distance Education." <http://www.ihep.com/Pubs/PDF/Quality.pdf>. (Accessed August 4, 2003).

Jacoby, Barbara. 1996. *Service-Learning in Higher Education: Concepts and Practices*. San Francisco: Jossey-Bass.

Journal of Scholarship of Teaching and Learning. <http://www.iusb.edu/~josotl>. (Accessed August 4, 2003).

Kassop, Mark. 2003. "Ten Ways Online Education Matches, or Surpasses, Face-to-Face Learning." *The Technology Source* (May/June) (online edition). <http://ts.mivu.org/default.asp?show=article&id=1059>. (Accessed August 4, 2003).

Keller, J. M. 1978. *Practitioner's Guide to Concepts and Measures of Motivation*. Syracuse: School of Education, Syracuse Univ.

Knefelkamp, L. Lee. 1990. "Seasons of Academic Life." *Liberal Education* 76 (3): 4–12.

Krathwohl, D. R., B. S. Bloom, and B. B. Masia. 1964. *Taxonomy of Educational Objectives: The Classification of Education Goals*. New York: McKay.

Kurfiss, J. G. 1988. *Critical Thinking: Theory, Research, Practice and Possibilities*. Washington, DC: ASHE-ERIC Higher Education Report #2, Association for the Study of Higher Education.

Kvavik, Robert B., and Michael N. Handberg. 2000. "Transforming Student Services." *Educause Quarterly* 23:2 (online edition). <http://www.educause.edu/ir/library/pdf/eq/a002/eqm0022.pdf>. (Accessed August 4, 2003).

Lucas, Christopher. 1992. *American Higher Education: A History*. New York: St. Martin's, 173.

Mapp, Karen L., and Susan Moore Johnson. 1997. Working Paper on Diversity at the Harvard Graduate School of Education. Cambridge, MA: Harvard Graduate School of Education.

McLaren, Peter. 1999. "A Pedagogy of Possibility: Reflecting Upon Paulo Friere's Politics of Education." *Research and Comments* (March).

Miller, Richard E. 1998. *As if Learning Mattered*. Ithaca, NY: Cornell Univ. Press.

Nakkula, Michael J., and Sharon M. Ravitch. 1998. *Matters of Interpretation: Reciprocal Transformation in the Therapeutic and Developmental Relationships with Youth*. San Francisco: Jossey-Bass.

National Institute of Education. 1984. *Involvement in Learning: Realizing the Potential of American Higher Education*. Washington, DC: National Institute of Education.

National Service Learning Clearinghouse. <http://www.servicelearning.org>. (Accessed August 4, 2003).

Noble, David. 1998. "Digital Diploma Mills: The Automation of Higher Education." *First Monday* 3 (1). <http://www.firstmonday.dk/issues/issue3_1/noble/index.html>. (Accessed August 4, 2003).

Noble, David, Ben Shneiderman, Richard Herman, Phil Agre, and Peter J. Denning. 1998. "Technology in Education: The Fight for the Future." *Educom Review* 33:3 (online edition). <http://www.educause.edu/pub/er/review/reviewArticles/33322.html>. (Accessed August 4, 2003).

Oakeshott, Michael. 1989. *The Voice of Liberal Learning: Michael Oakeshott on Education*, edited by Timothy Fuller. New Haven: Yale Univ. Press.

Regional Accrediting Commissions. 2000. "Best Practices for Electronically Offered Degree and Certificate Programs." <http://www.ncahigherlearningcommission.org/resources/electronic_degrees/index.html>. (Accessed August 4, 2003).

Ringenberg, William C. 1984. *The Christian College*. Grand Rapids: Eerdmans.

Senge, Peter M. 1990. *The Fifth Discipline: The Art and Practice of the Learning Organization*. New York: Doubleday.

Senge, Peter M. 2000. *Schools That Learn: A Fifth Discipline Fieldbook for Educators, Parents, and Everyone Who Cares About Education*. New York: Doubleday.

Stanton, Timothy K., Dwight E. Giles Jr., and Nadinne I. Cruz. 1999. *Service-Learning: A Movement's Pioneers Reflect on Its Origins, Practice, and Future*. San Francisco: Jossey-Bass.

Tagg, John. 2003. *The Learning Paradigm College*. Bolton, MA: Anker.

Terenzini, Patrick T. 1999. "Research and Practice in Undergraduate Education: And Never the Twain Shall Meet?" *Higher Education* 38: 33–48.

The Woman's Journal 21, no. 49 (December 6, 1890): 385.

Veysey, Laurence. *The Emergence of the American University.* 1965. Chicago: Univ. of Chicago Press.

W. K. Kellogg Foundation. 2000. "How Service Works." <http://www.wkkf.org/Pubs/PhilVol/Pub556.pdf>. (Accessed August 4, 2003).

MISCELLANEOUS TOPICS

Berry, Wendell. 1972. *A Continuous Harmony: Essays Cultural and Agricultural.* New York: Harcourt Brace and Jovanovich, Inc.

Block, Peter. 2002. *The Answer to How Is Yes: Acting on What Matters.* San Francisco: Berrett-Koehler.

Emerson, Robert M. 2001. "Fieldwork Practice: Issues in Participant Observation." In *Contemporary Field Research.* Los Angeles: Univ. of California Press.

Evans, Philip, and Thomas S. Wurster. 1999. *Blown to Bits: How the New Economics of Information Transforms Strategy.* Cambridge, MA: Harvard Business School Press.

Flew, A. G. N., ed. 1951. *Logic and Language.* Oxford: Oxford Univ. Press.

Gergen, Kenneth J. 1980. "If Persons Are Texts." In *Hermeneutics and Psychological Theory, and Psychopathology*, edited by S. B. Messmer, L. A. Sass, and R. L. Woolfolk. New Brunswick: NJ: Rutgers Univ. Press.

Greene, Maxine. 1995. *Releasing the Imagination: Essays on Education, the Arts, and Social Change.* San Francisco: Jossey-Bass.

Grudin, Robert. 1982. *Time and the Art of Living.* New York: Ticknor and Fields.

Hadot, Pierre. 2002. *What Is Ancient Philosophy?* Translated by Michael Chose. Cambridge: Harvard Univ. Press.

Heifetz, Ronald A., and Marty Linsky. 2002. *Leadership on the Line: Staying Alive through the Dangers of Leading.* Boston: Harvard Business School Press.

Kuhn, Thomas S. 1962. *The Structure of Scientific Revolutions.* Chicago: Univ. of Chicago Press.

Larsen, Jens Peter. 1972. *Handel's Messiah: Origin, Composition, and Sources.* New York: Norton.

Lorde, Audrey. 1980. *The Cancer Journals.* San Francisco: Spinsters Ink.

Miller, Sue. 2003. *The Story of My Father: A Memoir.* New York: Knopf.

Pregent, Richard. 1994. *Charting Your Course.* Madison, WI: Magna.

SOCIAL AND CULTURAL ISSUES

Cairns, Susan. 1990. "The Son of Man and God the Father: The Social Gospel and Victorian Masculinity," in *Meanings for Manhood: Constructions of Masculinity in Victorian America,* edited by Mark C. Carnes and Clyde Griffen. Chicago: Univ. of Chicago Press.

Chomsky, Noam. 1989. *Necessary Illusions: Thought Control in Democratic Societies.* Boston: South End.

Cross, William E., Jr., Linda Strauss, and Peony Fhagen-Smith. 1999. "African American Identity Development Across the Life Span: Educational Implications." In *Racial and Ethnic*

Identity in School Practices, edited by R. Sheets and E. Hollins. Mahwah, NJ: Lawrence Erlbaum Associates, 29–47.

Drucker, Peter F. 1994. "The Age of Social Transformation." *The Atlantic Monthly* (November): 73.

DuBois, W. E. B. [1903] 1996. *Souls of Black Folk: Essays and Sketches.* New York: Modern Library.

Eck, Diana L., and Devaki Jain. 1987. *Speaking of Faith: Global Perspectives on Women, Religion, and Social Change.* Philadelphia: New Society.

Engineer, Asghar Ali. 1990. *Islam and Liberation Theology: Essays on Liberative Elements in Islam.* New Delhi: Sterling.

Foulke, Mary. 1996. "Coming Out as White/Becoming White: Racial Identity Development as a Spiritual Journey." *Theology & Sexuality: The Journal for the Study of Christianity and Sexuality,* no. 5 (September): 22–36,

Gilligan, Carol. 1993. *In a Different Voice: Psychological Theory and Women's Development.* Cambridge, MA: Harvard Univ. Press.

Guinier, Lani. 1998. *Life Every Voice: Turning a Civil Rights Setback into a New Vision of Social Justice.* New York: Simon & Schuster.

Gutiérrez, Gustavo. 1988. *A Theology of Liberation: History, Politics, and Salvation.* New York: Orbis.

Hall, Peter Dobkin. 1982. *The Organization of American Culture, 1700–1900 : Private Institutions, Elites, and the Origins of American Nationality.* New York: New York Univ. Press.

Jacobson, Matthew Frye. 1998. *Whiteness of a Different Color: European Immigrants and the Alchemy of Race.* Cambridge, MA: Harvard Univ. Press.

Jenkins, C. A., and D. L. Gainer "Common Instructional Problems in the Multicultural Classroom." *Journal on Excellence in College Teaching* 2: 77–88.

Lind, Robin. 2002. "E-mail: Boon or Burden?" *In Trust* 13 (3): 22–23.

Mangabeira, Roberto, and Cornel West. 1998. *The Future of American Progressivism.* Boston: Beacon.

Putnam, Robert D. 2000. *Bowling Alone: The Collapse and Revival of American Community.* New York: Simon & Schuster.

Report of the American Commitments Project. 1995. *The Drama of Diversity and Democracy: Higher Education and American Commitments.* Washington, DC: Association of American Colleges and Universities.

Said, Edward. 1991. "Reflections on Exile." In *Marginalization and Contemporary Cultures,* edited by Russell Ferguson et al. Cambridge, MA: MIT Press.

Said, Edward. 1994. *Orientalism.* New York: Vintage.

Schor, Juliet B. 1992. *The Overworked American: The Unexpected Decline of Leisure.* New York: Basic.

Smith, D. 1989. *The Challenge of Diversity: Involvement or Alienation in the Classroom.* Washington, DC: The George Washington Univ.

Spencer, Stephen. 2001. *William Temple: A Calling to Prophecy.* London: SPCK.

Stafford, Tim. 1999. "The Criminologist Who Discovered Churches." *Christianity Today* (June 14): 35–39.

Steele, Claude M. 1992. "Race and the Schooling of Black Americans." *Atlantic* 269 (4): 68–78.

Steele, Claude M. 1995. "Stereotype Threat and the Intellectual Test Performance of African Americans." *Journal of Personality and Social Psychology* 69 (5): 797–811.

Steele, Shelby. 2002. "The Age of White Guilt: And the Disappearance of the Black Individual." *Harper's Magazine*, November.

Thich Nhat Hanh. 1992. *Touching Peace*. Berkley: Parallax Press.

Ware, Vron, and Les Back. 2002. *Out of Whiteness: Color, Politics and Culture*. Chicago: Univ. of Chicago Press.

Ware, Vron. 1992. *Beyond the Pale. White Women, Racism and History*. New York and London: Verso.

Watts, Craig. 2001. "Living with Diversity: Romans 14:1–9." *Preaching* 16: 35–37.

West, Cornel. 1993a. *Prophetic Reflections: Notes on Race and Power in America*. Monroe, ME: Common Courage.

West, Cornel. 1993b. *Race Matters*. Boston: Beacon.

West, Cornel. 1993c. *Beyond Eurocentrism and Multiculturalism*. Monroe, ME: Common Courage.

West, Cornel. 1999. "Christian Love and Heterosexism." In *The Cornel West Reader*. Edited by Cornel West. New York: Basic.

West, Cornel, and bell hooks. 1991. *Breaking Bread: Insurgent Black Intellectual Life*. Boston: South End.

West, Cornel, and Michael Lerner. 1996. *Jews and Blacks: A Dialogue on Race, Religion, and Culture*. New York: Plume.

Williams, Patricia J. 1997. *Seeing a Color-Blind Future: The Paradox of Race*. In The 1997 Reith Lectures. London: Virago.

Wlodkowski, R. J., and M. B. Ginsberg. 1995. *Diversity and Motivation: Culturally Responsive Teaching*. San Francisco: Jossey-Bass.

STUDENTS

Baxter Magolda, Marcia B. 1992. *Knowing and Reasoning in College: Gender-Related Patterns in Students' Intellectual Development*. San Francisco: Jossey-Bass.

Belenky, M. F., B. M. Clinchy, N. R. Goldberger, and J. M. Tarule. 1986. *Women's Ways of Knowing: The Development of Self, Voice, and Mind*. New York: Basic.

Bloom, F. E., A. Lazerson, and C. A. Nelson. 2001. *Brain, Mind, and Behavior*. 3rd ed. New York: Freeman.

Chickering, Arthur W. [1969] 1993. *Education and Identity*, 2nd ed. San Francisco: Jossey-Bass.

Clark, M. Carolyn. 2000. *An Update on Adult Development Theory*. San Francisco: Jossey-Bass.

Colomb, Gregory. 1988. "Where Should Students Start Writing in the Disciplines?" Paper presented at the Annual Meeting of the Conference on College Composition and Communication. Georgia: ERIC Document Reproduction Service, ED297341.

Gardner, Howard. 1983. *Frames of Mind: The Theory of Multiple Intelligences*. New York: Basic.

Gardner, Howard. 1993. *Multiple Intelligences: The Theory in Practice*. New York: Basic.

Gardner, Howard. 1999. *Intelligence Reframed: Multiple Intelligences for the 21st Century*. New York: Basic.

Gregorc, Anthony F. 1998. *Mind Styles Model: Theory, Principles and Applications.* Gregorc Associates.

King, Patricia M., and Karen Strohm Kitchener. 1994. *Developing Reflective Judgment: Understanding and Promoting Intellectual Growth and Critical Thinking in Adolescents and Adults.* San Francisco: Jossey-Bass.

Kolb, David A. 1984. *Experiential Learning: Experience as the Source of Learning and Development.* Englewood Cliffs, N.J.: Prentice-Hall.

Light, Richard J. 1990. *Explorations with Students and Faculty about Teaching, Learning, and Student Life.* The Harvard Assessment Seminars, 1st report. Cambridge, MA: Harvard Univ. Graduate School of Education and Kennedy School of Government.

Merriam, Sharan B., and Rosemary S. Caffarella. 1998. *Learning in Adulthood: A Comprehensive Guide,* 2nd ed. San Francisco: Jossey-Bass.

Perry, W. G. 1970. *Forms of Intellectual and Ethical Development in the College Years: A Scheme.* New York: Holt, Rinehart and Winston.

Schmeck, Ronald R., ed. 1988. *Learning Strategies and Learning Styles.* New York: Plenum.

Smith, Donna M., and David A. Kolb. 1986. *The User's Guide for the Learning-Style Inventory: A Manual for Teachers and Trainers.* Boston, MA: McBer.

Sousa, David A. 2001. *How the Brain Learns: A Classroom Teacher's Guide,* 2nd ed. Thousand Oaks, CA: Corwin.

Sue, D. W., and D. Sue. 1990. *Counseling the Culturally Different: Theory and Practice,* 2d ed. New York: Wiley.

Treisman, Uri. 1992. "Studying Students Studying Calculus: A Look at the Lives of Minority Mathematics Students in College." *College Mathematics Journal* 23 (5): 362–72.

TEACHING AND LEARNING

Allen, L. R. 1996. "An Instructional Epiphany." *Change* (March/April).

Angelo, Thomas. A. 1993. *A Teacher's Dozen: 14 Useful Findings from Research on Higher Education.* Washington, DC: Phase II Classroom Research Project, American Association of Higher Education.

Astin, A. 1991. *The American College Teacher.* Los Angeles: Higher Education Research Institute, Graduate School of Education and Information Studies, Univ. of California, Los Angeles.

Barnes, Linda L. 1999. *Variations on a Teaching/Learning Workshop: Pedagogy and Faculty Development in Religious Studies.* Athens, GA: Scholars Press.

Bean, J. C. 1996. *Engaging Ideas: A Professor's Guide to Integrating Writing, Critical Thinking, and Active Learning in the Classroom.* San Francisco: Jossey-Bass.

Bess, James L. 2000. *Teaching Alone, Teaching Together: Transforming the Structure of Teams for Teaching.* San Francisco: Jossey Bass.

Boice, R. 1996. *First-Order Principles for College Teachers: Ten Basic Ways to Improve the Teaching Process.* Bolton, MA: Anker.

Booth, Wayne C. 1988. *The Vocation of a Teacher: Rhetorical Occasions 1967–1988.* Chicago: Univ. of Chicago Press.

Boyer, Ernest L. 1997 [1990]. *Scholarship Reconsidered: Priorities of the Professoriate.* San Francisco: Jossey-Bass.

Brookfield, Stephen D. 1995. *Becoming a Critically Reflective Teacher*. San Francisco: Jossey-Bass.

Brookfield, Stephen D. 2000. *The Skillful Teacher: On Technique, Trust and Responsiveness in the Classroom*. San Francisco: Jossey Bass.

Brookfield, Stephen D., and Stephen Preskill. 1999. *Discussion as a Way of Teaching: Tools and Techniques for Democratic Classrooms*. San Francisco: Jossey-Bass.

Carnegie Foundation for the Advancement of Teaching. <http://www.carnegiefoundation.org/>. (Accessed August 4, 2003).

Chickering, Arthur W., and Zelda F. Gamson. 1998. "Seven Principles for Good Practice in Undergraduate Education." In *Teaching and Learning in the College Classroom*, 2nd ed. ASHE Reader Series. Edited by Kenneth Feldman and Michael Paulsen. Needham Heights, MA: Simon and Schuster Custom Publishing, 543–49. Reprinted from *AAHE Bulletin*. March 1987.

Chickering, Arthur W., Zelda F. Gamson, and L. M. Barsi. 1989. *Seven Principles for Good Practice in Undergraduate Education*. Milwaukee: Winona State Univ.

Christensen, Norman L. 1995. "The Nuts and Bolts of Running a Lecture Course." In *The Academic's Handbook*, edited by Leigh DeNeef and Craufurd Goodwin. 2nd ed. Durham, NC, and London: Duke Univ. Press.

Collison, George, Bonnie Elbaum, Sarah Haavind, and Robert Tinker. 2000. *Facilitating Online Learning: Effective Strategies for Moderators*. Madison, WI: Atwood.

Cross, Patricia, and Mimi Harris Steadman. 1993. *Classroom Research: Implementing the Scholarship of Teaching*. San Francisco: Jossey-Bass.

Daloz, Laurent A. Parks, et al. 1996. *Common Fire: Lives of Commitment in a Complex World*. Boston: Beacon.

Davis, Barbara Gross. 1993a. "Preparing or Revising a Course." In *Tools for Teaching*. San Francisco: Jossey-Bass.

Davis, Barbara Gross. 1993b. "The Course Syllabus." In *Tools for Teaching*. San Francisco: Jossey-Bass.

Davis, Barbara Gross. 1993c. *Tools for Teaching*. San Francisco: Jossey-Bass.

Davis, J. R. 1993. *Better Teaching, More Learning: Strategies for Success in Postsecondary Education*. Phoenix: Oryx.

Dick, Walter, and Lou Carey. 1985. *The Systematic Design of Instruction*. Glenview, IL: Scott, Foresman.

Eble, Kenneth E. 1988. *The Craft of Teaching*. 2nd ed. San Francisco: Jossey-Bass.

Edgerton, R., P. Hutchings, et al. 1993. *The Teaching Portfolio: Capturing the Scholarship in Teaching*. Washington, DC: American Association for Higher Education.

Erickson, Stanford C. 1988. "Decisions about Course Content." In *The Essence of Good Teaching*. San Francisco: Jossey-Bass.

Frederick, P. 1981. "The Dreaded Discussion: Ten Ways to Start." *Improving College Teaching* 29 (3): 109–14.

Frederick, P. 1995. "Walking On Eggs: Mastering the Dreaded Diversity Discussion." *College Teaching* 43 (3): 83–92.

Gardiner, Lion F. 1994. *Redesigning Higher Education: Producing Dramatic Gains in Student Learning*. Washington, DC: Graduate School of Education and Human Development, George Washington Univ.

Gerlach, V. S., and D. P. Ely. 1980. *Teaching and Media: A Systematic Approach*. 2nd ed. Upper Saddle River, NJ: Prentice Hall.

Graham, Charles, Kursat Cagiltay, Byung-Ro Lim, Joni Craner, and Thomas M. Duffy. 2000. "Teaching in a Web Based Distance Learning Environment: An Evaluation Summary Based on Four Courses." <http://crlt.indiana.edu/publications/crlt00–13.pdf>. (Accessed August 4, 2003).

Graham, Charles, Kursat Cagiltay, Byung-Ro Lim, Joni Craner, and Thomas M. Duffy. 2001. "Seven Principles of Effective Teaching: A Practical Lens for Evaluating Online Courses." The Technology Source (March/April). <http://horizon.unc.edu/TS/default.asp?show=article&id=839>. (Accessed August 4, 2003).

Halpern, D. F., et al. 1994. *Changing College Classrooms: New Teaching and Learning Strategies for an Increasingly Complex World*. San Francisco: Jossey-Bass.

Hannun, W. H., and L. J. Briggs. 1980. *How Does Instructional Systems Design Differ from Traditional Instruction?* Chapel Hill: School of Education, Univ. of North Carolina.

Hutchings, Pat. 1996. *Making Teaching Community Property: A Menu for Peer Collaboration and Peer Review*. Washington, DC: American Association for Higher Education.

Hutchings, Pat, ed. 2000. *Opening Lines: Approaches to the Scholarship of Teaching and Learning*. Menlo Park, CA: Carnegie Foundation for the Advancement of Teaching.

Hutchings, Pat, ed. 2002. *Ethics of Inquiry: Issues in the Scholarship of Teaching and Learning*. Menlo Park, CA: The Carnegie Foundation for the Advancement of Teaching. <http://www.carnegiefoundation.org/elibrary/docs/bibliography.htm>

Hutchings, Pat, and Marcia Babb. 2002. *The Scholarship of Teaching in Higher Education: An Annotated Bibliography*. Menlo Park, CA: The Carnegie Foundation for the Advancement of Teaching. <http://www.carnegiefoundation.org/CASTL/index.htm>

Hutchings, Pat, Chris Bjork, and Marcia Babb. 2002. "An Annotated Bibliography of the Scholarship of Teaching and Learning in Higher Education." <http://www.carnegiefoundation.org/elibrary/docs/CASTL_Bibliography.pdf>. (Accessed August 4, 2003).

Jenrette, M. S., and V. Napoli. 1994. *The Teaching/Learning Enterprise: Miami-Dade Community College's Blueprint for Change*. Bolton, MA: Anker.

Kraft, Robert G. 1998. "Group Inquiry Turns Passive Students Active." In *Teaching College: Collected Readings for the New Instructor*, edited by Maryellen Weimer and Rose Ann Neff. Madison, WI: Atwood. First published in 1985 in *College Teaching* 33 (4): 149–54.

Matthews, Roberta S. 1996. "Collaborative Learning: Creating Knowledge with Students." In *Teaching on Solid Ground: Using Scholarship to Improve Practice*, edited by Robert J. Menges, Maryellen Weimer, et al. (San Francisco: Jossey-Bass.

Mazur, Eric. 1997. *Peer Instruction: A User's Manual*. Upper Saddle River, NJ: Prentice Hall.

Merriam, Sharan B., ed. 2001. *The New Update on Adult Learning Theory*. San Francisco: Jossey-Bass.

Milton, O. 1978. *On College Teaching: A Guide to Contemporary Practices*. San Francisco: Jossey-Bass.

Mosteller, Frederick. 1989. "The 'Muddiest Point in the Lecture' as a Feedback Device." *On Teaching and Learning* 3: 10–21.

Nysse, Richard W. 1998. "Technology and the Classroom: Inevitable and Better." *Word & World* 18 (4): 419, 421. [Draft Version. <http://www.luthersem.edu/rnysse/TechnologyAndThe Classroom.htm>. (Accessed August 4, 2003).]

O'Reilley, Mary Rose. 1998. *Radical Presence: Teaching As Contemplative Practice*. Montclair: Boynton/Cook.

Palmer, Parker. 1993. *To Know As We Are Known: Education as a Spiritual Journey*. San Francisco: Harper & Row.

Palmer, Parker. 1997. *The Courage to Teach: Exploring the Inner Landscape of a Teacher's Life*. San Francisco: Jossey-Bass.

Palmer, Parker. 2000. *Let Your Life Speak: Listening for the Voice of Vocation*. San Francisco: Jossey-Bass.

Parks, S. D. 2000. *Big Questions, Worthy Dreams: Mentoring Young Adults in Their Search for Meaning, Purpose, and Faith*. San Francisco: Jossey-Bass.

Rice, R. Eugene. 1990. "Rethinking What It Means to Be a Scholar." *Teaching Excellence* (winter/spring): 1–2.

Rosell, Garth M. 1978. *Classroom Observation Form*. Published by the Case Study Institute and distributed by the Intercollegiate Case Clearing House, Cambridge, MA.

Rosenthal, Robert, and Lenore Jacobson. 1992. *Pygmalion in the Classroom: Teacher Expectation and Pupils' Intellectual Development*. New York: Irvington.

Salmon, Gilly. 2000. *E-Moderating: The Key to Teaching and Learning Online*. London: Kogan Page.

Schon, D. A. 1987. *Educating the Reflective Practitioner: Toward a New Design for Teaching and Learning in the Professions*. San Francisco: Jossey-Bass.

Schwehn, M. R. 2000. *Everyone a Teacher*. Notre Dame, IN: Univ. of Notre Dame Press.

Seldin, P. 1997. *The Teaching Portfolio: A Practical Guide to Improved Performance and Promotion/Tenure Decision*. Bolton, MA: Anker.

Seldin, P., and L. Annis. 1991/92. "The Teaching Portfolio." *Teaching Excellence* 3(2): 1–2.

Shulman, Lee S. 1989. "Toward a Pedagogy of Substance." *American Association for Higher Education Bulletin* 41 (June): 8–13.

Shulman, Lee S. 1993. "Teaching as Community Property: Putting an End to Pedagogical Solitude." *Change* (November/December): 6–7.

Shulman, Lee S. 2004. *Teaching as Community Property: Essays in Higher Education*. San Francisco: Jossey-Bass.

Shulman, Lee S., and Pat Hutchings. 1999. "The Scholarship of Teaching." *Change* (September/October): 10–15.

Stark, J. S., M. A. Lowther, and B. M. K. Haggerty. 1987. *Responsive Professional Education: Balancing Outcomes and Opportunities*. ASHE-ERIC Higher Education Report, no. 3. Washington, DC: Association for the Study of Higher Education.

Walsh, J. (2000). "The Keystone Project and the Effectiveness of Teaching in our Seminaries." *Seminary Journal* 6 (1): 8–17.

Weimer, Maryellen. 1993. *Improving Your Classroom Teaching*. Survival Skills for Scholars, no. 1. Newbury Park, CA: Sage.

Weimer, Maryellen. 2002. *Learner-Centered Teaching: Five Key Changes to Practice*. San Francisco: Jossey-Bass.

Weimer, Maryellen, and Joan Parret. 1988. *How Am I Teaching?* Madison, WI: Magna.

Winkelmes, M. A., and J. Wilkinson, eds. 2001. *Voices of Experience: Reflections from a Harvard Teaching Seminar*. New York: Peter Lang.

Wittich, W., and C. Schuller. 1979. *Instructional Technology: Its Nature and Use*. 6th ed. New York: HarperCollins.

Wolfe, Pat. 2001. *Brain Matters: Translating Research into Classroom Practice*. Alexandria, VA: Association for Supervision and Curriculum Development.

Wright, W. A., et al. 1995. *Teaching Improvement Practices: Successful Strategies for Higher Education*. Bolton, MA: Anker.

Zull, James E. 2002. *The Art of Changing the Brain: Enriching Teaching by Exploring the Biology of Learning*. Sterling, VA: Stylus.

THEOLOGICAL EDUCATION

Aleshire, Daniel. 2002a. "Character and Assessment of Learning for Religious Vocation." Presentation at a conference sponsored by the Association of Theological Schools, Pittsburgh, November 1–3. <http://www.ats.edu/programs/leader/leader/papers/aleshire/aleshir3.htm>

Aleshire, Daniel. 2002b. "Top Job? Make Friends, Raise Money," *In Trust* 13 (2): 24–25.

Amos, Katherine E., ed. 1999. *Theological Education* 36 (1). Issue Focus: "Educational Technology and Distance Education: Educational Issues and Implications for Theological Education."

Association of Theological Schools. *ATS Degree Program Standards*. http://www.ats.edu/accredit/degstand.rtf.

Association of Theological Schools. *ATS General Standards*. http://www.ats.edu/publicat/publitoc.html.

Baillie, John. 1939. "The Theological Course as a Preparation." *The International Review of Missions* 28: 535–48.

Bainton, Roland. 1957. *Yale and the Ministry*. New Haven: Yale Univ. Press.

Banks, Robert. 1999. *Reenvisioning Theological Education*. Grand Rapids: Eerdmans.

Beardslee, William A. 1966. "The Background of the Lilly Endowment Study of Preseminary Education." *The Journal of Bible and Religion: Theological Education Number* 34 (2).

Bellinger, Charles. 2003. "Theological Education and Distance Learning: A Working Bibliography." <http://libnt2.lib.tcu.edu/staff/bellinger/theo_distance_bib.htm>. (Accessed August 4, 2003)

Berling, J. A. 1991. "Issues in Achieving Pluralism in Faculty Development: The Challenge and Opportunity of Inclusivity." *Theological Education* 28 (3): 47–57.

Briggs, Kenneth. 2002a. "Looking for Leaders." *In Trust* 13 (4): 8–12.

Briggs, Kenneth. 2002b. "The Churches Drift Away." *In Trust* 13 (2): 6–9.

Brown, William Adams. 1920. "The Responsibility of the University for the Teaching of Religion." *Yale Divinity Quarterly*, 16 (4): 152.

Brown, William Adams. 1938. *The Case for Theology in the University*. Chicago: Univ. of Chicago.

Browning, Don S., ed. 1983. *Practical Theology: The Emerging Field in Theology, Church, and World*. San Francisco: Harper and Row.

Browning, Don. 1995. "The Nature and Criteria of Theological Scholarship." *Theological Education* 32 (1): 1–11.

Calahan, Kathleen A. 2003. *Projects That Matter: Successful Planning & Evaluation for Religious Organizations*. Bethesda, MD: The Alban Institute.

Chopp, Rebecca. 1995. *Saving Work: Feminist Practices of Theological Education*. Louisville, KY: Westminster/John Knox.

Dykstra, Craig. R. 1991. "Reconceiving Practice in Theological Inquiry and Education." In *Shifting Boundaries*, edited by Barbara Wheeler and Edward Farley. Louisville, KY: Westminster/John Knox.

Farley, Edward. 1983. *Theologia: The Fragmentation and Unity of Theological Education*. Philadelphia: Fortress.

Farley, Edward. 1988. *The Fragility of Knowledge: Theological Education in the Church and the University*. Philadelphia: Fortress.

Fisch, Thomas, ed. 1990. *Liturgy and Tradition: Theological Reflections of Alexander Schmemann*. Crestwood, NY: St. Vladimir's Seminary Press.

Fletcher, John. 1980. "Beyond Survival: The Coming Crisis for Theological Seminaries." *Alban Institute Action Information* (November/December): 6–10.

Fletcher, John. 1983. *The Futures of Protestant Seminaries*. Washington, DC: The Alban Institute.

Foster, Frank Hugh. 1888. *The Seminary Method*. New York: Scribners.

Gadamer, Hans-Georg. [1960] 1999. *Truth and Method*, translation revised by Joel Weinsheimer and Donald G. Marshall. New York: Continuum.

Gadamer, Hans-Georg. 1976. "The Universality of the Hermeneutical Problem." In *Philosophical Hermeneutics*, translated by D. E. Linge. Berkeley: Univ. of California Press. Originally published in 1966.

Gallagher, Shaun. 1992. *Hermeneutics and Education*. Albany: State Univ. of New York.

Gezork, Herbert. 1965. "An End and a Beginning." Commencement Address. Andover-Newton Theological School.

Groome, Thomas H. 1980. *Religious Education: Sharing Our Story and Vision*. San Francisco: Harper & Row. 184–232.

Hart, Ray. 1991. "Religious and Theological Studies in Higher Education," *Journal of the American Academy of Religion*. 59 (4): 715–827.

Hernandez, E. I., and K. G. Davis. 2001. "The National Survey of Hispanic Theological Education." *Journal of Hispanic/Latino Theology* 8 (4): 37–59.

Hodgson, Peter Craft. 1999. *God's Wisdom: Toward a Theology of Education*. Louisville, KY: Westminster/John Knox.

Holbrook, Clyde. 1991. "Why an Academy of Religion?" *Journal of the American Academy of Religion*. 59 (2). First published in *Journal of Bible and Religion*, 1964, vol. 32.

Hough, Joseph, Jr., and John B. Cobb, Jr. 1985. *Christian Identity and Theological Education*. Chico, CA: Scholars.

Hough, Joseph, Jr., and Barbara G. Wheeler. 1988. *Beyond Clericalism: The Congregation as a Focus for Theological Education*. Atlanta, GA: Scholars.

Jones, L. Gregory and Stephanie Paulsell, eds. 2002. *The Scope of Our Art: The Vocation of the Theological Educator*. Grand Rapids: Eerdmans.

Kelsey, David H. 1992. *To Understand God Truly: What's Theological about a Theological School?* Louisville, KY: Westminster/John Knox.

Kelsey, David H. 1993. *Between Athens and Berlin: The Theological Education Debate*. Grand Rapids: Eerdmans.

Kierkegaard, Søren. *Fear and Trembling and the Sickness unto Death.* 1954. Translated by Walter Lowrie. Garden City, NY: Doubleday Anchor.

Killen, P. O. C. 2001. "Gracious Play: Discipline, Insight, and the Common Good." *Teaching Theology and Religion* 4 (1): 2–8.

Klimoski, Victor. 2003. "Assessment and the Professional Character of Ministry." *Theological Education* 39: 35–52.

Mackay, John. 1956 January. "Some Questions Regarding Theological Education with Special Reference to Princeton Seminary." *Princeton Seminary Bulletin* 49: 3–12.

Mackenzie, W. Douglas, M. W. Jacobus, and E. K. Mitchell. 1911. *On the Education of the Minister and on the Training for Various Forms of Christian Service.* Hartford, CT: Hartford Theological Seminary.

McCarthy, Jeremiah, ed. 2003. *Theological Education* 39 (1). Issue Focus: "The Character and Assessment of Learning for Religious Vocation."

Miller, Glenn T. 1990. *Piety and Intellect: The Aims and Purposes of Ante-Bellum Theological Education.* Atlanta: Scholars Press.

National Conference of Catholic Bishops. 2001. *Program of Priestly Formation.* 4th ed. Washington, DC: United States Conference of Catholic Bishops.

Niebuhr, H. Richard, Daniel Day Williams, and James M. Gustafson. 1956. *The Purpose of the Church and Its Ministry: Reflections on the Aims of Theological Education.* New York: Harper and Row.

Niebuhr, H. Richard, Daniel Day Williams, and James M. Gustafson. 1957. *The Advancement of Theological Education.* New York: Harper.

Preheim, Rich. 2002. "Class Acts." *The Mennonite* 5 (17): 30.

Rosell, Garth M. 2002. "Renewing the Mind." *Conversations: Newsletter of the Lexington Seminar* (spring): 3.

Schleiermacher, Friedrich. 1988. *Brief Outline of Theology as a Field of Study.* Schleiermacher Studies and Translations, vol. 1. Lewiston, NY: Mellen.

Schuth, K. 1999. *Seminaries, Theologates, and the Future of Church Ministry: An Analysis of Trends and Transitions.* Collegeville, MN: Liturgical.

Schwehn, M. R. 1993. *Exiles from Eden: Religion and the Academic Vocation in America.* New York: Oxford Univ. Press.

Smart, James D. 1960. *The Rebirth of Ministry.* Philadelphia: Westminster.

Webb, S. 2000. *Taking Religion to School: Christian Theology and Secular Education.* Grand Rapids: Brazos.

Weber, Jerry Dean. 1997. *To Strengthen and Develop Protestant Theological Education: John D. Rockefeller Jr. and the Sealtantic Fund.* Ph.D. diss., Univ. of Chicago.

Weil, Simone. 1951. "Reflections on the Right Use of School Studies with a View to the Love of God." In *Waiting on God,* translated by Emma Craufurd. London: Collins.

Wheeler, Barbara G., and Edward Farley, eds. 1991. *Shifting Boundaries: Contextual Approaches to the Structure of Theological Education.* Louisville, KY: Westminster/John Knox.

Williams, Raymond B., ed. 1997. *Journal of the American Academy of Religion: Thematic Issue on Teaching and Learning in Theology and Religion* 65 (4).

Williams, Raymond. B. 2001. "Getting Technical: Information Technology in Seminaries." *Christian Century* (February): 14–15.

Williams, Raymond B. 2002a. "Reflecting Back and Looking Forward." *Conversations: Newsletter of the Lexington Seminar* 4 (2): 3. Excerpted from "A Teacher's Life: An Interview with Raymond B. Williams." Interview by Malcolm Warford, editor, with commentary by Lucinda Huffaker. 2002. In *Teaching Theology and Religion* 5 (4): 211–20.

Williams, Raymond B., ed. 2002b. *Teaching Theology and Religion* 5 (1). Special Issue: "Teaching with Technology."

Wood, Charles M. 1985. *Vision and Discernment: An Orientation in Theological Study.* Decatur, GA: Scholars.

Wood, Charles M. 1994. *An Invitation to Theological Study.* Valley Forge, PA: Trinity Press International.

Wright, Walter C., et al. 1999. "A Seminary Fishbowl: The Larger Curriculum." *Conversations: Newsletter of The Lexington Seminar* 1 (1): 5–6.

Ziegenhals, Gretchen E. 2002. "The Simple Gifts of Setting and Reflection." *Conversations: Newsletter of The Lexington Seminar* 4 (1): 1, 7

Participating Schools

1999

Austin Presbyterian Theological Seminary
Calvin Theological Seminary
Lutheran School of Theology at Chicago
Regent College
Virginia Theological Seminary

2000

Associated Mennonite Biblical Seminary
Claremont School of Theology
Eastern Baptist Theological Seminary
McCormick Theological Seminary
Seabury-Western Theological Seminary

2001

Bethel Theological Seminary
Church Divinity School of the Pacific

Luther Seminary
Pacific Lutheran Theological Seminary
United Theological Seminary of the Twin Cities

2002

Colgate Rochester Crozer Divinity School
The General Theological Seminary
Gordon-Conwell Theological Seminary
Lexington Theological Seminary
The Lutheran Theological Seminary at Philadelphia

2003

Lutheran Theological Seminary at Gettysburg
Methodist Theological School in Ohio
Phillips Theological Seminary
Pittsburgh Theological Seminary
Trinity Evangelical Divinity School

2004

Ashland Theological Seminary
Baptist Theological Seminary at Richmond
Lancaster Theological Seminary
Lutheran Theological Southern Seminary
Wesley Theological Seminary

2005

Bethany Theological Seminary
Eastern Mennonite Seminary
Episcopal Theological Seminary of the Southwest
Trinity Lutheran Seminary
Wartburg Theological Seminary

Contributors

DIAMOND CEPHUS is consultant for the Boston Public Schools and tutor in psychology and education at Harvard College. He has worked extensively in church programs for young people in New York City and is completing a doctorate at Harvard University where he has specialized in the contributions of critical philosophy to the understanding of issues of diversity and prejudice.

STEPHEN ELLINGSON is Assistant Professor of Sociology at Hamilton College. Previously, he was Assistant Professor of the Sociology of Religion at Pacific Lutheran Theological Seminary and Director of the Lilly Project on Congregational Ministry. His academic interests focus on issues of religious change and continuity, identity and meaning, and the relationship between religion and collective action.

SAMUEL ESCOBAR is Thornley B. Wood Professor of Missiology, Eastern Baptist Theological Seminary; well-known leader in international evangelical Protestantism. A native of Peru, he has served on the faculty of the National University of San Marcos in Lima and now lives in Spain while continuing to teach at Eastern Baptist.

VICTOR KLIMOSKI is Director of Life Long Learning, St. John's Seminary; former Dean of St. Paul School of Theology, St. Thomas University. Trained in adult education and theology, he consults widely on issues in teaching and learning in theological schools.

GLENN T. MILLER is Dean of Bangor Theological Seminary, where he also serves as Waldo Professor of Ecclesiastical History. He specializes in American religious history and is currently completing the second volume of a two-volume history of theological education in the United States.

RICHARD W. NYSSE is Associate Dean of Learning Systems and Technology and Professor of Old Testament at Luther Seminary. He has twice been book editor of *Word & World* (1980–84 and 1984–91).

GARTH M. ROSELL is Professor of Church History and Director of the Ockenga Institute at Gordon-Conwell Theological Seminary, where he has also served as Academic Dean. His research interests center in religious history, especially the American evangelical tradition.

JANE SHAW is Fellow and Dean of Divinity, New College, Oxford University where she leads the summer program in theological studies. In addition to teaching religious history, she is also a leader in women's studies at Oxford. She is currently completing a book on a modern religious movement in Great Britain.

GORDON T. SMITH is President, Overseas Council Canada. Previously, he was Vice President for Academic Affairs and Associate Professor of Spiritual Theology at Regent College, Vancouver. He has also served as a missionary in the Philippines. His research and publications focus on spiritual theology and the spiritual life.

JERRY L. SUMNEY is Professor of Biblical Studies, Lexington Theological Seminary. His primary interest is in the theology and writings of Paul and Paul's contributions to the formation of contemporary Christian congregations and ministries. He is the editor of the *Lexington Quarterly*.

MALCOLM L. WARFORD is Director of the Lexington Seminar, Research Professor at Lexington Theological Seminary, and former President of Bangor Theological Seminary and Eden Theological Seminary. He has also been a member of the faculties of St. Louis University and Union Theological Seminary in New York.

RAYMOND BRADY WILLIAMS is Charles D. and Elizabeth S. LaFollette Distinguished Professor in the Humanities, Emeritus, Wabash College; Founding Director, Wabash Center for Teaching and Learning in Theology and Religion. Trained as a New Testament scholar, he has also published widely on Hinduism and religious pluralism in the United States.

MARY-ANN WINKELMES is Associate Director of the Derek Bok Center for Teaching and Learning at Harvard University, where she also serves as a

Lecturer in Extension in the area of art and art history. Her educational interests focus on the nature of pedagogy and curricular change.

GRETCHEN E. ZIEGENHALS is Director of Women's Studies, Georgetown College; former Assistant Editor, *The Christian Century*. She is the editor of *Conversations*, the newsletter of The Lexington Seminar.

Index